LIBERATE

I0023976

The Empowering Guide to Grassroots System Change

Paul Deslauriers

NRG Publishing

P.O. Box 606

Makawoa, HI 96768

Acknowledgment:

Ongoing Support: Kathleen Cardella

Line Edit: Patricia Neri

Cover Design: Bill Greaves

1. Community Organizing

2. Social Change

3. Political Reform

ISBN 978-0-9771833-5-7

Free Weekly Resource Guide
for
Grassroots Organizing and System Change
www.LiberateGuide.com

Paul Deslauriers is also author of

- *Grassroute Guide: A Road Map to Community Empowerment*
- *Bearer of Light: A Catalyst for Global Change*
- *IN THE HIGH-ENERGY ZONE: The 6 Characteristics of Highly Effective Groups."*

Visit www.NRGpublishing.com

Book Content

Appendix: Catalyst for Change

Introduction

Right now, we have an unprecedented opportunity to change the systems that exploit the masses and that fuel the ultra-rich. We have a timely opportunity to bring about uplifting and supportive change for 99% of the population by rewiring a few critical pieces. Because of the blatant dysfunctions within our government, monetary, health care and education systems there is a growing awareness that something is terribly wrong and people are willing to take action.

The time is ripe to act

A new paradigm is blossoming. We have redefined how we connect as a global society through the internet and cell phones. Hierarchical structures are less relevant than they were. New tools and solutions are available from science, economics, and organizational development. This shift opens clear paths for the system change we need. *Liberate* is a catalyst and a comprehensive, proven how-to for that peaceful and uplifting transition.

A bright future waits with system change

We can all have nutritious food, clean abundant water, unpolluted air. We can all develop our potential, pursue fulfilling work and earn a fair wage. We can have free education, and medical care. We can eliminate debt and have a monetary system that serves our community. All this can be realized by rewiring our systems.

The main barrier is the formation of beliefs

Our manipulated unconscious beliefs are the primary mechanism keeping us on a road leading to modern day enslavement. Propaganda, social engineering, and even chemical suppression help sustain this veil of delusion. *Liberate* explores the formation of these beliefs and their impact; it is a guide to awaken from the delusion and propaganda that shape our perceptions and what appears real and true. When the veil is lifted we can listen to a deeper truth.

Truth will set us free

The truth can be liberating as well as shocking. Four appendices in *Liberate* provide foundational information to end the deception. When we wake up to the facts about our government, media, military, corporate, and monetary systems, we can see which parts are evil and corrupt and withdraw support. Also, there is a deep truth about our nature that is a powerful change agent, that we all can participate in.

The Law of Attraction is a powerful creative tool

Your endeavors will succeed if you persist holding your goal in mind and engage the law of attraction. If you hold joy, you will attract what brings more joy. The laws of attraction and information fields are important mechanisms to support the needed change or anything you want

A proven process provides a roadmap that accelerates a peaceful change

The 16 points of awareness and change applies locally to a small group as well as a nation. At the essence of the process is a deeper truth common to all group endeavors. The process is very relevant to today's society. Engaging true stories illustrates the process that is accessible to anyone who would like a bright future.

Effective organizing tools can develop any group initiative

We must come together if we are to be the power behind the change. As we unplug from corrupt systems, it is important that grassroots organizations are in place and functioning to replace needed services. There are many organizing processes and insights provided in this guide with many application examples.

Group energy amplifiers can power change

High-energy grassroots systems are developing all around us and are strengthening regional resources, exchanges, and investments. The science of group energy fields and the integration of specific core values can support any group activity or organization to function at a high level. This is the next frontier and an evolution we are now living.

Understand Elite system wiring that controls our society

The distinctive wiring characteristic of the Elite system is its consolidation, centralization and control of power into the hands of the few. The hierarchical structure is slow to respond, inefficient and serves the self-chosen privileged few. It breeds divisiveness, manipulation and fear. These systems suppress the potential of citizens while increasing control by the power brokers.

There is a trigger that will quickly change the Elite wiring

Any system has a trigger that when changed has a cascading effect throughout that organized system. The systems of the elite are primarily controlled by the monetary system and within that system is a trigger for monetary reform and the cascading effect that can reform all systems.

Rewire to Common Good systems

The Common Good system is wired to spread local empowerment to the many, resulting in rapid and diverse responses. It generates a greater ownership and participation in the local community development. *Liberate* provides engaging real life stories that illustrates a clear rewiring process.

We may face bumps and roadblocks along the way

Factions within the government and these elite systems are fearful of citizens organizing; they realize it will precede the downfall of their exploitive ways. I was the coordinator for 287 grassroots groups focused on exposing the evil of those who rule the US government. This provided ample experience of their divisive strategies. The strategies of these anti-organizing groups and counter measures are presented in the text.

Grassroots systems change is unstoppable

Grassroots systems change is non-violent, decentralized, self-propagating, uplifting, inclusive, territory-capturing, adaptive, flexible, minimally confrontational, and liberating. Such a widespread movement is impossible for the power brokers to suppress or co-opt. Liberation is unstoppable.

Be empowered and part of the evolution underway.

This book is a catalyst and a comprehensive, proven how-to for that peaceful and uplifting transition.

Chapter 1

A Journey of Discovery

The foundation of this book is built on a universal essence. It touches a deep truth affecting all of existence and our individual and collective ability to change our social systems. This universal essence provides a perspective that contradicts much of what we are led to believe.

This essence is energy's vibration and resonance. Its nature provides a clear path to change the oppressive systems we live under. Its nature gives form to our universe. Its laws determine our ability and capacity for success in any venture. Applying these principles is vital for the system change that lies ahead.

These principles shook me to my core and changed the course of my life on several occasions. To me, they are more than concepts for they have been part of my journey as an engineer, oceanographer, environmental consultant, director of a yoga community, organizational development consultant, activist, and grassroots organizer. For thirty two years I worked as a systems engineer restructuring the way organizations function to bring out their potential.

This first chapter uses my life experiences to illustrate important principles and tools. These are later built on by local organizing experiences and proven strategies to help rewire our society to serve the common good.

These strategies require seeing a new perspective and awakening to a deeper truth. My journey has been directed by one burning question, a quest for a fundamental truth. What is the nature of energy? Fifty years later I understand its nature as a true guide for rapid system change.

A Commitment to the Journey

My dad and I were driving through the Rhode Island countryside on a late spring day in 1967. He was at the wheel. In our quietness, I was reflecting on how to tell him about my decision to leave the Catholic seminary. For four years I had lived and studied in the cloisters of Our Lady of Providence. But by now it had become clear to me that the priesthood was not my path.

I still had a deep urge to explore the life of spirit. But I needed some new framework, some way that I could make sense of the mystery that seemed to lie at the root of religion and the aspiration of heaven.

My high school physics class had given me the first glimpse of my new path. The teacher wrote on the blackboard with chalk flying and wide sweeping movement: "Everything around us, including ourselves, is made of energy."

Everything?

I remember looking around the classroom at the desks, the chalkboards, my classmates—all made out of the same stuff. Made out of something invisible, and yet real-beyond-real. Something that seemed to have spiritual qualities, and yet it had never been mentioned in catechism class. Something tangible and scientific that could be studied. I was seventeen at the time, and new ideas were dawning in my mind. I sensed that I had encountered a deep truth, and I wanted to pursue it. But I wasn't sure where the pursuit would take me. So how could I explain this to my dad?

We drove past large fields on either side of the road. The fields had been recently plowed, the wide landscape turned up rich and brown. On the right side of the car the sun was gleaming. On the left dark clouds were churning up a storm. The sky was pumping with energy.

I just blurted it out: "Dad, I decided to leave the seminary. I don't think this lifestyle is for me."

As always, my dad was accepting and supportive. He listened attentively to my reasoning and nodded at my conclusions. Then he asked, "What do you want to do?"

Before I could answer, a bolt of lightning shot across the sky. It struck a stand of trees at the edge of a nearby field. A deafening clap of thunder ripped through the air as a wave of energy shot through me.

It was as if nature itself was prompting my answer. I pointed to the spot where the flash of lightning had hit the earth and said with a conviction that came from the core of my spine, "I want to understand that."

"What?" he asked.

"Energy. All aspects of energy."

I didn't know what else to say; I didn't know where this path would lead me. All I could do was sit there feeling the conviction—a knowing.

Dad had a puzzled look on his face. My comment didn't really make sense in terms of choosing a profession. He glanced over to where the lightning hit, and then he turned to me with a smile. "You've got my support whatever you decide," he said.

I had the support of many others who influenced this journey to understand all aspects of energy. Understanding the nature of this all-pervasive energy and applying its principles can help us quickly change these dysfunctional systems and live a more fulfilling life.

Energy Flow Through Systems

In college I learned about energy in a practical, applicable way. I earned a bachelor's degree in electrical engineering and a minor in marine ecology. Science, engineering, and ecosystems shared a common foundation.

The energy that makes our universe is always vibrating. The frequency of this vibration affects the form created and results in the great diversity around us. Just as the color red vibrates at a lower level than higher vibrating purple, everything is colored with vibration. The vibration can change based on the system it operates in.

Energy's electromagnetic force can activate intricate circuits etched in micro detail. Electrical energy can be amplified or dissipated. There is a flow through circuits that results in a wide range of uses. The circuitry and resulting electrical system define the expression of that energy to accomplish incredible tasks.

7

Likewise ecosystems have a range of connections that affects the biological productivity and well being of its inhabitants, measured as the biological energy flows through the system. Eugene P Odum pioneered the concept of how the interdependence of divergent ecosystems is the basis of how the earth functions. His followers looked at the energy flow of a variety of ecosystems and the circuitry that affected it. Some systems had high productivity. More evolved systems shared interdependence and mutual support that allowed them to thrive.

This interdependency became very clear to me while I was working for the marine zoology department at the University of Rhode Island. We researched the impact of lobster fishing along the Narragansett coast. In areas where the lobsters were over-fished, their main prey, crabs and sea urchins, flourished out of balance. The seaweed and kelp that the prey fed on were soon depleted. Then the sea urchins either moved on or starved to death, leaving the system devoid of the life that it once had.

The more advanced sustained ecosystems were based on cooperation and mutual support versus competition and survival of the fittest. Two different approaches to ecosystems reflect the two divergent roads we can chose to travel. There is the Darwin approach that emphasized low vibrating ecosystems that are based on "survival of the fittest." Our society can interpret it as a corporate slogan that "greed is good." Elisabeth Sahtouris, an evolution biologist, had the approach of a more evolved and sustained ecosystem based on mutual support and collaboration. Coral reefs to forests function as a whole in this way. She has used the way natural systems are wired and function to help us apply sustainable approaches to our economy.

The circuitry of ecosystems can be extended to organizations or societal systems. Energy gets amplified or dissipated depending on the type of system it functions in.

Everything is Interconnected and Unpredictable

Small changes can have far-reaching impact on the evolution of any system. Just out of college, I was doing research for Massachusetts Institute of Technology (MIT) as part of a massive oceanography project involving fourteen countries. It was an amazing opportunity to meet the notable oceanographers I had read about in my classes. The scientists felt that if they understood the larger ocean currents, they could predict long-range weather patterns. But it wasn't that simple.

I was at the hub of the operation at the Bermuda Biological Station with 1969 technology. Every day they would radio the coordinates of a wide range of current markers at different depths in the northern Atlantic Basin. They simultaneously would send the data to me where I would record the movement of the current markers. I couldn't make any sense of it, as some markers were moving at 2 knots in one direction, and 50 meters deeper the marker would go in the opposite direction. Some would shoot off and stall. After three weeks the chief scientist went over my data and mapping and then called all 14 vessels to Bermuda for a meeting.

We found that small eddy currents could abruptly change the course of the larger, weather-producing ocean flows. And these smaller eddy currents were unpredictable.

The same unpredictability applied to our observations of the atmosphere. Meteorologists made the assumption that weather is a cause-and-effect phenomenon: winds rise, clouds form, and rain falls. But we discovered that very small, undetectable changes in a weather system lead to unpredictable consequences. Knowing the weather pattern now is no prediction of what it will be even a couple of days hence. They concluded that accurate long-range weather predictions are not possible. Tiny disturbances can produce exponentially divergent behavior. Chaos can occur at any time.

The same thing occurs in any group field. The repercussions of small shifts have the potential to create big shifts in the energy field. The same thing happens in life. You meet a person who creates a connection that opens a door, and your career takes off. You miss a train, and then meet the love of your life.

Each of us is a dynamic system. Our evolving future is uncertain. No matter how determined we are to increase probability, some degree of uncertainty always exists. We all must be able to adapt to life's uncertainty.

Pollution in Ecosystems

When the oceanographic study ended, my next professional work involved studying the ebb and flow of energy and pollution within coastal ecosystems particularly along the Atlantic basin. There were two projects: the first was studying the air/sea interface. I would collect samples in a special sterilized boat. I would get launched off and row away from the vessel and collect samples of the air/sea interface. They would later take these samples for trace deposits of chemicals and pollutants that would affect the plankton at the base of the food chain. Even out in the vast ocean, as I sampled from Barbados to Africa, the air pollution settling all across the Atlantic began to make me more conscious on how we affect our planet.

My other study was sailing in the Sargasso Sea and netting clumps of seaweed that drift in the ocean. Within the seaweeds, were little critters that would be part of that self-contained mini ecosystem. Live little fish, barnacles, clams, and clumps of tar from oil spills. The study showed the holistic impact of pollution on these ecosystems.

After two years as a research assistant, I was hired by an engineering consulting and research company based in Columbia, Maryland. At the same time I went to graduate school and earned a master's in mechanical engineering with an emphasis on ocean engineering. The company asked me to head a new division dedicated to environmental issues. This part of the business grew rapidly. I received significant research grants and supervised oil spill research and response for governments, oil companies, and native cooperatives, including being one of three scientists on the U.S. National Spill Response Team. The more I worked, the more I learned how humanity and catastrophes impact ecosystems.

We live in systems that can vibrate high and prosper, or tumble down. If they do go down, how can they be resurrected, how can we support the recovery of the systems? Pollution work reflects connectedness, repercussions and impact on systems. It shows ways of recovery when a system has been badly damaged.

In a similar manner, any system can get polluted and it will impact all aspects of the system on some level. How do we contain pollution, and eliminate it from the system it is contaminating, while doing the least amount of damage? How can we reverse its effects? As you will see, we are dealing with widespread pollution that has permeated all aspects of our social systems. Many methods apply not only to our ecosystems, but also to our social systems.

Waking to a Vast Power

One night Janet, a dear friend, asked me a crucial question. "Have you ever experienced the Holy Spirit?" she said.

For some reason, the question stopped me in my tracks. I tried hard to come up with an instance. I thought right away of the seminary, of Gregorian chants filling the chapel with a powerful uplifting vibration. Other images surfaced. An incredible day surfing in Hawaii. Sailing in the Caribbean. The bliss of being with a lover.

"Nope," I said.

She laughed. "Well don't you think that you should? Shouldn't it be part of your research? After all, there must be a lot of energy in the Holy Spirit."

She told me: "If you pray for that experience, sincerely pray, it will happen." She seemed quite sure of herself. And I—for some reason that was beyond idle or even professional curiosity—felt attracted to her suggestion. So I did pray.

One week later I was doing my daily yoga practices—I had just gone into a spinal twist and was holding the position when a burst of energy shot up my spine. When the sensation reached the crown of my head, I had an experience that changed my life forever. Imagine that you are in an airplane rising through dark clouds and suddenly, unexpectedly, you pop into the clear skies above the clouds. A veil is whisked away. I was sincerely seeking an awakening beyond the framework of religion, beyond the images of my imagination. Then one evening, the concept turned experiential.

I walked through that door. It hit me on a cellular level. It was not a glimpse, but a full emersion into a dimension beyond this one. I felt, inwardly saw, and was bathed with energy that filled my mind's eye with a brilliant white light. My consciousness broke through the clouds of physical existence. It was something real, not imagined, I was not hallucinating. My entire being was washed in energy; an orgasmic opening that filled me with bliss, a blessed awakening.

It was an energetic connection to a consciousness beyond my earthly experience. I awoke to another realm. In that awareness I experienced a connection with an all-powerful being, which I cannot describe. It is an experience. It is a place beyond duality where the words that categorize things do not exist.

It was what I had been searching for without knowing it—not a person or a place, but an emotional, energetic connection, an innate connection with spirit. Surging through me was a blissful, rejuvenating, awesome energy.

"And I tell you, Ask, and it will be given you; seek, and you will find; knock, and it will be opened to you. For every one who asks receives, and he who seeks finds, and to him who knocks it will be opened." Luke 11:9-10

I can claim to be one of the 80% of Americans who have had an experience of connecting with this universal energy. So my story is not special or unique, but our experiences help ground the lofty conversation.

Changing Form

The next day I went to work full of excitement. I remember telling my friend Norm that I had encountered something much vaster than our physical world. He thought I was nuts. I told the president. I told all the technicians who worked for me. Everybody thought I had a screw loose.

From that moment my life shifted, a new awareness of a spiritual reality set in. A new set of priorities took hold of my life. Over the next few weeks I changed. Work became less important. A new passion was filling my heart and mind. I plunged myself into the study and practice of yoga. I shifted to a light, whole-food diet, mainly fruit and vegetables.

I decided to stop doing environmental work. My associates were shocked. I sold my sports car and bought a Scout International truck. I sold my furniture and bought a twenty-eight-foot Argosy trailer. All I knew for sure was that I had to get out of the office and follow a deeper calling. Where to go, I wasn't sure. I figured that I should immerse myself in nature. But mainly I just had to get on the road. Break out into a free form. Find what I would find. So, packed with all my toys—surfboard, skis, boat—I set out on my journey.

For a few months I kicked around the North and South Carolina coast, working with some professors I knew from my pollution work. I studied coastal erosion, sea turtle migration, and estuary productivity. In late September, after the summer crowds had gone home, I drove out to Yellowstone Park and camped at the foot of the Grand Tetons. There was a light snow, the first of the season. A full moon made everything glisten. The peaks were awesome. I remember thinking that here in the wilderness I would find what I needed. And I did. It just wasn't what I expected.

That night I was reflecting on my situation as I climbed into the trailer. During my meditation I felt the emptiness of the space. I thought about the fact that I was all alone, isolated. Although I felt closer through silence and prayer, I needed to interact with others. To experience spirit is to experience interconnectedness.

I suddenly realized that I was in the wrong place. I had a revelation: It doesn't matter where I am or what I do, I thought. What matters is my connection to the higher vibration. Being in an environment, community, or group that was dedicated to a similar path seemed the most supportive way to maintain that connection.

I needed an ecosystem of my own, an environment dedicated to uplifting my spirit. Just as a plant needs the right soil, water, sun, and temperature in order to flourish, I needed the right setting so that I could grow into this higher energy. I needed an incubator of spirit.

It can be healthy to change form; this is especially true when you have a deep calling to shift your course. It is stepping into the unknown. As we move into system change, some may find a new form will bring greater happiness.

Community as an Incubator for Growth

My interest in energetic systems led me almost inevitably to an interest in yoga. In my mind, yoga was the study of energy as it circulated in my own body. I was thrilled to discover that the basic laws of energy and matter, the same ones I had learned in those physics classes, had been set down six thousand years earlier by ancient yogis. They saw that all matter is made of energy coming from a dimension beyond our physical reality, and this energy has a specific behavior.

And I knew the place to go. My yoga teacher in Maryland had told me about Kripalu many times. Once I had even gone there, to the woods of northeastern Pennsylvania, to attend a yoga retreat. It had been a week full of powerful experiences and insights. Directed by a charismatic leader named Amrit Desai, Kripalu was the largest residential yoga community and personal growth center in North America. During my retreat they asked me to join their community. The next morning I called their main number and announced that I was coming to stay. ".Great," they said. I got into my truck and drove in a beeline from the Grand Tetons to Sumneytown, Pennsylvania.

Kripalu has changed locations since the late seventies, but this was its original community, a cluster of old stone buildings set in the pinewoods at the end of a dirt road. I parked my trailer behind the men's bunkhouse, a wooden structure built to provide basic shelter for the twenty-five or so male residents. This is where I slept for the next few years, in a bunk in a room with seven other men. The entire community rose every morning at 4:15 for a jog, yoga, and meditation. There was something special about laying my yoga mat down with others at this hour, day after day, year after year. The men became my brothers and the women my sisters. We washed dishes, gardened, and did other projects together. We went to inspirational talks and sharing sessions six nights a week. We had agreed, each of us, to make this collective spiritual experiment as a community.

Kripalu showed me that groups can generate powerful energy fields. We residents formed an interconnected web, and our shared energy made all of the discipline and practices much easier. I was uplifted, supported, and rejuvenated. We could create this effect because the Kripalu community had a single mission—to be in what I now call the "high-energy zone." This mission shaped the activities of the community, what we ate, and the way everyone worked. It created clear alignment among the nearly two hundred residents. It

14

gave us a foundation that touched everyone's core values and yet was bigger than all of us. This was lesson number one in my education about group fields: the power of creating a shared and uplifting vision. Such a group knows the interconnectedness described by quantum physics and by ancient yogis.

Truth Beyond Diversity

After settling into the community, I called my friends and associates. They told me that several of my old clients were trying to track me down to work on environmental projects. In fact the timing was perfect. I needed a source of income, and here was work that I could do from my trailer parked behind the men's dorm. So I started a consulting company that operated out of one of the largest yoga retreat centers in the United States. I did projects for the Environmental Protection Agency, Exxon, The National Oceanic and Atmospheric Administration, and the U.S. Coast Guard. I worked about six hours a day, and the rest was dedicated to yoga practices and community life. It was an ideal situation.

This life continued for a couple of years. Then the consulting work pulled me away from Kripalu for a time. During the early eighties, the hot area of concern for environmentalists was the pristine landscape of Alaska. In 1981 a consortium of fourteen oil companies and other clients asked me to start an office in Anchorage. So after much contemplation, I left the safe confines of my spiritual community and within six months found myself in Anchorage with nine employees.

Still mindful of the unified community from which I had come, I now found that my client base was anything but unified. It included native Alaskan groups, two state agencies, four federal agencies, and nearly all of the oil companies operating in the state. People often asked me how I could manage such a diverse group of clients. In my yoga-trained mind, however, I found myself looking right past their separating biases and interests to find a deeper truth.

By seeking verifiable data, questioning stories, and listening with an open mind allows critical thinking. To be relentless in expanding access to factual data and seeing it without preconceived concepts was part of the process. The idea for Marine Consultants was to be a clear a mirror of truth as we possibly could.

I found a great value in working with such diversity. The wide disparity of viewpoints among my clients forced me to expand my own views and to search even deeper to find the underlying truth. My consulting firm developed a reputation for finding solutions outside of special-interest positions and preconceived answers. And from this point on, my work has operated on the following principle: embrace diversity and focus on the underlying truth. It is a process I continue to use and one that is crucial for the needed system change.

Confronting Belief Systems

At age twenty-eight, I was owner and president of a growing consulting company with nine employees. However, success just seemed to cause more stress. I often worked late into the night by myself. Even though I had seasoned professionals on staff, I was carrying all the weight. Finally, I could no longer ignore the fact that I simply wasn't delegating enough. I had a pattern of mistrust, a habit of not including others. This pattern interfered with openness, and with teamwork.

As I reflected on the pattern, I saw that it had taken root during my teenage years. Back then the impact of the belief was slight and negligible. Like a stick in a slow stream, it caused barely a ripple. But as the stream picked up speed—as my business and employees all amplified my pattern—the stick began sending out larger and larger eddies. The pattern became apparent.

When I was fourteen, I had a lawn mowing business. I took care of twelve lawns. Once I hired a kid to help me while I went away to camp. He did a bad job. I had just come back from cleaning up the kid's mess and apologizing to my clients when I ran into my dad. I loved and respected my dad. Here's what he said: "If you want something done right, do it yourself."

His comment became my conviction. It buried itself in my subconscious mind and took root as a belief. Now, for the first time, I could see it.

Awareness of the belief, along with my realization that the belief no longer served me, was the first step toward uprooting it. Then I took active measures. I got support from my staff. I developed delegation skills, encouraged entrepreneurship, and expanded my trust. I let go of the conviction that I had to do everything myself. Within a month the pattern was essentially gone.

Once installed, a belief functions as part of our perceptions and therefore filters out everything that does not fit it. In this way, beliefs blind us. Over time we become our beliefs. They become our frameworks for thinking, feeling, functioning, and relating. They shape our intentions. They create our "sense of reality."

But our belief systems are often acquired falsely. We hang onto misinterpretations and misconceptions about ourselves, others, and life itself. This is a glimpse of how our reality is primarily shaped by these unconscious beliefs that filter our perceptions and actions. Our subconscious beliefs are where the primary battle is waging for system change.

Organizational Pollution

I began my professional career by looking outward at the natural environment, studying the effects of pollution and disturbance on the energy and health of the ecosystem. But when I tried to get to the source of the pollution, I found that I had to turn 180 degrees, so to speak, and look inward at the health of the company that had hired me.

I became sensitized to what I consider a deeper, more pervasive pollution than oil spills – the dysfunction that permeated the politics and the inner workings of the various organizations I was working for. Like its counterpart in the natural world, this pollution was blocking energy pathways, short-circuiting natural rhythms, and creating problems far beyond the immediate locale. It prevented groups from dealing with real issues and attaining their goals. I realized that the true cause of dysfunction in group systems was not to be found in the obvious place, out where the trouble was expressing itself. The source was behind the repercussions.

It was a pollution I was ill equipped to handle. The problem and dynamics seemed overwhelming as I had worked in the hierarchy of many large corporations and saw the mazes set up to lead to nowhere.

That is when I received the call from Amrit Desai, the leader of Kripalu. He asked if I would like to co-administer the Sumneytown ashram where I had previously lived. The organization had purchased a large facility in western Massachusetts and would be moving the majority of the residents to this new center. About sixty people would remain in Pennsylvania.

I accepted his offer. In doing so I was giving up an excellent income and some prestigious work. This wasn't a rational choice, but I never doubted it for a minute. My interest had shifted to the human ecosystem, and I wanted to further develop myself. The decision simply felt right.

Principles of Group Energy

At the Pennsylvania facility, I began directing personal growth activities for the residents and guests. I studied, practiced, and taught not only yoga postures but also the philosophy of this ancient science. It was during this period when my ideas about energy began to come into focus. The fundamentals had been laid out thousands of years earlier by pioneers of the science of yoga. These ideas had been refined by my graduate study of physics and tempered by my environmental work.

The real proof came to me as I further integrated these natural laws in my own life. I noticed a change in myself. My mind grew less cluttered. I could recognize the sources of stress and unhappiness. I became a better listener. My relationships deepened. I felt alive and energetic and connected to something bigger than my previous more shallow existence.

I began to articulate the principles of energy. I began to apply them in my workshops. It didn't matter to me whether the workshop focused on stress management, personal growth, or relationship building. The same principles applied because at our essence everything is energy.

I became aware of the link between a group's energy field and specific group values. High-energy systems are wired in such a way that actually reflected the behavior of quantum energy.

Six characteristics came clearly into view working with groups—leading workshops on yoga, personal growth, and relationships. (Alignment, Relational, Diversity, Possibility, Openness and Synergy). Chapter 7 will explore theses behaviors of energy and how they provide a road map to creating high energy groups.

These programs created temporary group fields that typically involved up to 120 participants and lasted three to five days. I found that if the six characteristics were integrated into the group fields, participants had high-energy experiences, they felt revitalized and transformed. They were able to see their issues and blocks from a more expansive consciousness. What I witnessed in the group response was confirmed later by the participants' anonymous evaluations.

Group Energy Fields

While ashram director I lead personal growth and yoga retreats. The deeper objective was for participants to have personal growth breakthroughs. In these three and seven day programs our team of facilitators were able to develop a high vibrating group field, where there is a sense of connectedness, acceptance, and community. While in that group field it is much easier to see the low vibrating patterns and beliefs that keep on sabotaging goals. Personal growth and breaking through to a more expanded consciousness is much more probable in this type of group setting.

In 1985, I married Christine, a senior workshop leader at the Massachusetts facility. We began leading workshops together, my program offerings expanded with my partner. In time I gave nearly three hundred programs, which were designed around the principles of energy that are set forth in this book.

The workshops became our laboratory. We saw over and over that when the participants' behavior aligned with the nature of energy, they felt rejuvenated and uplifted, had significant breakthroughs, and felt they got much greater value from the workshop.

I received valuable lessons through these programs. One lesson I learned early on was the importance of openness. At first I felt that I had to design programs in which every minute was scripted. Soon though I realized that I couldn't predict what would emerge from any particular group field. I learned to throw away the design and walk into each group field with an open mind. My role in part was a midwife helping to birth individual and group transformation.

We would assure a safe environment. This is essential for an open group field. "Be open; stay formless"— this was another characteristic of energy that fully revealed itself during this period of personal growth workshops. I began to see that subtle blocks and negative projections from any of the participants tended to bring down the energy in the group. So we developed activities to create openness. For example, in our couples workshops we had the participants pair up with strangers and tell each other "the most challenging aspect of your relationship," then listen with unconditional acceptance—staying open not only to their words but also to their emotions, not interrupting to "fix it," allowing the partner to dig down to the roots of the challenge. These were always powerful exchanges. Within five minutes people were getting a grip on the issues in their primary relationships.

We exercised these characteristics of energy in designing the workshops. We deliberately created interconnectedness by getting participants to interact a lot with each other. We struck a dynamic balance in our scheduling, which included work, play, socializing, and exercise. We stimulated diversity in people's thinking. We promoted a sense of possibility by believing in people's potential. In short, our workshops functioned in the high-energy zone.

But the workshops had a built-in limitation. They lasted only three to seven days. Because the group field formed and dissolved within that brief context, it was difficult for us to effect permanent changes. People would experience a peak "aha!" then, leaving the group, would gradually lose some of the insight that they had gained.

Participants in the couple's workshops generally fared better. Couples reported to us that they not only retained the positive changes in their relationships, but also grew and gained new insights. The difference was that the couples came to us with an existing group field (a partnership), and continued it after. I realized that a sustained group field, like living in an ashram or having a supportive group of people where you work, can greatly impact your well-being.

That's why Christine and I said yes when we got requests to bring our process away from Kripalu to benefit other groups—

businesses and grassroots groups for example. We were being handed opportunities to work with group fields that sustained themselves, that outlasted the brief period of a workshop.

Energy Shifts for Organizations

Would the same concepts apply in the ongoing, workaday world of a functioning group? Would our concepts help businesses respond and grow? Would they create more uplifting workplaces? Do these basic energizing characteristics apply to any group field? We set out to get some answers.

In 1986 Christine and I began a consulting company called NRG (pronounced "energy"). Our mission was to apply the energizing formula to business organizations.

A business's road to the high-energy zone often requires challenging work to break dysfunctional patterns that go against energy's nature. Leaders have to face their own energy-draining behaviors. They have to address conflicts. They have to retool systems that short-circuit productivity, creativity, and responsiveness. And yet we found that whenever a group aligns itself with the energizing characteristics, magic happens.

For example, we worked with a production company ranked fifth in its industry. It lacked technical competitiveness, and it had been operating in the red for the previous six years. After we helped the company change its primary dysfunctional patterns, it shifted into the high-energy zone. Within a year its revenues tripled. It quickly became the innovative leader in its industry. Within two years it was dominating the industry worldwide, more than double the size of its nearest competitor.

We preferred to focus on industries that shape consciousness. The theory being that our efforts would generate a greater positive impact in society.

Television broadcasting companies and advertising agencies were our primary market. For a while we were the most active consultants for these industries in the United States. We also worked with a broad range of industries including automotive, entertainment, airline, hotel, restaurant, and manufacturing. Regardless of the form or niche of the business, these same energizing characteristics pointed the way to developing the optimum environment for creativity, well-being and growth.

Organizational Circuitry

After working for 28 years serving hundreds of organizations in their development, four tools and perspectives were invaluable to support any organized system or group. I have used them in mergers, sibling dynamics in family-owned businesses, successful companies' evolutions, rescuing failing companies and organizing groups to resolve community needs. If we utilize these tools wisely we can transform and grow any organized group endeavor. We will apply them later in the text.

Any organization of people develops with the weaving of three types of patterns: personal behavior, group structure, and interpersonal relations. The circuitry of any sustained group is formed by the interplay of these three patterns with amplifiers and triggers. These dynamics affect the efficiency, productivity, and creativity of the group.

Personal Patterns: Whenever people engage in group activities, they engage their personalities, which they express in their behavioral patterns. For example, a person's level of concern for others will be noticeable in her or his actions. She will be a good listener or a poor one, sensitive or insensitive, assertive or passive, skilled or unskilled. These are her personal patterns of behavior.

Structural Patterns: In grassroots communities the need for effectiveness, efficiency, quality and directions is evident when taking strategic actions. Roles, responsibilities, and procedures need to be defined. Scheduled meetings, tasks, and goals help direct the interactions. The structure needs to accommodate a balanced approach to optimize community power.

Interpersonal Patterns: Interactions within the group form interpersonal patterns. When we interact, we begin to form opinions. We might hear gossip, hype, PR, or interpretations of peoples' behavior. We start to believe certain things about others. Stories of heroics or someone's good nature affect our perceptions of others in a positive way. We all too easily construct negative boxes around people. If enough people in a group habitually see the same negative box around someone, then the group gets locked into a fixed perspective. More people begin feeling the same way, and soon the mistrust is part of your group's circuitry. Even though the original gossip was false, the interpersonal pattern becomes real.

Thus personal, structural, and interpersonal patterns can be woven into the dynamic circuitry of a group culture. Each pattern can be energy–gaining or energy–draining. Some patterns have more impact on the group circuitry than others.

The real "stuff" of an organization's culture is its personal, structural, and interpersonal patterns. These patterns can be influenced by adapting values. The patterns are how the culture actually functions. These give an organization its character, reflect its actual values, and ensure the reproducibility of its efforts. These patterns give form to its living dynamic circuitry.

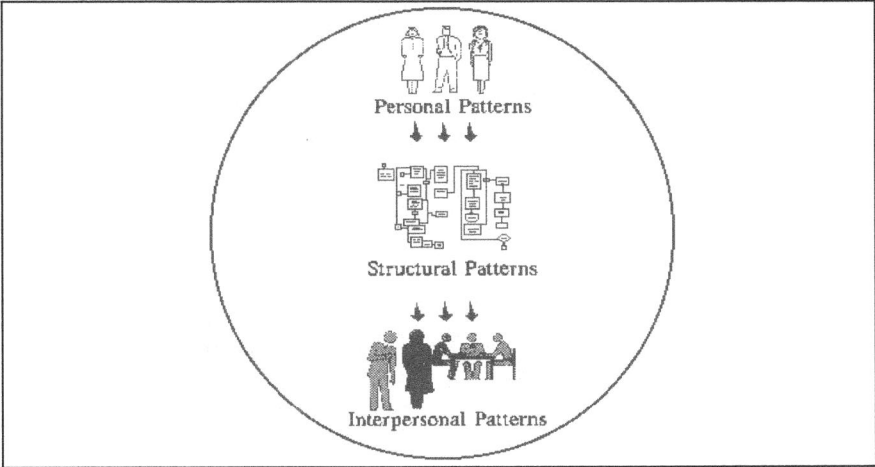

Amplifiers: Also, within this circuitry are what I call amplifiers, which one finds in any hierarchical structure. Those who have and hold the most power authority and influence have their personal patterns amplified in the group. They impact the group energy in a holistic way. They feed the group's potential; but if they are blocked or dissipate potential, they can starve it. If you're organized around a hierarchy, then look at the behavior and action of this empowered group or individual. They provide the major influence of your culture over time. That is why triggers are nearly always associated with those patterns that are amplified.

You will see later how important this point is, for these elite systems are hierarchical, and those who pull the strings have a particular psychological make-up that is amplified and permeates the systems. We can see the values that they hold, and these values shape policy, drive decisions, and give the structure and systems their characteristics. This insight points to the cornerstone ready for removal.

The Roots of Patterns: The most effective way to change a pattern is to go to the root of what is holding it in place. When the root of the primary dysfunctional pattern is transformed the entire system or organization changes its form. The root is often a belief that becomes an unquestioned command. This root can hold and reinforce a dysfunction. It is what is fixating our present systems.

Personal growth therapies all focus on patterns, and they all approach change by trying to get to the root of the pattern. They may not agree on methodology, they may not agree on whether that root is mental, physical, chemical, or emotional, but they all agree that transforming the root is the direct route to change. Most of our behavioral patterns are rooted in our beliefs. Our beliefs feed our behaviors just as roots feed plants. The roots are invisible just as our beliefs are often unconscious.

Dysfunctional patterns can become reassuringly familiar like background noise. We can be blind to alternatives that are more suitable and productive. We let opportunities pass us by. Unconsciousness locks us into cultural patterns that reduce the group's potential to thrive. Then they become difficult to discern through our own personal filters and the group-induced cultural trance.

Trigger for Optimum Growth: Any organization or system can rapidly grow and prosper by transforming a single cultural trigger that is so pivotal to success that it can cascade into improvement on many fronts that will affect growth indefinitely. What is fixating the root of the primary dysfunctional pattern in any human system is often erroneous beliefs held by someone in power. The trigger for my consulting company in Alaska was a belief I took in from my Dad twenty years earlier.

These triggers exist in the culture of all organizations and once transformed result in improved teamwork, creativity, professional development, efficiency, and profitability. The kinds of key domino-growth triggers I refer to can be found in an individual, a team, or structure, and could be the root trigger for your organization's advancement.

For virtually all organized systems, there is a primary trigger that sets the dysfunctional tone throughout the group. You can change symptoms of a primary dysfunctional pattern—but unless the primary pattern is transformed at its roots or disempowered, the dysfunction and its repercussions will remain. That is why *Liberate* goes to the trigger of lasting change.

Lifting the Deceptive Government's Veil

I was attending a book conference in Maui. My publisher wanted me to present my upcoming publication on organizational development.[1] I was about to leave for the airport on 9/11/2001 when I received a call from my girlfriend in Massachusetts. She said the US is under attack and all flights were canceled. It seemed like she was describing a movie. I was staying at a remote part of the island where we had no TV and I immediately got in my car.

I drove to Charlie's Bar in the town of Paia at 9 am, with a 6-hour difference from the East Coast. Charlie's had an array of TVs above a long carved wooden bar. When I walked in, I saw the horror on the flat screen. Because of the time difference they were showing clips of repeats.

I sat down next to a young couple in tears; they were from New York, on Maui for their honeymoon. We watched in shock as they showed people jumping from the Twin Towers. The honeymooner shared that he was a bike messenger and that the World Trade Towers was his main route. "I probably know some of those people jumping."

When the TV showed the second plane hit the building, I jumped up from the bar stool distraught; standing next to me was a tall man, in his forties. He was well-dressed with expensive trousers and a silk shirt not typical garb for a funky local bar in the morning.

When the TV screen flashed to a speech by George Bush, this man blurted out with anger, "See that beady eyed son-of-a-bitch. He knew! He knows. He's a part of it; this is part of bigger scam."

I looked at him with a puzzled and stunned look and asked "What did you say?" Sure that I didn't hear correctly.

He looked at me straight in the eyes, "That's right. You heard me. I'm telling you the truth. I am part of a special CIA division. I was sent here to chill out because I couldn't take what was going down today."

He continued, "I don't know why I'm telling you this, I see your shock." Then he said, "Look at me in the eyes, you know I'm telling the truth."

In his eyes I saw a steadiness and conviction I could not deny.

Then he added. "If anyone of my associates finds out that I told you this, I'm a dead man." He paused and pointed to me, saying "and so are you."

My head was spinning. I went blank. I didn't know what to say. I couldn't take it in. It was too big of a leap for me. I would not believe there are those in the US government who would do such an evil thing to these people I saw suffering on the TV.

I heard a rumbling noise, turned toward the TV and saw the first tower collapsing. I stared for a moment at the spectacular collapse in ten seconds. When I turned around, the man was gone. It was too weird for me to grasp. I only told my girlfriend after I flew back to Massachusetts, still not being able to accept what I was told.

Nearly two years later, when I saw the movies *Fahrenheit 9/11* and then the early cuts of *Loose Change* that I finally started to understand what I was told on that day was truer than the "official" government story. Having earned a masters degree in Mechanical Engineering, I could not deny the scientific facts.

Then I began to investigate the CIA, the Federal Reserve, the Military Industrial Complex, and governance. In many ways it was empowering to more fully grasp how I was being manipulated. I encourage you to read the appendix. Exposing the truth is not meant to elicit fear but to be a catalyst for uplifting change.

Back at my house in western Massachusetts, I showed documentaries, followed by discussions, on the 9/11/2001 attacks and the corrupt system. Then I formed a bond with two dedicated men. We rented a high school auditorium, advertised, and ninety people showed up to watch several videos that questioned the Bush administration's story. We showed 2 public movies every month at different locations. Our group distributed over 12,000 DVDs during our first year. We had a core group of over forty dedicated activists and began doing joint projects with fourteen other activist groups in New England; we went to Washington, DC, to lobby Congress.

Question the government story take time to watch a video by Richard Gage of Architects and Engineers for 9/11 truth or a lighter approach by James Corbett on You tube, "9/11- the truth in 5 minutes." Irrefutable facts provide powerful insight to break through the delusion. Use truth as a catalyst for action, seek truth with uplifting solutions, and you will be uplifted also.

The truth can set you free. However, truth can involve confronting beliefs and propaganda instilled since birth. To question the politicians, the bankers, and the media heads is to question those who have taken authority and power into their own hands to create exploitive systems. But in our optimism we thought if we exposed the truth, citizens would demand reform.

Grass Roots Organizing for Social Change

This led to my involvement in 9/11 truth.org. In 2006 I became the coordinator for 287 grassroots groups in the US and 62 international focused on exposing the truth of 9/11. Through these communities, we invoked a collective power and authority to transform this grave danger. We were inspired by Gandhi and Martin Luther King. At first many of us felt that 9/11 truth is the Achilles Heel of the corrupt military/industrial/government/media complex that presently holds so much power. We thought all we had to do is expose the truth and the system would transform.

Most of us did not realize the power of subconscious beliefs scripted by the government and the media. Take for example the twisting of the words "conspiracy theory", the label for those who questioned the government's story. Many media outlets turned it into "Conspiracy Nut", which even went as far as "terrorists". The result was that it immediately turned people off from listening as you were labeled and discarded as some crazy person in their internal dialogue.

Challenges mount even higher. The movement had succeeded in getting over 60,000 signatures from Manhattan residents demanding a reinvestigation into 9/11. This far exceeded the 38,000 signatures to put this on a ballot. A judge intervened declaring a reinvestigation to be irrelevant and a waste of tax payer money as the government has published the "official story". Change through the system is mostly futile. When I spoke with honest politicians, like Denis Kucinich, he stated that the existing government/legal system is wired so that no significant change can happen from the bottom up.

There were government agents also actively trying to shut down grassroots operations by infiltrating groups, mostly in cities where there are a lot of new faces. There are no huge numbers involved, it doesn't take many. In New England I knew of six government saboteurs focused on the 9/11 truth movement.

The other problem was focusing on this horrific story that many people were too afraid to hear, or it was too big of a leap. The energy of that negative focus was permeating my being. As the coordinator for so many groups, I was fed a constant stream of information describing the atrocities happening around the world because of these elite few. That focus on what was wrong was draining. It was affecting my attitudes, my health, my finances, my friendships, and my joy

This negative energy was somewhat appeased by our group of relations and friendships being formed. So we saw the solution lied in developing community. It was through community that negative energy was appeased to a certain extent. But still the negative focus was draining. That is when our local Berkshire 9/11 Truth group saw the solution involved a different strategy.

It became clear to all of us that we needed to focus on uplifting community solutions rather than expounding on the horrors created by this small group of very wealthy people. So uplifting community solutions became the focus instead of trying to expose what is wrong. That does not mean we turn our heads from truth, it is not the main drum I march to.

I still consider myself a truth advocate; I am now seeking to change the system through grassroots initiatives that serve the local community vs. pointing to the worst abuse of the Elite System. 9/11/2001 was the catalyst that got me involved. The truth is a catalyst for action. Now I focus on what is possible, not what is wrong.

Community ReStart

Community ReStart, originally named Co-Act, began in 2008 with forty members of the previous 911 Truth group in Berkshire County in Western Massachusetts. The mission was to create grassroots initiatives that address the local community's greatest unmet needs. The function of these grassroots initiatives would allow us to disengage from the Exploitive Systems and move into Common Good Systems. It illustrated a process for providing effective solutions starting with no more than the intention to work collaboratively to resolve the issue.

At Community ReStart we held 120 consecutive weekly meetings at my house. Participants even plowed my mile-long road in a snow storm to have the meeting. We began with a potluck meal. Over a weekly feast, we connected on a personal level. Each meeting had a topic relevant to community issues and needs. We would often have presenters and local experts. Then we would be in a circle for brainstorming accessing our collective intelligence. This was where our strategies were born. In a setting of openness and collaboration, everyone respected and trusted this group intelligence.

Our active focus of helping to resolve local community needs through meaningful grassroots engagement has been at the heart of our service. The inception of our initiatives comes from Community ReStart's creative brainstorms that generate group intelligence that point to solutions to community needs. Over the past 7 years Community ReStart has developed:

- The Pearl Street Center: a day center for the homeless and unemployed
- Berkshire COTS: an emergency cot shelter during winter
- Supportive Housing: affordable sober housing
- Transport Web: transportation access study
- Berkshire Hydro: hydroelectric for local towns
- Time Banks: barter exchange system
- Work Force: employment opportunities
- Food Net: fresh produce to pantries and meal sites

The success of a grassroots venture is as much about the spirit and the relationships within each enterprise as it is about economics, marketing, and product. When the barriers between team members have dissolved, there arises one mind. It's actually a single intelligence that works collectively with people who serve the community good.

To make lasting societal change we need to utilize the collaborative spirit and the deeper laws that help govern energy and consciousness. We also need to access organizing principles that will support the development of systems outside of the existing corrupt ones. Local community resources and their connections help develop self-sustained and prosperous systems that benefit the community instead of the elite few.

We are faced with a system-change issue that does not require force, anger, opposition, or violence; it requires some grassroots development and a simple refusal to participate in corruption. Grassroots systems can quickly develop to allow unplugging with minimal disruption. Resources can be rewired to serve the community. Now is a time to awaken and end the tyranny behind our governance.

Chapter 2

Awakening

The primary challenge we face in system change is within each of us. This is where the primary battlefront lies. The skirmishes are for the control of your subconscious beliefs that shape perceptions that can lull society into fabricated illusion. Beliefs can help humanity reach its highest potential or bring it to its own enslavement.

Beliefs can be planted without our knowledge or consent. These distorted beliefs act as filters that narrow and delude our perception. They can be shaped by social engineering involving a wide range of media, particularly television. We can be lead to believe anything including the false perception that we are powerless to change these corrupt systems.

Awakening is an internal process. It is shining light on darkness that has been set in our subconscious by ignorance and manipulation. Breaking through begins with an internal process that confronts belief systems about government, money, and well-being.

This chapter explores this battlefront. The impact of the subconscious beliefs in shaping our perception is profound. It can manipulate US taxpayers to support imperialist wars in Afghanistan, Iraq, Sudan, Libya, and Yemen. Syria is in its sights. Removing false beliefs allows awareness of the tyranny being committed so that we can end it. Understanding the formation mechanisms of these beliefs can help us un-form them from the subconscious. We are more able to facilitate our own awakenings.

An awakening can occur at any moment, any time we realize a deeper truth, any time we release beliefs that delude us and dissipate our potential, or when we connect with a power much bigger than ourselves. When that experience or realization is integrated, a completely new perspective on life appears. We see life through a different lens and feel at a different frequency. Often it is accompanied by some life change.

A teacher writing on a blackboard, "everything is made of energy," awoke something inside of me, as did a visceral connection with a universal energy and consciousness. The events of 9/11/2001 generated a shocking awakening. My awakenings also showed me not to focus on what is wrong, but what is right and uplifting change. Each of these awakenings challenged beliefs and concepts that have been part of my make-up and the collective unconsciousness. It was as if I was living in a dream infused with misinformation and then I awoke. I hope I keep on awakening. The journey of social change starts right where you are, awakening from within.

The Primary Block to Awakening.

Underneath all we think is all we believe. These beliefs shape our thoughts, direct action, and form our perception of the world we live in.

By far the most opaque blinder we have to truth, the biggest block to accessing our true potential lies within each of us. The structure of our conscious illustrates the most fundamental step to awaken for lasting uplifting change. Ancient mystics saw that underneath our actions are the beliefs that in some way direct our thoughts and perceptions. According to modern day psychologists like Carl Jung, this unconscious layer shapes over 90% of what we perceive and forms a collective standpoint to make our awareness of our world.

"Who looks outside, dreams; who looks inside, awakes." C Jung

Layers of Consciousness

Awareness

Conscious Awareness is what we see and are aware of in the moment.

Non-Conscious Awareness processes our feelings and body functions that come into conscious awareness when we focus on them, like the sensations in your right toe.

Pre-Conscious Awareness is when we want to access knowledge, memories, language or information.

Unconscious

Unconscious Personal Beliefs are accumulated many ways including manipulation and distortion to make you believe what is true or not true.

Collective Unconscious Beliefs come from our family, friends, community, and larger groups like nations, and are influenced by collective agreements that can be manipulated. A cultural conditioning is part of this.

Super Conscious

Sub Super Conscious involves a connection outside of our confined awareness where intuition and insights awaken.

Super Conscious Mind is a high vibration connection with Universal Consciousness.

The unconscious false belief systems act as a barrier to the super-consciousness. It is like looking down in a lake. If the surface has turbulence, like an unfocused awareness, you cannot see very deep. If the water column is murky, like a subconscious filled with false beliefs, you will not see to the depths where the super consciousness lies.

That is why personal growth often involves the letting-go of low vibration beliefs like self doubt or blaming others for your circumstances. It is the peeling away of false perceptions that block a deeper awakening. I welcome bringing these dysfunctional false beliefs within me to my awareness so I can let them go and have a less obstructed connection to a higher consciousness.

Understanding the influence, formation, and elimination of beliefs provides a key to ongoing awakenings. Question your beliefs. They are not fixed. You put them there or unconsciously allowed them there; you can remove them.

Changing our beliefs of the existing exploitive systems is the most important step toward changing our societal systems. So allow yourself to question your beliefs about our government, legal systems and this "War on Terror." Who is really behind the US military/industrial complex and the invasion of foreign nations? Why is the Federal Reserve owned by private bankers with ties to Goldman Sacs and Wall Street? What has happened to our privacy? What has happened to our governance and the disenfranchisement of its citizens?

Beliefs

Under all we think and perceive is all we believe. Underneath what we can access to our awareness lays the vastness of the subconscious. It is cluttered with complexes of experiences, decisions, and information.

A belief is a deeply-rooted complex established with conviction. Our beliefs shape not only what we do, but also how we see. They color how we perceive the world. Beliefs guide our thoughts, actions, and emotions. They do this whether we are aware of them or not.

Our beliefs operate powerfully in our lives. They affect our biochemistry, perceptions, digestion, glands, immune systems, and all aspects of our being. They have the power to make us sick or healthy. We cannot help but act according to our beliefs and live them as our conceptual centers. When we hold a false belief, as I did in my consulting company, it can have harmful consequences.

Our subconscious is fertile grounds to form an array of beliefs. As we take in our day-to-day experience, we are bombarded by outside messages specifically designed to impact and shape our beliefs. Unconscious beliefs can be developed by those who control the media, religious, government and monetary systems.

These outside influences can program beliefs and create a new "reality" which is based on distortion and lies. In this way a dream has been woven by the Elite. It is a dream world fashioned around unsustainable material consumerism, oppositions, fear, and a false American Dream.

As a society, we need to awaken to the manipulation that herds us down a road of subjugation. The real battlefield is the subconscious and the erroneous beliefs that enslave us. The elite's dream world reinforces fear, debt, separation, anger and violence. Likewise, these contracted energies make our subconscious denser and our connection with a higher consciousness is dampened. The belief-forming mechanisms of social engineering are described in Appendix C.

We need to replace this low consciousness and contracted energies with an uplifting vision and strategic action to make it happen. Feed beliefs that cast a bright light onto our future. Darkness cannot exist in the presence of light. For our well-being, our beliefs should be energy gaining, not energy draining.

If you believe that the storm trooper police of the Elite will come and take you away and you are constantly on the alert for their presence, then you drain your energy with fear and probably delusion. Beliefs that contract your energy are energy drainers.

Other beliefs like those from Gandhi focused on the power of love and forgiveness. He would teach others to develop local self-sufficiency while peacefully unplugging from corrupt systems. The belief in love and helping our fellow humans is uplifting and energizing. There are many beliefs that uplift and support us, beliefs like a healthy self-esteem or the vision of accomplishing a community project.

If the formation of beliefs can fuel the "War on Terror"; why not use beliefs for noble purposes? If beliefs are part of our make up and how we function in the world, why not use it constructively. A belief in the power of love can change a person and society for the good. We can use the power of beliefs to fuel initiatives for a peaceful transition, from exploitive to common good systems.

The real battlefront is the false beliefs that deceive us and prevent us from seeing a deeper truth. The analogy of battle is appropriate as these opposing forces are invading the subconscious to deceive us into giving our wealth and well-being to a few self-proclaimed leaders. This invasion allows a sinister agenda to unfold. From the manipulation of the subconscious, we have become partially enslaved in the elite's dream world and most of us don't know it.

We must understand the landscape of the battlefield to avoid pitfalls. Our subconscious can be crafted to take action that harms us, our family, and nation. We can be lulled into a cultural trance. It all starts with the formation of beliefs.

The Formation of Beliefs

Most people's subconscious is forming and reinforcing beliefs on a daily basis. We are flooded with undigested input, many reinforcing a crafted message that settles into our mind. This input creates clusters or complexes of images, and emotions that can form beliefs. Beliefs can be behind reactions, behaviors, and perceptions that go on with little conscious awareness. In this way, we become manipulated.

The majority of citizens in Nazi Germany were led to believe the deception of their glorious future until the deck of cards fell. The .01% pulling the strings knows the subtle tools of propaganda used back in Germany and have developed it since. They control the media so they can spin whatever they want to make impressions. To implant false beliefs you model the process based on belief's natural formation.

Belief Formation

1. A major event occurs or a constant reinforcement of a message.

2. We interpret the event and make a decision: This is what I need to do to succeed or to take care of myself or to make sense of it.

3. We have a feeling of certainty about that decision.

4. We look for and find further proof that we have made a good decision. We ignore or deny evidence to the contrary.

5. Our belief begins to dictate the world we co-create and experience.

Implanting False Beliefs

1. A good example is the 9/11/2001 attack of the Twin Towers, Building 7 and the Pentagon, and the resulting "War on Terror." During the first hours of a major trauma the emotional upheaval can be directed into forming a powerful belief. The constant shocking images of the planes crashing into the towers, people jumping to

their deaths, the towers' collapse, the rubble, the pentagon attack, and the patriotism it sparked were fertile grounds to plant a belief.

2. The perpetrators had a conspiracy theory of the attack already staged and ready to broadcast. On that day they ran several mock drills with foreign CIA operatives staged as terrorists. The media began blaming Al Qaeda shortly after the second attack. The CIA operatives already had their story made up to deliver during the time of trauma when beliefs are most powerfully formed.

3. Over the days that followed a constant reinforcement of their story was portrayed. A great sense of unity and shock was genuinely felt. And the media kept on reinforcing their story while eliminating things from the public's eyes like the collapse of Building 7, the explosions that occurred as the towers collapsed, or that a plane never hit the Pentagon. They broadcasted a message of certainty about a story made up by its architects.

4. Further reinforcement for the War on Terror came when US military grade anthrax was found in Washington DC. They managed to shut down Congress and kill several people. Blamed on terrorists the alerts continued daily. The constant barrage in the news made the nation ready to fight this "War on Terror." The Congress and Senate easily passed the Patriot Act that was in the making for years. This gave unprecedented rights to control and intrude on US citizens, but we accepted the abuse from them to fight against something they had created.

5. The beliefs now dictate that we pay for crippling military industrial complex expenditures. Trillions of dollars have been transferred through this made-up nonsense to justify the Elite's global aggression and thievery. But the controlling Elite got us believing that Osama held up in a cave in a remote part of Afghanistan made a major blow to the financial and military might of the US. That we must attack innocent people, make their countries a living hell filled with death and destruction, and plunder their resources. And that we are justified in this act based on a false belief.

The beliefs crafted by the Elite to justify their "War on Terror" were based on a cataclysmic event. But a reinforced message can also generate untrue beliefs that steer the course of your life. My personal life story is a good example.

I was brought up in the Roman Catholic faith and was influenced by the beliefs of the Church. My school teachers were Catholic nuns, brothers, and priests through to college. My belief in their beliefs led me to join the seminary to be a priest. But I shed those handed down perceptions as I more fully understood the lifestyle and organization. After four years in the seminary I took a different path when I realized my beliefs about the church were not true for me. A whole new perspective and possibility opened when I released a limiting belief and became more empowered in the process. However, for my first 17 years those beliefs influenced my character, relations, and decisions.

Once we integrate a belief, it becomes an unquestioned command to our nervous systems. It dictates our actions and shapes our perceptions. It filters the energy we put out, and it interprets the energy we take in. We unconsciously validate the ideas springing from it. It generates a fixed pattern of behavior.

Once installed, a belief functions as part of our perceptions and therefore filters out everything that does not fit it. In this way, beliefs blind us. Over time we become our beliefs. They become our frameworks for thinking, feeling, functioning, and relating. They shape our intentions. They create our "sense of reality." We need to replace the beliefs that keep us participating in a system that fuels evil.

When you believe, you can resolve community needs locally. When you believe, you can be joyous and partake in the abundance that surrounds us. When you believe there is hope. When you believe you can, you can. There is a reason for this insight described in the next chapter.

Interpretations of Events Shape Beliefs

But our belief systems are often acquired falsely. Repeated messages from the government, corporations, and media generate a perception that may be meant to hide the full truth. We hang onto misinterpretations and misconceptions about systems, others, and life itself.

For ten years, I led workshops that explored the way personal beliefs shape relationships. In one of these, a woman said that her primary belief about relationships was *"you can't trust men—they are out to get you."*

With some coaching, she uncovered the root experience of that belief. One day when she was 12 years old, she was visiting her cousin in her uncle's bar. That day she got cornered in the back room by one of the regular patrons. He grabbed her and planted a wet kiss on her mouth. She pushed him away, disgusted, walked out, and never told anyone. But she made a decision. She formed a belief that shaped her actions thereafter.

In this very same program, there was a man who touched me deeply by his loving interactions within our group of sixty participants. He exuded love. I could feel it coming from his heart.

During one of the breaks I asked this man what he had done to be in this loving energy space. He looked at me with a smile and showed me his forearm, where there were numbers tattooed. He told me, *"During World War II my parents, sister, two brothers, and I were all taken to Auschwitz. I was the only one to survive. While regaining my strength after I was freed, I had time to reflect on this experience. At times I felt anger and the discord of hate. But I saw how this negativity was impacting my recovery."*

"Then I drew on another experience, reflecting on the love my family shared before being imprisoned. When I would envision my family, I would recall love and openness, and a surge of energy would enter my heart. I made a decision to hold that expansive energy of the heart versus the contracted energy of hate. So, I made a decision: live what my family taught me, not the hate of the prison camp. And that has been the belief I live on a daily basis."

One person suffered a forced kiss and chose to shut down her heart. Another suffered atrocities and chose to keep his heart open. It's not the events that create our beliefs. It's our decision to interpret the events that makes all the difference.

We can interpret the events created by the parasitic elite in a way that shuts down our heart and dampen our spirits. Or we can be like the Auschwitz prisoner who used the experiences as a way to focus on the power of love.

Reconstructing Memory and Beliefs

Memory is a sequence of rearranged data that shifts every time it is retrieved. Memory pieces together similar experiences, desires, justifications, and imaginations in the reconstruction mix. So the reconstruction is never like the actual experience and becomes further distorted every time it is recalled.

Proteins are the building blocks of memory. If you block proteins from forming, you block memory. Likewise, when you recall you also use proteins. Every time we access a memory it is reconstructed with proteins. Every memory is built anew when accessed. Protein inhibitors can block memory formation and recall.

You can also create new memories after the incident. Memory is malleable. Media can be used to shape these memories for a purpose. Every time you recall, you reconstruct the memory with slight changes. Keep on adding false information in the aided re-call, you get a reconstruction that outside architects want. Our media and TV are particularly an important part of reconstructing memory to fit the elite's purpose.

We can distort memories of previously experienced events. We can be easily coached to recall things that are not there or hide things that are there. With this level of access to our subconscious beliefs, we can have our primary filters altered by the media.

Elizabeth F. Loftus, an expert in memory recall, notes several cases that exposed this human back door. In 1986 Nadean Cool, a nurse's aide in Wisconsin, sought therapy from a psychiatrist to help her cope with her reaction to a traumatic event experienced by her daughter. During therapy, the psychiatrist used hypnosis and other suggestive techniques to dig out buried memories of abuse that Cool herself had allegedly experienced. In the process, Cool became convinced that she had repressed memories of having been in a satanic cult, of eating babies, of being raped, of having sex with animals and of being forced to watch the murder of her eight-year-old friend. She came to believe that she had more than 120 personalities, children, adults, angels and even a duck, all because Cool was told she had experienced severe childhood sexual and physical abuse. The psychiatrist also performed exorcisms on her, one of which lasted for five hours, and included the sprinkling of holy water, the use of a cross with screams for Satan to leave Cool's body.

When Cool finally realized that false memories had been planted, she sued the psychiatrist for malpractice. In March 1997, after five weeks of trial, her case was settled out of court for $2.4 million. Nadean Cool is not the only patient to develop false memories as a result of implanted memories.

In Missouri, in 1992, a church counselor helped Beth Rutherford to remember during therapy that her father, a clergyman, had regularly raped her between the ages of seven and 14 and that her mother sometimes helped him by holding her down. Under her therapist's guidance, Rutherford developed memories of her father twice impregnating her and forcing her to abort the fetus herself with a coat hanger. The father had to resign from his post as a clergyman when the allegations were made public. Later medical examination of the daughter revealed, however, that she was still a virgin at age 22 and had never been pregnant. The daughter sued the therapist and received a $1-million settlement in 1996.

Loftus's research into memory distortion goes back to the early 1970s, when she began studies of the "misinformation effect." These studies show that when people who witness an event and are later exposed to new and misleading information about it, their recollections often become distorted. In one example, participants viewed a simulated automobile accident at an intersection with a stop sign. After the viewing, half the participants received a suggestion that the traffic sign was a yield sign. When asked later what traffic sign they remembered seeing at the intersection, those who had been given the suggestion tended to claim that they had seen a yield sign. Those who had not received the phony information were much more accurate in their recollection of the traffic sign.

Misinformation has the potential for invading our memories. After more than two decades of exploring the power of misinformation, researchers have learned a great deal about the conditions that make people susceptible to memory modification. Memories are more easily modified, for instance, when the passage of time allows the original memory to fade.

False messages are being constantly woven to create images and construction of a fake reality. For example, the CIA's involvement in developing Al Qaeda, ISIS and the drug trade is well documented and it is their made up chaos that justify their existence. See CorbettReport.com on topics related to Al Qaeda, ISIS. Therapists could stir up such opposition from their patients to their parents when their reasoning is totally made up. We are dealing with a barrage of distortions that create a false cultural trance that can easily pit neighbor against neighbor, nation against nation.

Waking Up from Cultural Trance

The distortion and reshaping of memories and the fabrication of misleading beliefs are the major weapons of the elite few to keep the masses in line with their deception. The veil of delusion is thick. Familiarity makes our behaviors subconscious. The routine of thoughts and behavior creates a trance. We go on automatic pilot. It's like the frog that is put in a pot of water without a lid. Gradually the pot is heated to a boil. If the pot is heated slowly enough, the frog will remain in the pot, even though it could easily leap to safety. However, because it is unconscious of the slowly changing conditions, it allows itself to be cooked.

In the same way, we are sometimes immersed in dysfunctional patterns that slowly kill off our potential. In our trance we forget we can change our environment. We stay put as the dysfunction boils away our creativity, our potential, and our spirits. The ability of a group to allow itself to be boiled away, to adapt to dysfunction, underlies cultural trance. We can easily jump out of the pot if we chose to.

In a physical trance, we lose voluntary movement and our actions become unconscious. In a cultural trance, we accept and perpetuate the environment without question. George Ivanovitch Gurdjieff, the Russian philosopher, called this cultural trance a "false personality."

We are shaped and reshaped by our cultural context. We actually construct many habits of our thinking and perceptions to reflect the consensus of what our cultures deem important. Ordinary awareness aligns itself to fit the culture. We start to assume that our cultural context is in fact reality.

The two most prevalent causes of cultural trance are complacency and leadership's suppression of change. A cultural trance is reinforced by a defeatist acceptance of "fate," particularly when people believe they do not have the power to change. People often feel and understand their trance but are fearful to speak up. As time passes, the dysfunctional pattern fades into the background, filtered from people's conscious awareness. In the end, what may not be normal becomes the norm.

What are some of the reinforced beliefs that paralyze much of the population from being involved with demanding change? Here is a partial list of the many untrue beliefs in the US that discourage us from making change.

Untrue Beliefs Preventing System Change

The United States stands for democracy and freedom and its leaders are guided by what serves its citizens, no need for concern.

- Any change of the system must be made through the existing corrupt exploitive system.
- We must sacrifice our freedoms and rights to fight this global "War on Terror."We must comply with what the government wants for the "good of all."
- We are dependent on the Federal and State government for our safety and well-being.
- The 99% is disempowered to make changes on a grassroots level.
- The Elite's systems are too vast, confusing, and compartmentalized to understand, let alone change.
- The Federal Reserve and the business of printing money are owned by the Federal Government.
- What we get from TV and the print media is fair and balanced and no need to question what we are told.

Transforming Beliefs

Questioning assumptions and convictions are healthy. Personal growth involves confronting and transforming self-limiting or destructive beliefs. Our growth as community and nation requires removing the distortions implanted in our collective subconscious. Perceptions, behaviors and judgments are fixated by beliefs and they can be transformed. If you put them there you can remove them. Below are insights into the formation of these beliefs and effective methods for changing them.

Transforming Dysfunctional Beliefs

1. Question the premise of the belief: How did it form, what decisions did you make? You may have been led astray. You may have made a decision about an event that happened when you were five years old. You may believe the government propaganda. Dysfunctional beliefs are founded on false premises.

2. Recognize what you're getting, which is nothing: Realize the repercussions of the dysfunctional belief. What have been the consequences? The quickest way to change a belief is to associate it with pain and suffering.

3. Focus on joy and love and the low vibration beliefs will drop away as they are not being fed the energy that sustains it.

4. Create an "empowered belief": Align a new belief with the greater truth of who you are and what you would like your community to become. An empowered belief is an affirmation, and is the antithesis of the dysfunctional belief. The empowered belief should be:

- expressed in the present tense

- stated positively about changing yourself, or creating a vision

- said in a way that evokes deep feeling and passion within you

Example: *"I, Paul am joyously developing successful grassroots initiatives."*

5. Identify Support: Get support for your empowered belief and utilize this reinforcement. This support can come from family, friends, business associates, a grassroots group or a higher power.

<u>Tools for Change</u>

- Start with a different belief that supports what you want

- Reinforce your belief by getting others involved to support your new belief

- Pain is the ultimate tool for shifting the old belief. Look at the facts and the pain and suffering induced by the old way.

- Model from other successes.

- Use positive affirmations to attract what you want

Help people embrace the reality of what we are facing. For example, help them let go of a belief that those in charge of government, military, and monetary systems have the people's welfare and the Common Good in mind. People are further confused by believing in mainstream media as a source of reliable and balanced information. These two organizations then reinforce messages like the "War on Terror." Once you change the flag-waving, media-distorted beliefs about democracy and liberty and see what we have done to Afghanistan, Iraq, and Libya, killing and displacing millions, and pillaging resources all for the benefit and amusement of an elite few. Your awareness expands, you transform beliefs,

A Consciousness Shift

When we see through distorted collective unconscious and personal beliefs several facts come more clearly into light especially if you are familiar with the appendix. First, we are not bound to support systems that exploit the masses based on deception. Tomas Jefferson encouraged radical house cleaning of government to remove corruption. It is feasible through a decentralized, but connected grassroots effort. The most important point for hope is the application of an ancient secret of creation discussed in the next chapter. Here a few points to support a belief that we can peacefully change the system.

Affirming System Change

- The systems created by the Elite only function because the 99% participate. Refuse to utilize or support Elite Systems, you cut off the flow of energy and it dies.

- Growing number of citizens are pulling back this veil of delusion and realizing the wealth disparities and hardships stem from Constitutional violations the citizens have the power to remedy.

- Awakening from this delusion can be as easy as turning on a light switch; it is a dark fear. It disappears in the light of truth and experience.

- We are sovereign Beings and the only one above is the Creator. The *"Laws of Nature and of Nature's God"* entitle us our Liberty. No man or government rules over us against our will, we are free. This is the foundation of America, which is founded on the principles laid out in the Declaration of Independence.

- New localized systems can develop rapidly through collaboration around community needs. They are free from the shenanigans and control by the Elite.

- The community, through collaboration, has the power and resources to develop new initiatives without the conventional means of money.

- Through grassroots organizing of the 99% we can become a force that is much greater than the Elite Systems controlled by a fraction of 1%.

- There is something bigger than system change that is unfolding. It is a shift to a higher energy and consciousness on this planet.

You can affirm change and support it through a shift in your thought pattern. We have talked about letting go of dysfunctional beliefs and we can also strengthen new positive beliefs. Affirmations can quicken the transition to Common Good Systems as it clarifies and reinforces what you want.

Action

Free yourself from dysfunctional beliefs and the distortions of propaganda. Replace it with the understanding that you are empowered to make change. One person can change a nation. Gandhi and Martin Luther King showed a path for system change. Although it may require awakening the masses to embrace and integrate system change, it starts with you. All you need to do to start is believe.

Belief Reminders

- Under the patterns of behavior, under all that we think, lives all we believe.

- The events of our lives do not determine our realities so much as the decisions that we make about those events. These decisions can form beliefs.

- Most of us treat a belief as if it's a thing, when really it's just a feeling of certainty about something that can be manipulated. We think that "this is the way life is," when often it's not.

- Our beliefs become unquestioned commands to our nervous systems. They write the script for our perceptions.

- They have the power to expand or destroy the possibilities of our present and future. Beliefs shape intention and action.

- Beliefs can be planted and manipulated, like the "War on Terror." Also our memory can be influenced to change its recall. So we may have many false beliefs.

- Whenever we believe something, we no longer question it. Question your beliefs. Question your group's beliefs.

- Breakthroughs in awakenings are triggered with a change in energy-draining beliefs.

- Believe in and think about what you want. Visualize and affirm the change. Be the change you want to see.

Chapter 3

Directing the Creative Force

The Force Behind it All

When scientists probed into matter, they found a primordial energy, Quantum Energy, the smallest discrete unit of physical matter, it's like tiny vibrating strings. An energy about 100 billion times smaller than a proton, is the essence that makes the physical realm we perceive.[2] These energies combine in a relational field that has a toroid shape, to make sub-atomic particles, like the electron.

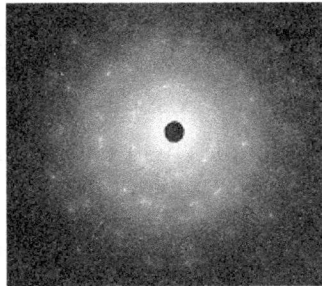

Diffraction rings around an electron

Everything around us is energy vibrating at the various frequencies in a relational field with other energy that gives distinction to our Universe. Just as the different frequencies within the Light Spectrum gives us distinct colors, so do the spectrum of quantum vibration gives our universe distinction. In addition, our thoughts and emotions have a distinctive frequency. We live in a pulsating, vibrating physical realm. Everything that exists, in the air, in dirt, in water, and in our bodies, is energy vibration in motion at different frequencies.

When physicists studied the behavior of this energy, they discovered something about reality that shook the scientific community at its roots. They discovered that this fundamental energy exists outside of our three dimensions of space and one dimension of time. In other words, this universal energy has one foot in our four-dimensional reality and its other foot in another dimension(s).

This discovery translates to you and me in this very moment. The energy making our physical reality links to another dimension. We are right now connected to an unseen dimension beyond our normal awareness. We are part of both, but identify with this physical plane. Even if we are unaware of the connection, the laws of this linked dimension apply to us as we are not separate. We are made of this energy, and the laws and behaviors apply to you and me or any endeavor.

Werner Heisenberg, a Nobel Prize winner in physics, described quantum waves as *potential energy*. He said of their discovery: *"introduced something standing in the middle between the idea and the actual event, a strange kind of reality just in the middle between possibilities and reality."*[3]

Potential: The inherent ability or capacity for growth, development, or coming into being. Capable of being, but not yet in existence.

Throughout this book I will use *potential energy* to refer to this omnipresent force, also called the quantum wave, the super-string, and the quantum field. Other cultures use their own names. In Polynesia, they call it *mana*; in China, it is *chi*; in Lakota, *wakan*; and in India, *prana*. The six-thousand-year-old Samkhya philosophy from India named it *prakriti*. Regardless of the name, it is the same potential energy.

Mystics throughout time have listened deeply to their inner nature to gain awareness of this all-pervasive energy. For millennia, spiritual leaders have been teaching that the physical world, including you and me, comes from this source energy, and that it has a particular nature. Now modern scientists have confirmed it. As they grasped the nature of potential energy fields, the old Newtonian, mechanical approach to understanding the world went to a deeper level. Now the new, though ancient, knowledge has launched a revolution.

David Bohm described our universe as an island on this vast ocean of primordial energy. The very underpinning of our universe is a field of energy. It is a vastness beyond the scope of words or imagination to depict. Einstein's equation $E=Mc^2$ is a recipe for the amount of energy involved in creating the appearance of mass from this vast ocean. Matter is always interacting with this infinite ocean.

Dr, Bohm concluded that, *"quantum theory indicates the need for yet another new order, which we call "enfolded" or "implicate." One of the most striking examples of the implicate order is to be seen by considering the function of the hologram, which clearly reveals how a total content (in principle extending over the whole of space and time) is "enfolded" in the movement of waves (electromagnetic and other kinds) in any given region. We then come to the notion that the quantum theory indicates that this implicate order is not merely a dependent or fortuitous feature of the content, but rather, that it should be considered as the independent ground of existence of things, while the ordinary explicate order is what should be considered as dependent."*[4]

We are inherently connected to something much bigger than our physical universe. The manifestation of our universe is dependent upon the underlying implicate order. This connection is ongoing, even though it may not be on the radar screen of our awareness. Through this connection, we can access unbounded potential. But the rules are different because you are operating in the implicate order.

Consciousness Shapes Energy

Part of that implicit order is the power of consciousness in shaping potential energy to create information fields. One field is around us all the time as your conscious and mostly subconscious shapes your aura. This aura is primarily an information field imbued with our consciousness. The aura information field keeps on recreating who you are as the cells in your body are replaced every seven years.

"What we are today comes from our thoughts of yesterday, and our present thoughts build our life of tomorrow. Our life is the creation of our mind." Buddha

Consciousness shapes the potential energy that makes our physical existence. Six thousand years ago, Bronze Age sages were contemplating the transition of the all pervasive potential energy into physical form. For these Sankhya mystics, it isn't only energy that exists beyond our physical dimension. There is also consciousness. It is independent of energy, but merges with it in the physical realm. When consciousness merges with potential energy it creates an information field.

Information fields inform potential energy to unfold and manifest. It unfolds in numerous ways. In fact, the word Sankhya means "enumeration of energy." It is the study of how energy and consciousness emerge. Consciousness has an idea, and potential energy responds to the idea by attracting and creating physical events and things.

Scientists in the field of quantum mechanics have discovered that the moment they inquire into the nature of subatomic particles, what they are looking for happens. If they want to find an electron with no spin, they find it. If they think about an electron with no velocity or no momentum, then the electron they study will acquire those characteristics.

This responsiveness was demonstrated in John Wheeler's delayed choice experiment conducted in the early nineties. The experimenter decides at the last moment whether or not to insert a mirror that would measure either the wave or the particle. As soon as the experimenter makes the choice, the photons seem to respond instantly and retroactively. The delayed-choice experiment has been verified in the laboratory at a retraction time of a few billionths of a second. [5]

Wheeler concluded: "*Nature at the quantum level is not a machine that goes its inexorable way. Instead, what answer we get depends on the question we put, the experiment we arrange, the registering device we choose. We are inescapably involved in bringing about that which appears to be happening.*"

Hinduism, Buddhism, and Taoism all claim that a transcendent consciousness, rather than matter, is the framework of all being. Consciousness ultimately shapes reality. Our individual consciousness is actualized through our beliefs, what we think about most of the time with an associated feeling behind it. We become co-creators with others in this emergent reality.

Our thoughts hold power. Why not use that power wisely, in a way that helps co-create Common Good Systems. Awaken to your power. Affirm uplifting beliefs about yourself and your community.

Life Is an Interplay of Energy Fields

Objects fall to the ground because they are affected by the earth's gravitational field. The earth exerts a gravitational force on the moon and does the same to the earth. The two fields push and pull each other in a way that creates a stable energy system or field. By Newton's third law of motion, these forces are of equal strength and in opposite directions. The earth with its north and south poles generate a toroidal shaped field.

The fact that the electromagnetic field can possess momentum and energy makes it very real and usable. Energy fields are not phantasms. Resonance within the field holds a stable vibration and cohesion. Stable resonance can generate form. It is integral to the creative process. Electromagnetic fields, when harnessed, power computers and light bulbs. Tesla showed by tapping into the electromagnetic field of the earth he was able to harness its clean abundant free energy. So the oil barons and banksters burned down his facility, destroyed his work and notes, and made sure his invention died with him. But this technology will again surface.

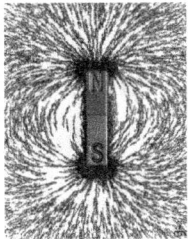

Fields are states of space filled with interconnected energy creating invisible structures. In "superstring" physics, the torus is known as the "perfect" shape. We ourselves are fields of energy with a similar form. Each atom of our being is charged with energy, and each cell has a field. This energy is constantly transmitted through our nerves and synapses. Layers of electromagnetic energy, surround our physical body at all times. These layers include our aura field shaped and colored by the vibration and information they hold.

Different fields exhibit different behavior and rules. For instance, electromagnetic force includes both positive and negative expressions. Why then, as far as we know, is there no such thing as

53

negative gravity? Nuclear force has a strong and a weak expression. But why do these function only within the nucleus of the atom, while electromagnetism and gravity are infinite in range?

We don't know why. But we do know that these fields serve specific functions.

The Distinct Nature of Fields

Electromagnetic Field: Infinite in range, it carries the light from stars and holds together the atom. It governs the laws of chemistry. The forces of electricity and magnetism cause a charged body to be attracted to, or repelled by, other bodies.

Gravitation Field: The universal attraction of all mass particles toward one another is the weakest of the forces. Gravity has infinite range and always attracts, never repels. This force that causes an apple to fall and keeps our feet on the ground is the same force that guides the galaxies in their movements throughout the universe.

Weak Nuclear Force Field: The nuclear force helps power the sun and presides over the phenomenon of nuclear decay.

Strong Nuclear Force Field: It binds particles together to make protons and neutrons. Without it, there would be no atoms and the universe would be a fog of potential energy.

Information Field: Formed from consciousness and follows the implicate order where the field is non-linear and responds instantaneously regardless of distance and it attracts similar frequencies and manifestations. Like attracts like. It can condition space and affect fundamental spin characteristics of subatomic particles.

In the United States, information fields are hardly mentioned, but look around at their impact. In our society, machines produce and people supervise them. The main productive force is actually the information. The success of a product is not its mass production. The phone, steam engine or computers does not depend on the labor that produces the machine but on the state of social knowledge and engagement. This information field generates a market and sales, and affects distribution and integration of the technology. Similarly, a new information field can help bring about the system change our planet so desperately needs. Its emergence requires our knowledge and connection with others.

In the quantum world, the only reality is relationship. Potential energy comes together in relationship to make quantum fields, which in turn combine to make up atoms. These quantum fields of potential energy are the building blocks of our universe. They combine to form atomic fields, which in turn form molecular fields, then cellular fields. Our thoughts create an information field that amplifies when aligned with others.

Our relationships—in other words, our group energy fields— are also real. They are experienced. We sense and feel the "vibes" of others. This group energy field is a powerful tool described in Chapter 7. The effective use of personal or group information fields is very important in the success of any endeavor.

The Law of Attraction

We are all subject to the same underlying nature. And its deeper nature is a part of us and the creative process. Our subtle thoughts and the more dense beliefs also vibrate at a particular frequency creating an information field. In fact, we are always vibrating with our feelings and consciousness. These vibrations extend out from us. This subtle energy travels unobstructed through things we consider physically impenetrable, after all it's all energy. Our information fields are extending out attracting our reality.

We are literally a broadcast tower sending out energy vibrating at a certain frequency. This vibratory energy we send out attracts a similar energy vibration. It seeks a vibration match. We actually beam out and attract what we are feeling and thinking about most of the time.

We are all Vibrational Beings. Every thought that we think is vibrating at a very personal frequency . . . and by the powerful Law of

Attraction whatever energy we extend is the energy we attract. Like attracts like, in this subtle energy realm, it functions in the implicate order.

Each and every component that makes up our life experience is drawn to us by the powerful Law of Attraction's response to the thoughts we think, and our feelings. Our money and financial assets; our body's state of wellness, how we are treated, work satisfaction, and rewards— the very happiness of our life experience in general—is all happening because of the story that we tell and the beliefs that we hold.

To a certain extent the story that we are led to believe, that we then repeat as true, helps attracts that reality. The war on terror is an incredible story. If we follow fear-generated news, watch movies and shows that evoke fear and violence and dwell on it, we will attract a vibrational match. If we chose to believe in and focus on joy and new ways of framing our societal structure, we will help attract that. The information field we generate contributes to the change and attracts new systems that serve the Common Good.

When we acknowledge our power, and then ask ourselves, "*What is it that I do want?*" we begin a gradual shift into the telling of our new story and into a much-improved point of attraction. The realization that something is not as we want it to be is an important first step. However, once we have identified that, the faster we are able to turn our attention in the direction of a solution, the better.

"The significant problems we face cannot be solved at the same level of thinking we were at when we created them." - Albert Einstein

The problem is a different vibration frequency than the solution. It is a different consciousness and that shift happens when you see the vision of change and believe you can make it happen instead of dwelling on the problem. Focus on what you want versus what you don't want.

A great way to check what you are thinking is to check what you are feeling. If you are happy, you are focusing on what you want. If you are annoyed or angry, you are often focusing on what you don't want.

A belief is nothing more than a chronic pattern of thought, and we have the ability to begin a new pattern, to tell a new story, to achieve a different vibration, to change our point of attraction. We can generate a new information field. The Law of Attraction is responding to our vibration frequencies, and we can change our frequency of attraction. It can start simply by visualizing the lifestyle we desire and holding our attention upon those images. We attract what we feel and think about most of the time.

When it is asked with heartfelt feelings, it is always given. We think we are asking with words, or even with action, and sometimes we are, but the Universe is not responding to our words or our action. The Universe is responding to our vibration, our information field made of our emotions and consciousness.

Attracting a Vibration Match

The spectrum of color is associated with specific frequencies and vibrations. At the lower vibration it is red. At the highest vibration the light is white. In a similar way our energetics can vibrate at a higher level -- into the white light. By energetic, I am referring to a measurable, experiential energy vibration always present within us, whether we are conscious of it or not.

Our energy vibrates at different levels like the electromagnetic spectrum. We are always vibrating. Moods and emotions are our feeling sense of it. When our energy is vibrating at a high level we feel uplifted, love, and expansive. Our vibration more closely aligns with the high vibrating potential energy. In that emotional state of unconditional love we become more of a vibrational match with the threshold of our physical universe.

That is why Jesus emphasized love so often in his teachings. "Love the Lord your God with all your heart and with all your soul and with all your mind.' 'Love your neighbor as yourself.'

Love is a vibration that is concentrated in our heart, which permeates our entire energy field. That vibration is a key to unlock a door to a higher dimension. Just as potential energy is in a relational field, we become consciously aware of the oneness we share.

Our mind field can also resonate at a variety of levels. Valerie Hunt measured the Electromagnetic Field of the brain with sensitive equipment developed by NASA to monitor astronauts in space. She found a significant vibrational shift occurred with a shift in consciousness.

EXHIBIT 20
CONSCIOUSNESS SPECTRUM SCHEMA
ORDINARY REALITY

O-Hz   200 KHz
(ELF ------→ ----------------------------→ --------------------------- →(EHF)

P
O
W
E
R

Grounded Material
Consciousness States

ALTERED REALITY

Metaphysical - Psychic
Hypnotic - Channeling States

TRANCE REALITY

Trance State

MYSTICAL REALITY

ALTERED   TRANCE   COSMIC

LEGEND
Horizontal: Frequency Pattern of Reality)-Hz (extremely low frequency)
to 200 Hz (extremely high frequency)
Vertical: Quantity or Power of Energy

The vibration of Mystical Reality went beyond the capacity of the equipment to measure this energy. If our emotions can be expansive, as with the vibration of love, so can our consciousness. We all have the capacity to deeply connect with our Super Consciousness.

Our feelings act as a compass as we engage the Law of Attraction. Think of what you want. In your mind's eye visualize your desire manifesting. Notice how you feel. Feelings of joy, love and happiness reflect what you want.

Now think about what you don't want. Visualize a worst case scenario. Now notice your feelings. The lower vibrations of fear, anger, hurt are usually present. We can easily fall into habits of repeating negative stories and feeling bad. We will attract more of the same.

If we take responsibility for our systems we become empowered to change them. Instead of what is wrong, look at what can be. The idea is to work on feeling happy. Nurture a positive attitude. Be grateful for something in your life. You get back the vibration you put out.

The Power of Possibility Thinking

"No pessimist ever discovered the secret of the stars, or sailed to an uncharted land, or opened a new doorway for the human spirit." Helen Keller

I noticed at an early age there are two basic categories of people: "energy drainers" and "energy gainers." The energy drainers see their glasses as half-empty. They are always coming up with reasons why something won't work. When I was around them, they pulled me down. Then, there were the "possibility thinkers". Their positive outlooks always inspired me.

When we take on a positive outlook, our energy is uplifted even in the face of adversity. When we refuse to see possibility, we cripple our own energy and limit what we are able to accomplish. When we acknowledge the unlimited potential we are surrounded by, we see the creative ability of an unblocked consciousness. We can't help but be positive.

As a business consultant, I have assessed the behavior of hundreds of managers. I have seen their decisions, actions, and characters magnified by the group that empowers them. Some of them spun the group energy down, and some spun it up. The "up" managers had at least one thing in common—they all saw inspiring possibility in their teams. These successful managers saw themselves as encouraging people to let their highest potential unfold. Managers who were always on the lookout for problems, oddly enough, seemed to encounter many more problems. Managers who prided themselves on being "problem solvers" had more problems.

Think of the people who have inspired you—teachers, managers, mentors, and chance encounters. Were these people possibility thinkers?

Children who receive positive messages of love, support, and encouragement develop more of their potential than children who hear ridicule and abuse. Seeing and acknowledging possibility in children boosts their natural self-esteem—in other words, their mental health and energy.

One advertising agency learned that the best way to launch a nonprofit environmental protection organization was to start envisioning possibility. The agency's first ad campaign centered on a long list of problems and reached the conclusion that people should have grave concern for the environment. That year, the organization raised a modest $6 million. The next year the same advertising agency with the same ad budget focused on the possibility of a healthy, vibrant environment and what that would mean to future generations. They raised $18 million.

For seven years while working at a center for the homeless and unemployed called the Pearl Street Center, I noticed people's attitudes and their resulting life's circumstances. Those who were surely, negative and complaining seemed to attract a lot of terrible life experiences like being beaten up, a continuous chain of abusive partners, not able to find work, and health woes. Those who were positive saw this as a temporary situation, found work and uplifted their circumstances fairly quickly.

Having a negative reaction to something is normal and ok. It's what you choose to do after having the negative reaction that is most important. Are you complaining about it, writing about the negative experience, telling ten friends, thinking about it constantly? All this time you are giving attention to what you don't want, causing you to include it in your vibration and to attract more.

The Law of Attraction brings you what you think about. It is your creation. Every intention is an invitation for the universe to respond. The Law of Attraction is totally neutral — it doesn't filter what you ask for. If you think about what you want, you get it. If you think about what you don't want, you get that too.

We all have the ability to control what thoughts we hold onto. What could be more just than the powerful Law of Attraction responding equally to everyone who holds a thought over time? This is also saying that you are the creator of all of your experiences, even the negative ones. You are not a victim. By taking responsibility for our life, we can take responsibility for change.

Taking Responsibility

According to the Law of Attraction we are responsible for creating our reality. We can deny responsibility and blame others for what shows up in our life. In the process we become disempowered, we are the victim of something out of our control and it is *"their fault."* Perhaps you get to feel righteous in this victim's stance.

As this book uncovers the mass deceptions we live under, you may ask *"How can I be responsible for this mess?"* There are several possible answers. One that I like is that we have allowed this situation to escalate to create a catalyst big enough to bring this planet together and push it toward an evolution. We have drawn this collective experience for our growth.

Another is that we have allowed ourselves to be deluded on a subconscious and societal level. We have allowed the .01% to create turmoil and hardship. Our society has been lulled into a trance. We simply need to wake up to the deeper reality that surrounds us. We need to take responsibility to wake up.

We also need to take responsibility for what we share in common including our schools, parks, roads and libraries. Taking responsibility for our community is an important part of restoring balance. The citizens have the final say. It allows us to say from our heart, *"As community, we are in control; we are empowered to not cooperate with corruption and evil."*

When we accept the fundamental spiritual understanding that *"you are the creator of your own reality,"* blame is irrelevant. How can you blame someone for what happens to you when you have a hand in creating everything that makes up your reality?

This is a tough realization for those being introduced to this. It's hard, too, for advanced learners. It means you have to take responsibility for everything that happens to you — good and bad. It's so much easier to point a finger and be a victim when something goes wrong.

Dwelling in blame has consequences. Blame inherently carries a victim frequency. It attracts more circumstances and events that will make you feel even more like a victim. That's the Law of Attraction. Allow an incident to make you feel like a victim and you'll soon have plenty of other opportunities to reinforce that feeling.

What if you deny responsibility for what you experience? What if you say, "*Something out there is causing these problems, and I'm only noticing what they are doing to me.*" You are not listening to the lessons coming to you through this experience.

The key to mastering the Law of Attraction is responsibility. You accept personal responsibility for everything in your life. If you perceive it, you've manifested it. Whatever you give your attention to will expand.

How do you learn to stop thinking about what you don't want? Accept responsibility for attracting it. Realize that changing the internal script will also change the external one. There comes more awareness to what your internal dialogue dwells on. This raises your consciousness and makes you more capable of successfully applying the Law of Attraction to get what you do want.

By assuming responsibility for creating your reality, you also assume the power to change it. You can consciously put more energy into thinking about what you do want. Some of those negative thoughts will still pop into my mind, but I don't dwell on them.

Taking responsibility is about empowering ourselves with the knowledge that we are the ones running the show, and all we need to do is be more deliberate about our focus and the emotions we hold. Make your life a deliberate attraction; attract more of what you want and less of what you don't want

Create a Vision for Change

"We are what we think. All that we are arises with our thoughts. With our thoughts we create the world." —Buddha

We can navigate troubled waters through the power of vision. We are drawn to what we envision and we attract others and resources who align with it. It was the method of navigation the ancient Hawaiians used to sail to remote islands in the middle of the Pacific Ocean. They "saw" in their minds eye the destination and their intuitive compass guided them. If we are to get somewhere, we need to know where we are going. We can co-create a bright future if we first envision it. Later the intuitive compass will be discussed.

Vision

- Vision comes from the Latin *videre*, to "see." The more visual and identifiable the vision is, the more compelling it will be.

- A compelling vision touches something in the hearts of all the participants, one that resonates with their values.

- An expansive vision, something beyond the actual person or organization, serves and supports society in a positive, uplifting way.

- Regardless if the vision is compelling or expansive, it should inspire in a unified way.

- Vision is always evolving; it is an expression that grows.

Vision cannot be dictated; it can only emerge from a coherent process of reflection and conversation. For that dialogue to occur, an open environment is required, one that is safe, where differences can be accepted.

Taking charge of our lives begins with clarity of vision with specific goals. Where do you want to go? If you don't know where you are going, you probably won't get there. Planning is the way we envision and create a future of our own choosing. It is based on setting and accomplishing goals that further our interests and fulfill our deepest intentions and commitments.

Tips on Vision and Goals

"Failing to plan is planning to fail." (Alan Lakein)

A goal is a specific desire, intention or vision you choose to focus your creative energy.

- The willingness to choose and to accept the consequences of your choices is the basis for personal responsibility and freedom. It is the recognition that you cannot go in all directions at once, and the willingness to channel your energy in the chosen direction.
- Choose your future or it chooses you. Goals are dreams with deadlines.
- The creative process of guided change starts with a clear picture of the desired positive outcome.
- The clearer and more well-defined the vision or goal, the more able you are to accomplish it.
- Images of desired outcomes move and inspire people toward successful accomplishment.
- The higher or more noble the goal, the more energy you get to accomplish it. The big picture is deeply inspiring. Go for a vision of greatness.
- True goals come from the heart, are personally compelling and recognizably yours.
- Go for it. Goals that are 50% believable and represent a stretch are most empowering.
- Written goals work best.
- Intention precedes method and action.

When your goals, thoughts, actions, and emotions align with the task at hand, you become present and reduce energy dissipation. Your entire energy field becomes more coherent. The same principle applies to group energy. If a group has conflicting intentions, it is weakened. As phrased in the biblical proverbs:

"Where there is no vision, the people perish."[6]

In the same way, groups need vision or their energy scatters, factions form, and their potential perishes. They easily can breed divisiveness as a key unifier is missing. There is no ability to give feedback on progress or course corrections because there is no course.

Think of a time when a group you were in was united in a common focus. That common focus was acquired through openness, dialogue, listening, and reflection. Visions that tap a group's power align with individual aspirations. They articulate goals, support the common good, share a power to inspire and elicit commitment. In this way, with everyone on board and aligned they generate a cohesive group energy field. This is when a group can make incredible achievements in team sports or community development.

Building a shared vision requires creating processes in which members of the group, at every level, in every role, can speak about what really matters to them and be heard. A true shared vision cannot be dictated; it can only emerge from an integrated process. This integrated process requires a safe environment. It means eliminating barriers, censoring, and reprisals. It means encouraging forums where the dialogue of co-creation can flourish.

While conducting organizational development work for twenty-one television stations, I asked employees when the station had functioned at its highest level, when it had been the most unified, creative, and responsive. I asked, *"Was there ever a time when the pettiness stopped, when teamwork was job number one?"* In every station, the answer was the same. Everyone remembered the big news event, the one that brought everyone's focus together and created a bond that still resonates. An example of this bonding took place at a Los Angeles TV station when the 1992 earthquake hit. The quake humbled everyone with its 7.1 power. It caused sixty-eight deaths, nearly four thousand injuries, and close to $7 billion in damage. Suddenly the TV station had an urgently focused vision: *"Help the community respond. Rally relief. Communicate the need."*

The previous rivalries between the engineering and news departments disappeared. Everyone put in long hours. The period was stressful and meaningful. People in the group felt that their efforts mattered. They were involved in something much bigger than everyday quarrels. They were all immersed in a single intention. They felt united as a team.

You don't need a tower-cracking tremor to create common intention in a group field. A good group organizer can get the same result. Leaders, like earthquakes, focus the group's vision and align people with a common goal. However, they themselves must first align to the same vision and values.

There are a growing number of issues that are much bigger than an individual, and they affect us all. Quality food, air, feeding those in need, reforming any aspect of a corrupt system within our country, all call on us to the greater need.

Either a personal vision or group vision requires contemplation and reflection to assure you are behind the overall goals you or a group hold. When issues arise, it is important to focus on the vision. See and address the problem. But don't let the vision of the problem replace the vision of the goal. So when you want to develop, evolve, and grow, either on a personal or organizational level, there is an intuitive guidance always available to support your heartfelt journey toward what you want.

The Guide of Intuition

Before Doppler radar and the Weather Channel, there was the lone hunter who could feel the changes in the weather and know how to respond. If we're at all sensitive to the intuitive sense, we can rely on this type of communication, one that is not linear. It is a holistic communication. We sense it on a cellular level.

This communication is transmitted through our feelings or images. Many are aware of the feelings that come up from being connected to the web of energy around us. You have probably noticed this when people have simultaneous thoughts as you. You think of them and the phone rings with them on the line. These "spooky actions at a distance" make us aware that connections are subtly present. We can also intuit a group's interactions, needs, and directions. We can access information fields.

66

In other words, we each have a network of neurons fired by electrochemical transmissions. This feeling network is a highly developed communication system that receives external information and transmits it internally. Without this complex mechanism, we would be unable to respond to the outer world and we would be unable to keep our inner organs functioning and healthy.

Researchers have estimated that a hundred million nerve pulses reach our central nervous systems every second. From this vast amount of data our brains construct messages. These messages that come together do not result from rational thinking. They are intuitive.

Logical thinking engages a portion of one of our brain's hemispheres, but intuitive thinking involves our total being. When we use intuition, we sense what to do on a cellular and energetic level. It is an energetic and conscious response to what is emerging.

Intuition involves receiving and listening on a subtle energetic level to messages that come from our surrounding environments. It is an ever-present telephone line sending us communications from those with whom we share connections. This also includes connection with our vision and mission.

A Harvard University study asked CEOs how often they used intuitive judgments to make decisions. Sixty-five percent said that their best decisions were made by intuition. In the past, the notion of using one's intuition may have been viewed as fluff. But in today's high-energy, fast-paced, information-burdened business environment, intuition has become an essential tool for success. In times of danger, we tend to give our intuitions the credit they deserve. Our "gut" sense can guide us.

When a decision can mean initiative development, jobs, profits or even life or death, it is intuition that guides most of these decisions. It makes sense when you consider that everything is energy, we are all interconnected, and we sense this larger energy field with our feelings and consciousness.

When we transmit what we want, there is a feedback that comes back to us. It is the response from our personal transmission guiding us to what we should do. So broadcast what you want and be receptive to feelings and messages as you respond to what is unfolding.

Ways we receive Intuition

- **Visceral:** A gut feeling. People who are street-smart, for example, instinctively know how to avoid danger.

- **Imaging:** Information that comes in images or metaphors. This was the main creative access for Einstein.

- **Inferential:** An accumulation of little clues over time that suddenly blooms into a creative flash.

- **Subliminal:** Messages that hit us right before drifting into a dream state. Dreams or daydreams help us envision previously unnoticed clues or insights. This was Edison's primary creative mode.

- **Environmental:** Cues from everyday life. A flat tire may tell us not to take a trip; a computer crash may tell us it's time to rest.

Our intuitions become strong guiding lights when we acknowledge the reality of what is possible and the uncertainty of the actual path. We can be guided by the energetic connections, however subtle, that exist between us and the emerging creations of which we are a part.

Intuition is subtle and can easily be distorted or blocked through our personal attractions or aversions. These personal wants or fears can be counter to the belief and vision you hold. Your intuitive message gets distorted by having history which makes objectivity of the subtle intuitive message more difficult. The more clear your intention the more clear your intuitive reception will be and the greater your ability to respond to the opportunities coming your way.

As an example, when I began a project as an organizational development consultant, I would emphasize my intention was to serve the growth and betterment of the organization. I made it clear that the project wasn't about my getting future contracts, placating the leaders, or having any other agendas. When we eliminate our attractions and aversions we are more receptive to the true message, instead of a false projection based on what we want.

Don't lose sight of your destination, and hold positive expansive emotions. From the feeling you extend, you also receive a response that is a feeling sense. This feeling response when honed properly provides guidance to manifest your initiative. This intuitive guidance becomes a compass among the many challenges.

As a business consultant, I used my intuitive sense often. For twenty-eight years in this profession, it was my compass, and it never failed me. Intuition is what I would consult when steering an organization through challenges and changes. You access something more intelligent than your rational thinking.

Once you get a clear message, it is important to act on it. Without action, it is as though you ignore the insight and it can get weaker next time. That intuitive voice gets stronger as you consistently respond to the guidance. You develop this communication tool by listening and responding to it.

Utilizing information fields, the law of attraction and intuition requires we look within. Based on the consciousness and energy we hold, this process is not separate from us. Are you ready to take responsibility and take constructive action to change things? It is not an easy path. My personal story in the next chapter illustrates the challenge as well as a process for system change.

Chapter 4

Local Solution with Global Strategies

This chapter illustrates the application and power of the tools presented in the two previous chapters. It is a true story that portrays one of the most painful experiences of my life. It illustrates the manipulation of consciousness and the law of attraction. It shows the struggle not to succumb to the dark side. It is a story of trust, deception, propaganda, awakening, information fields, community, strategic action and success that applies both on a local and national level. It provides a roadmap and insights for system change, a guide for the journey ahead.

1) Beliefs of Trust:

This story began in 2009 when Community ReStart explored escalating homelessness and unemployment in Berkshire County, Massachusetts. During a weekly meeting, we had housing experts and social service experts describe the conditions for this growing population.

Unemployment, homelessness, and other economic stressors were affecting over 20% of Berkshire County residents. In Pittsfield, the largest city in our county, had a population of 44,000. There were 1,663 receiving unemployment benefits; however, the number doubled when you consider the unemployed not receiving benefits and those on disability.

There was no day facility for these people. When I interviewed 73 unemployed residents in Pittsfield, the major issue was disenfranchisement. Everywhere they went they were booted out. Many people became homeless when they lost their jobs, or had medical bills that financially ruined them, or were immersed in addiction or mental illness, or the bank took over their house.

Regardless of the circumstances they became stigmatized like the "untouchables" from the old cast traditions in India.

In 2010, those who controlled the purse strings in the City of Pittsfield had a vested interest in keeping the social service system as it was, and some held the philosophy "if you make it comfortable for the homeless, they will stick around."One state rep suggested we ship them off to the next district. Tied into this "good old boy" network were the two major funding sources for Berkshire County.

Despite the opposition from the "good old boy" network and funding barriers, we felt that the power of community and compassion was stronger. Without a penny of start up funding, a small group of dedicated people started an initiative that began with compassion and collaboration.

The new interim Pastor Sharon Grant [7] had worked with the homeless in the past. She also saw how this would align with their outreach ministry. In 1996 the church set its direction as an urban ministry. This decision was supported by the success of its Tuesday evening suppers and the desire to expand services to the downtown community. As of 2010 nothing had been done, so Sharon asked if Community ReStart would make it happen. Our non-profit organization developed, owned, and managed the project and the church provided the space. Sharon's partnership was invaluable in helping to provide a valuable service.

Pearl Street Day Center

The entrance was on Pearl Street and the image of a rough grain of sand turning to a gem in the proper setting was a good image for our initiative. The Pearl Street Center provided a needed solution and vision. We brought together unused and underutilized resources. This gave birth to the first center in Berkshire County for the homeless and unemployed or underemployed.

The Pearl Street Center in its first year of operation had 4,100 visits and over 11,400 services. It was a beautiful facility in the heart of Pittsfield. The Center was meeting a burning need. We provided phones, shower facilities, mail service, computers, coffee and snacks all free. We provided an important community service, all

for $4,000 for the entire year, using the community as the major resource.

I cringe when I hear people say, *"We can't do the initiative because we don't have enough upfront money to make it happen."* That means those who control the money supply must approve and support your project. The government, large corporations, banks, and foundations often control the distribution of funding. These needs for upfront money stem from the beliefs handed down that are flawed. It stops needed grassroots initiatives from getting off the ground. Often projects are considered based on profitability, (if they make money), versus the good it does for the community. We managed to pay all our bills and do a lot of good.

For three years, our partnership became stronger as we provided 32,000 services per year to the most vulnerable people in our community. The volunteer-based program kept on growing, and many of the staff were former clients.

Minister Sharon Grant was planning her retirement, which resulted in a search for a minister with a social service background to support what we were creating. The church selected Howard Fox to take over Sharon's place. The church spoke highly of him and he was part of the ethics board for the New England Chapter. I called his old church and heard praise of him. He had helped to establish a shelter for vets and was involved with that state's Food Bank.

I unconsciously transferred the trust I had with Sharon to Howard who always wore his cross and collar. He was bright, and understood the legal maze and language having been a corporate lawyer for sixteen years before becoming a minister. I was brought up with priests in my childhood, which influenced my seminary stint. So the cross and collar still held a belief of trust and confidence.

Howard began working with me on several projects. I found him to be very competent. I enjoyed our conversations and he certainly said the right things that resonated with me. I thought my relationship with the church was moving on where it left off with Sharon.

Trust is a belief that provides a sense of assurance and safety. It provides a foundation to build things. Like with any belief system, it helps shape perception. However, beliefs can create blinders, be manipulated, and misguided trust can hide harmful acts.

2) Exploring the Organizational System

Before I go into the relationship with the new pastor at this church where we had the Pearl Street Center, I feel it is important to lay out the picture of Community ReStart and what was at stake. It also provides some insight as to what a few socially minded people can accomplish on a grassroots level.

The organization started in 2008 with no money, just volunteers serving their community. All of our initiatives began by helping to resolve unmet local needs. A snapshot of the organization in April 2015 and its services follows.

Supportive Residency Program

Community ReStart's five buildings provided affordable, clean and sober housing with a range of support that empowers people and facilitates responsible citizenship. The program being developed included:

- Affordable community-based residences
- Residencies free of drugs, alcohol, and smoking
- Single, private rooms with shared common areas
- Employment, if needed, for qualified laborers
- Healthy nutrition provided through our three gardens
- Weekly Personal Growth workshops
- Weekly facilitated resident meetings
- Personal coaching to support positive change and goals
- Community service options

Community ReStart's Houses

11 Faulkner Place

19-21 Faulkner Place

211 Francis Ave

217 Francis Ave

213 Francis Ave

Personal Growth Workshops

Community ReStart was providing workshops that focus on building social, interpersonal and professional skills, how to get a job and keep it, and various other success-building techniques. For our residents it was a basic building block for community living. A series of workshops were offered every week for residents and open to the public.

Pearl Street
Day Center

The Pearl Street Center, previously mentioned, provided a place of support, rehabilitation, and community for those who were homeless, unemployed, or under-employed. For that year the Center provided 33,000 services to our poorest residents. The Center served between 30 and 60 clients per day, five days a week.

Food Net

Since its inception in 2009, FoodNet has provided up to 21,000 pounds of fresh organic produce yearly to local Berkshire pantries and meal sites helping to serve over 90,000 meals per year. Our three gardens and greenhouse provide ample opportunities to get involved. Our network with farmers and distributors extended food access beyond our gardens.

The Food Net provided produce to as many as eight meal sites. This nutritious food went to approximately 500 low-income participants who used these meal sites and 62 young mothers and their babies. We also served the cooks at these meal sites through education on preparing different types of fresh produce. We were facilitating monthly meetings with 14 local pantries and meal sites to coordinate our food service.

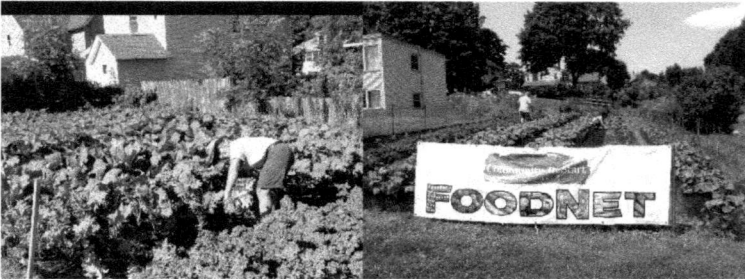

Work Force

Developed for the unemployed or underemployed, Work Force provided immediate work and income from temporary, permanent, full- or part-time employment. It was ideal for residents who needed work and ways to build their resume. This program matched competent workers with customers who were looking for affordable help. A wide variety of tasks could be accomplished, such as moving, cleaning, yard work, painting, or any labor. Prospective workers were CORI-checked and their ability appraised through our volunteer program. Qualified workers received rotating work assignments. At the time, we were sending out about 20 workers per week. This provided a stepping-stone from the long-term unemployed to permanent part-time and full-time work. We also were developing entrepreneurial businesses like an ongoing computer repair business at the time.

As a grassroots organization, we were growing. We were receiving large donations from our community. We had just received approval for a $50,000 grant and a house donation. Our income required a more sophisticated bookkeeping system. In the process of delayed filings, we temporarily lost our non-profit status. I did feel angst over that gap. At that time, we had a competent CFO getting our new accounting system set up and working on our financial filings.

The organization that had only good intentions to get it started, now blossomed into a social service agency addressing several needs of the community. Our members were proud of Community ReStart's many accomplishments.

3) Empowerment and Manipulation

Community ReStart needed a revised board to reflect the range of issues we were facing. As Executive Director, I was given the task to recruit new board members.

Meanwhile, my trust grew as I sought Howard's counsel on many occasions and found him insightful. I thought Howard's legal background would be of use because of property donations by banks. I knew how important this position was and I believed in him. I invited Howard to be Board President and he accepted.

Shortly after becoming board president, Howard acquired his own separate non-profit corporation. When I heard of it, I didn't give it a second thought because of my belief in trust.

Howard was charming and had a powerful presence. But at the time I didn't realize I was being duped. People can learn to use those skills to manipulate others and cast false impressions or hide some agenda. It is a skill that can be developed.

Howard learned those skills and honed them in a courtroom, as inflections and innuendos can have an impact on a jury. That skill can be used repeatedly to penetrate the subconscious and implant a range of misinformation. Having someone held up with trust, in a vaunted leadership position, amplifies their words to penetrate the subconscious. It is constantly used by mainstream media, as those in esteemed positions twist the truth with repeated messages, to serve some hidden agenda. When Howard began to repeat false information ... the false is believed to be true.

I had no suspicion of his plans at the time. I showed Howard respect and would constantly speak positively of him, furthering my endorsement of him. My belief system of trust blinded me to the divisiveness that had begun around me.

Howard also targeted four of the eight board members whom he felt he could persuade. The other two board members would immediately see through his scam and were avoided. So he started to meet individually with these board members. His backbiting and criticism was kept from my sight but I started to be aware of repercussions.

During this period, I began hearing complaints from some of Howard's parishioners who in the past praised our work highly. When I would enquire about a theft, or someone was treated poorly by one of the staff, or some mismanagement of a resource, I found the accusations to be false.

I guess you can call it "fake news," stories meant to deceive for a specific purpose. It is a strategy used often in today's media. However, it's the perception that registers, and reinforcing statements of a false impression penetrate the subconscious. It forms beliefs that color perception.

4) Divisiveness and Secrecy

Howard began to form his team with people who had connections with Community ReStart. Mark Christopher, a former volunteer at Community ReStart, created a partnership with Howard to develop his new non-profit. Mark was recently let go from Community ReStart because of his poor treatment of clients and questions about pilfering donation money. I found it disturbing that he moved into the attached office to Howard. I expressed my concern about Mark. He seemed to have an ax to grind and I felt divisiveness would ensue. Howard assured me it wouldn't and that he needed a volunteer with Mark's skill set.

He also hired our Work Force, part-time manager, Kevin Jones who was also a resident at one of our houses and helped manage our five properties. Without my knowledge the three started a venture called CR Workforce. The similarity to the name of Community ReStart's Workforce was no coincidence.

Unannounced to me, Howard had a meeting with Community ReStart's major donors. Howard approached them for funding to CR Workforce. Jim Conroy and his partner, who donated our buildings, started to become aware of the divisiveness that Howard and Mark were brewing. Both donors warned me something was not right.

Community ReStart's WorkForce had a contract with the City of Pittsfield to work on cleaning up the city's blighted properties. Mark Christopher stepped in and tried to take over the contract from the city for his CR WorkForce in an underhanded way. He met with the city declaring he and Kevin Jones would be running the projects. Mark informed me it was a done deal and that he now had the contract.

I met with Howard and confronted him with what had just happened. They backed off, and Howard blamed Mark for the miscommunication. I still did not equate that Howard would lie to me as I held onto the belief of trust. This is an example of how the obvious is hidden under beliefs. However, my trust was waning.

5) Sabotage and Slander

Our operations started to sputter. Our rent and program fees were not coming in and bills started to mount. Kevin Jones who collected money from some tenants said they were not paying rent. Suddenly we were over $6,000 short on our rental properties and our reserves were dwindling. We had a momentary shortfall with unexpected building repairs, but the repairs would be resolved with a $50,000 grant we were to receive.

Our sober residency program was managed by Kevin. After Howard hired him, I went to the house unannounced and found Kevin with two drunken residents on the back porch. Although Kevin was not drunk, the others were alcoholics whose stay was based on their maintaining sobriety. I put them on the wait list for a rehabilitation program for 45 days. They could return if they went to regular AA meetings. They refused to go to the program. Then they refused to leave the house with Kevin and Howard's encouragement.

This is when Howard cranked up the gossip. Word of mouth and social media projected how the programs were being mismanaged. As Executive Director, I was responsible for the operations. The short falls in our income and the difficulty with bills fueled more blame and accusations.

When investigating the missing money, I spoke to the tenants and program participants who had significant balances. When they said they had given the money to Kevin and showed me the receipts with his signature, it amounted to $6,300. I confronted him and gave him the time he requested to produce the missing money. The money never came, just more stories.

I fired Kevin, and he removed his belongings from our office and moved in with Mark and Howard. Despite the pending court case, he remained the foreman of their business. I set out to evict Kevin with his two buddies who snubbed treatment. They all refused to leave our house, peed on the floor and trashed the place. The sheriff's department got involved. This further stressed our financial situation.

Howard called a special board meeting to discuss financial concerns and what he referred to as *"significant management issues."* Being Board President, he had the right to hold a special meeting.

I had a sense of dread as I walked into the conference room. There was a heavy energy that seemed to weigh me down. My greeting with a smile was met with castaway eyes from the board members. Then my gut felt tight when Howard walked into the room with a very stern look.

He announced that there were very serious issues occurring and that the viability of the organization was at stake. He started by displaying financial information I had not received and said that we would have difficulty paying the mortgage and insurance on our buildings. That our clean sober housing program was not working. That I was the one to answer to the board, and that I was the one overseeing finances. When I tried to respond, a board member started to say I should find something else to do and leave the city. It was becoming clear I was being set up.

Howard said that I was jeopardizing the organization and that my behavior was reckless. He went on a rant blaming me for the financial problems, having alcoholics overrun our houses, and saying that the Pearl Street Center was a flophouse. Full of righteous conviction he said *"No one likes you; no one wants to work with you."* Then with his veins popping on his neck and with a red face declared, *"You must be removed from the organization."*

Howard timed it so that one of the other board members who saw through his scam was not present. This left Jim Conroy and me who understood his intentions. His months of backstabbing and working the four board members paid off. During the meeting any time I tried to explain what occurred, they would not listen but talked over me. Even when I showed we were not in financial difficulty because of the grant and donations we were receiving. No matter what I said, Howard had assured the mindset of the board majority. They kept on hammering home that I must be removed.

I had not realized the scope of Howard's plan until this point. I was shocked that he could turn people against me in such a vicious way, people who respected me at one point in time. When I brought up what was becoming more apparent, that Howard was attempting to take over the organization, I was hit with a wave of opposition. How dare I accuse *"Reverend Howard,"* a man of God, of such wrongdoing? *"He is trying to save the organization because of your mismanagement."*

Then Howard demanded I leave the room as part of the Board Protocol while they discussed my fate. As I sat in a room down the hall the shock of this betrayal began to sink in. I clearly got that Howard was out to destroy me through slander, and blame me for sabotaging the organization. I got to feel what a false flag attack is like.

I was in a state of shock. I saw now whom I was dealing with. It was a sudden unveiling. I was "blind sided" by Howard. What kept me blind to his harmful blow was my belief in the mask he wanted me to see.

I was called back in the room and I sat down to hear their judgment. Howard announced he wanted me out of the organization immediately. The other board members wanted to give me until October for a reorganization plan that they would consider. It was decided that the CFO would be in charge of the management and would report directly to Howard, who would oversee the organization through this "crisis." I would report to the CFO, who was deaf.

This was so upsetting and overwhelming that I sat there in shock after everyone left except for Kathy Cardella, my girlfriend, who was the sign language interpreter for our CFO. The gravity of my situation began to weigh me down. When I got up I felt dizzy and nauseous.

The vision in my left eye began to shut down. It was like a lens of a camera slowly closing. My periphery vision went black. I braced myself on the wall. Then my vision narrowed to a tiny pinhole. I felt weak sliding down the wall, collapsing to the floor and lost sight in my left eye. The ambulance came as I lay on the floor literally dazed by just what happened. While I lay in a hospital bed, Howard continued his takeover attack.

6) False Flag Attacks

Just before this, I had all the final paperwork ready to accept a $50,000 grant from Wells Fargo as well as a four-apartment building on a half acre close to our other buildings. The board had made all approvals for the grant the month before with all documents signed and ready to mail. Instead, while I was in the hospital, Howard confiscated it before it went out.

The grant would have been more than enough to handle our short fall due to the sabotage of Howard's employee. In addition, it was an important step for our housing program as we were developing affordable housing stock for those committed to their recovery from addictions.

Our main donor and sympathetic board member had worked with me on assessing the Wells Fargo grant and building. We had architects explore options and we had gardens planned for the Food Net. We saw that $20,000 would allow us to meet our obligations of the grant. The remaining would strengthen our finances. Jim Conroy and his partner, a former bank president, saw it as a solid plan to address our housing stock.

I knew Howard was sabotaging our financials to blame it on me. But I didn't think he would go this far. Without any consultation with me, Howard had convinced the board majority to cancel the $50,000.00 grant from Wells Fargo Bank. The board had approved the grant at $25,000. I even negotiated another $25,000 donation. It was in the works for 7 months. While I lay in the hospital, it all dissolved.

This shows the power of his influence when he labeled the grant as *"a glorified Ponzi scheme and seriously reckless."* We were receiving a cash grant and a four-apartment house; there was nothing to his unsubstantiated assertions. He did not communicate with the two board members involved in the project. He focused on talking with the four other board members he had control over. For Howard to make a decision to cancel the grant that we needed, after all the requirements of the grant were met, showed his malicious intent.

I could not rectify it. I later called my contacts at Wells Fargo. They said they would not consider us again because of the rude treatment, threats and cancellation of the contract by the board President and CFO.

Howard convinced the other four board members to not question him, and they were resigned to do his bidding. Through creating false perceptions, then weaving his story and assuming control, he made a direct attack on the survival of the organization. The board is analogous to the congress and senate who approve harmful acts to democracy and liberty.

7) Awakening

In the hospital after the MRI and range of blood and eye tests, I found I suffered a type of aneurism in my left eye. As I lay still in the emergency room, my eye sight began to return. I was wheeled into a semi-private room. By then the dizziness had subsided, and about 90% of vision in my left eye returned. After my consultation with the doctor, it appeared that only slight permanent damage was done to my vision. It was a great relief and good news that I could share with Kathy who was by my side.

During that evening as I lay still in my hospital bed, I began to reflect on my situation. For seven years, I had poured myself into this organization never receiving any financial compensation for working forty-hour weeks. We were serving over a thousand people a month and that was my payment. The organization I poured myself into was in the process of being taken over. Howard had control of the board, and legal control over the organization. He knew the game and he was about to use it to remove me in October.

I knew the organization would not survive with Howard, Kevin, and Mark at the helm. Community ReStart was based on volunteerism where people are inspired to participate by the organizers and by how fulfilling their work is. There is nothing inspiring about deception, manipulation and theft.

I now saw for the first time the type of person I was dealing with. Awareness is both powerful and scary. I was no longer blind to the slick pastor who loved quoting the bible. I was able to remove my beliefs of the church and previous pastor. I could now see the strategy, approach, persona and actions. Now many strange incidents made perfect sense. Now I could see Howard's orchestration of dark energy of divisiveness, slander and secrecy.

I was waking up to a nightmare. The board president had taken administrative control of the organization. He undermined me through slander and actually creating problems and blaming me for them. He heavily influenced four board members. It was all "legal." From any perspective, it looked bleak. Howard's plan was leaked out by Mark Christopher bragging out loud, *"I kicked Paul out of the organization and we are taking over the initiatives and assets under our new Corporation."*

In many ways, it was similar to when I woke up through the 9/11/2001 attack to the true terrorists and the controlling deception and manipulation by the elite few. I found it interesting how similar tactics were used to create deception, slander and manipulation to take what was not theirs to take.

I do believe in the law of attraction, I take responsibility for what unfolds in my life. In that way I am never the victim and everything comes to support what I want if I maintain a high vibration. So why would I want this?

At this point in time it hit me why I attracted this to myself. The image was clear. The week before Mark Christopher moved in Howard Fox's office, I was going through the draft of this book, thinking that I needed a compelling story to illustrate the challenge and solution to this global dilemma. I was looking for a story that would explore the challenge of becoming "aware." I needed a story that would show a path to get out of the corrupt control and manipulation of the government and legal system by using higher principles. I needed something to mimic the dire situation. I never thought the story would hit home like this.

If ever I was to use the principles I so deeply believe in, now was the time. It involved shifting my beliefs so I could listen to reality. I could use nature's laws to effectively change the apparent bleak situations to co-create a bright future. Utilizing the Law of Attraction, and the responsibility that comes with that, was my first reflection. I knew legally I had little to stand on because he controlled the board. I also realized that truth, love and light eventually overcome darkness. But for me to manifest this I had to address my own darkness. Facing my reaction of hurt and anger were to be part of my spiritual practice.

I was about to do battle. It was a war I did not want. I don't like putting myself in situations of conflict. Yet this organization was like a child to me, a big part of my focus for seven years. It was serving the most vulnerable people in our society. I knew its success could help our societal transition to Common Good systems. To get the organization back, I needed to use higher principles.

It's taking a stand, holding a sword of Truth and Light. But it takes a high energy and vibration to possess and hold the sword. It takes clarity to swing the blade that does not harm, but instead transforms. A spiritual warrior can wield the sword that no dark force can withstand. Light overcomes darkness.

To be a warrior requires preparation. I contemplated my next steps. That night with monitors beeping near my hospital bed, I felt a deep commitment to take on the challenge ahead.

The doctors wanted to keep me for an extra day for more tests and observation. Kathy and I booked a cottage on the shore of Cape Cod, Massachusetts, as the doctors recommended a 10-day rest. This was my time also to prepare as a spiritual warrior.

8) Hold a Sword of Light

When Kathy and I arrived at our small clean cottage, I was weak and my stomach was bothering me. I was not motivated to do too much more than rest and enjoy the beautiful day. My thoughts moved far away from the drama of Howard Fox. The disengagement was important in my healing.

By disengagement I mean not only no emails or phone, but also no internal mind chatter about what occurred. My thoughts and awareness instead were focused on the distant horizon, seagulls, seals, and rolling waves. If thoughts came about Howard, I would refocus to the here and now and the beauty around me. I knew by unplugging I would gain a new perspective and stay away from low vibration energy.

Meditating on the warm sand, the healing sun on my skin, being along the ocean was like an old friend who had just the right healing balm for my wounds. My past of spending my summers growing up on Narragansett Bay, being a lifeguard, an oceanographer, and an oil spill scientist studying coastlines brought all those parts of me alive. It was a great way to get out of the drama.

There were huge schools of herring swimming along the shore with seals stirring up the school's movement. Kathy and I went on long kayak paddles along the shoreline. She was another reason for my rapid healing. She was nurturing and loving with a great sense of humor and playfulness. Kathy was the perfect companion for my hiatus.

My energy returned and my head cleared. I was grounded in my resolve to create a solution and I knew I could not do it when my energy was down, when I felt beaten. I needed to heal my wounds and gain my strength to be a warrior.

On the seventh day after the Board meeting, I felt a strengthened energy stirring inside of me and I felt I was ready to explore my next steps. It is hard to see lofty visions and have an expanded consciousness if your energy is contracted. I needed to explore a solution from a place of well being. If I saw it through the eyes of fear and gloom, I would only attract what I feared. Now I was in a very different place from a week ago.

The model of a spiritual warrior is Gandhi. He held the vibration of love and non-violence and was able to transform a nation. It is a commitment to hold that high vibration connection even if crucified. The spiritual warrior holds love and forgiveness in the face of cruel unjust attacks. The commitment to love must penetrate the subconscious and dissipate beliefs that justify anger or an "eye for an eye."The energy of anger and revenge only attracts more of the same. Even with that knowing, I had waves of anger rise up.

I reflected on how a parent would respond to a pedophile minister molesting their child. It is easy to evoke anger when you think of the devious minds that would destroy an innocent life for their immediate perverted pleasure. I felt like my child was being harmed. On a collective consciousness level it is easy to swing into rage and retribution. In so doing I would lose my sword and means to shed light on darkness.

I didn't want that constricting, poisonous energy poring through me. It dampens my spirit and connection; I am the one who suffers if I go to the dark side. The low vibration breaks my connection; I even shut down my immune system.

To attract the blessing of Light and its mighty sword I must be connected to the Light and that means holding a high vibration. I had seen the destructive power of holding dark energy and it's never good.

Provoking anger was a strategy used by contracted saboteurs sent in by the CIA to disrupt 9/11 truth groups. Their strategy was to get people angry, mistrusting, and generate divisiveness. Slander, backbiting and sabotage were their major weapons. Similar to what Howard used. Leaders who were positive and had an attitude of non-reactive acceptance of what the government was doing, fared much better than those who reacted with anger and fear.

I worked with 9/11 truth activists who were outraged by the activities of this banking/government/industry/military complex. They held that rage inside them. They would alienate themselves, get sick or their group would fall apart. There were saboteurs who used emotional attacks to evoke a low vibration response and thus the group would lose their connection and cohesiveness.

When I was facilitating grassroots groups, I would emphasize not to provoke or respond in anger. I would help direct the members to take that energy stirred and use it to fuel positive strategic actions. Let the actions come from Truth and Light, which can be difficult to discern normally and near impossible when you hold a low vibration.

.   I lacked evidence to clearly show Howard's intention. I was dealing with a corporate lawyer, so I would have to start gathering data. Part of my tactic was not to react when provoked by him. What normally happens is that the provokers keep on escalating their destructive scenarios to elicit a reaction. So my strategy was to record Howard's increasing destructive scenarios as a way to show his behavior and expose his true intentions.

I was ready to return. I had no idea what Howard had waiting for me. My heart was open and I had a sword of Light ready to cut through darkness. I knew I had to be strategic and I looked at the situation as a four-dimensional game of chess. The fourth dimension was time. I was ready to take a warrior's stand and plan things strategically over time.

My intuitive guidance warned me of the level of slander I was about to face. Now that Howard's secret undermining was revealed to me, he knew how I would respond. I was facing a formidable opponent. I had to be clear about myself, as he would try to cut me and the organization down in many ways.

The way false flag attacks work is that first; someone creates a problem, and then blames it on a country, an organization or a person who has what they want. They then use the false blame as an excuse to invade, torture, or kill their opposition. Then they steal what they want. It is an evil we do not associate with ministers, "proclaiming God's word" or government officials sworn to protect democracy.

The morning I returned from Cape Cod, I received an early phone call from a friend saying there was a disturbing article in the paper. It said that Howard Fox is intervening because of financial difficulties within Community ReStart. The article went on to say that Reverend Fox is stepping in to help *"save the organization and the miss-management by Paul Deslauriers."*

Another friend called saying there were a bunch of nasty posts about me and Community ReStart on face book. The perpetrator was Bill Summers, a former tenant who stiffed us for two months rent and was caught smoking pot in our clean sober house. After vacating, he later broke into our house and was caught in bed with a girl with drugs; we had to issue a no trespass on him. He now was part of Howard's team. Bill considered himself a social media expert.

The afternoon of my return, I had an executive administration meeting. There were four desks in a big office with a round conference table in the middle. My office manager and Kathy arrived. Kathy's presence would provide an extra witness to Howard's next plans.

Howard then arrived with the CFO and our grant writer who were both Board members. I wasn't expecting Howard to be part of the executive meeting. That is when he declared, *"Community ReStart was in financial default. As Board President I have the right to intervene and take over the organization, it is a public asset and in this crisis, I need to oversee things."*

I asked Howard to leave, as this was an executive team meeting, there are clear boundaries for the board president that he was crossing. That is when he said, *"This is no longer your executive team, it's mine."* I looked at the three members, their eyes were down cast, as if they wanted nothing to do with this confrontation. In my absence, it appears he asserted control. Then he went on how he is now taking over CR and transferring and merging it into his Development Corporation.

I saw how he was provoking me to react. He had a smirk on his face and watched me intently, thinking that I would have a melt down so he could claim I am incompetent and irrational. He actually announced he was taking charge of the properties ($380,000 in assets) and put them under his own Corporation. He and Mark would take over Work Force and the Food Net. Then he went saying, *"I'm not sure what I will do with Pearl Street Center."*

A spiritual warrior is grounded, especially when provoked. Let feelings come up for they provide intuitive connections. However, stay the witness to the feelings, and do not let the emotions carry you away. Howard was provoking an emotional reaction. Little did Howard realize that I was playing a game of chess. I was amazed at the boldness of his statements and moves. He must have thought his cross and collar made him invulnerable.

I calmly responded, "I have one month to present my transition plans to the board. This decision was made during our last board meeting and it remains. I have been acting according to the Board's directions, and there has been no board meeting to change this decision."

Then I enthusiastically presented a small part of my transition plan. I had two managers to take over aspects of the operations. The first person was a housing expert who was my manager when I ran the Cot Shelter. The other person was a gardening instructor and farmer. She would bring in two grants and double our gardens. I was truly excited about my plan and expressed it at the meeting.

I could see my up attitude, despite what he just pulled, was the opposite reaction he was expecting. I didn't give many details but it was enough to let him know that I had a solid plan to counter his move. So I used that enthusiasm as a way to provoke Howard, which it did.

Howard, with a scowl, raised his voice and said, "I *am taking control of the organization; your plan won't work and I need to address the organization's crisis.*"

With a smile, I said, *"I disagree. I understand what you are up to."*

He stood up red faced, angrily pushed his chair, and left the room.

9) Understand the Oppressor ... Be Strategic

Not long after the meeting Howard closed down the Pearl Street Center without letting the staff or clients know. I was shocked; this had been an important service that hundreds of people relied on. I was flooded with calls begging not to close the facility. This further exemplified my helplessness at this stage of the game. Why would he act so aggressively to shut down a needed service? The motivation eluded me, so I did some digging.

I discussed the dynamics with two close friends who were respected psychologists. Their response was the same, *"you realize you are dealing with a Psychopath."* They then explained the nature of psychopaths and Howard's actions fell into place.

A psychopath can be defined as a person who has Antisocial Personality Disorder. This disorder is characterized by a disregard for the feelings of others, a lack of remorse or shame, manipulative behavior, unchecked egocentricity, and the ability to lie in order to achieve one's goals. Psychopaths can be dangerous. So it is best to avoid them, but in my case I was caught in his grasp.

They are con artists who always have a secret agenda. They are great at charming people, because they know how to get what they want. This type of charmer knows how to make people feel special, to ask people the right questions about themselves, and to shape their thinking. They are skilled actors whose sole mission is to manipulate people for personal gain. Howard certainly did that to four board members.

Psychopaths possess a strong mental acumen and can perform well in academics/skill without cracking a book. However, they use their intelligence in order to manipulate and hurt people, instead of helping them. Their extreme intelligence is part of what makes them so dangerous, because they will often be several steps ahead of people who are on to them and are able to cover their tracks. Howard was very smart.

They are "cold-hearted" and calculating. They carefully plot their moves, and use aggression in a planned-out way to get what they want. If they're after more money or status in the office, for example, they'll make a plan to take out any barriers that stand in the way, even if it's another person's job or reputation. Howard followed his calculated plans well.

If the person is a true psychopath, then everything in their world is about them and their plan. In my case, Howard angrily blamed me for the stress he felt over his struggle to take over Community ReStart, which actually happened. No consideration at all for what he had done to the organization, its clients, or me.

Psychopaths are willing to hurt whomever whenever if it means that they will achieve their goals. Many psychopaths are highly successful in corrupt systems that value this behavior. You will see in the next chapter how they influence the systems we live in. They even become president.

Psychopaths like to prey on the strongest people they can deceive unseen. They create slander to discredit any opposition. They can be delusional to the point where they believe that their lies are the truth. This is what happened to Howard as he kept on repeating his negative stories.

Howard used people like puppets. Like many psychopaths, they will also have a huge sense of entitlement, thinking that they deserve for others to create amazing things for them, without consideration for their wellbeing. They don't care about others, just wish to use them.

There are two key strategies that can be used in confronting psychopaths. They are based on a psychopath's two biggest fears: Fear of losing control and exposure.

The fear of losing control means that they cannot dominate like they imagine. The loss of control is a fear that his house of cards is collapsing on itself. So removing some of Howard's assumed power would strike at his fear and became one of the strategies.

Psychopaths also have a fear about being exposed. When strong people are around, they are afraid to get caught. They fear exposure because it breaks the veil of their charismatic charm. This is how they win people over, by manipulation, compulsive lying, and deception. They are chameleons and are capable of being anything to anyone, depending on what the person wants. The psychopath is the master of illusion and depends on not being found out

If you were to expose him, he would lie, and would discredit you, say anything about you to remove the likelihood of you being credible. He would say things like 'you are crazy' or anything to show himself in a good light, and you in a bad one.

It was best not to expose Howard directly in the newspaper because he can manipulate that perception. If you expose him directly, he will make you pay. It is never a good idea to expose a psychopath. The outcome would be lies, smear campaigns. It would add fuel to the fire.

He claimed that our organization was doing poorly financially and as Executive Director it was my responsibility that the books were not being balanced. The proof was in the balance sheet, and if I tried to explain the source, Howard would position it as my blaming others for my failures. His statement as board president, *"he was forced to remove me to save the organization because of financial mismanagement"*, is based on manipulated half-truths that allowed Howard to weave an image. It is the same strategy used by the .01% but on a far greater scale. The approach to deceive and manipulate perception is similar.

Howard Fox was masterful at playing the legal and deception game. There are ways to make legal claims to take what is not yours and ways to make immoral acts legal. Having been a corporate lawyer for 16 years before taking on the guise of the cross and collar, he knew the language and how to create a façade. But as long as he maintained a veil of illusion with these four board members and manipulate their perception, he could "legally" do what he wanted to the organization. The same strategy is being used on a global scale.

I did not know how this injustice could get resolved with his legal claims. My intuitive sense told me to keep on compiling data. It was mounting, and Howard kept adding to it.

10) Gather the Facts

Shortly after the Executive Meeting I received an email from Howard announcing a special emergency board meeting the following day. Before the meeting I was shown a different email to five board members: he wrote, "After Paul's recent outburst to staff and me, I am ready to vote him out as Executive Director today". The outburst never happened. Kathy, who was at the meeting he referred to, was amazed that he would write that when he was the one who got agitated.

When the board meeting began, Howard and two members he had coached said that I needed to move on and let Howard take over. Then Howard made up stuff about his need to be in charge. When I tried a rebuttal, Howard talked over me. I also saw it was futile because he had the majority in this forum.

The board did not fire me that day as Howard wanted, but would wait for them to consider my transition plan. The board went along with Howard to silence me and not allow me to represent Community ReStart. I had to report to the CFO who reported to Howard before making a public statement.

Within days, his partner Mark Christopher was claiming to be the property manager of Community ReStart's real estate and that they were taking over the five buildings under his Corporation. I found our Food Net sign crumpled and stuffed in the trash can by the Pearl Street door. Over the 6 years of serving Pittsfield, I have never experienced such negative energy.

I knew I was taking the stance of a spiritual warrior, but the slander took another level of absurd. It made me reflect how he was expressing the worst of who he was and then projecting that on me. Despite my reflection of Howard's mental state, I was hurt.

Consulting with lawyers there was little I could do as long as he had the majority of the board's ears. I felt that if one other board member would reconsider what Howard is up to, it could sway the tide.

I carefully constructed a legal brief with the help of friends with legal backgrounds. The ten points documented Howard's deception and attempt to take over Community ReStart. It included 32 pages of back up proof. I had a legal clerk and an investigator help put the proof and points down very methodical. I had my case and was ready to put it out.

I sent a copy to the board including Howard the day before the board meeting, the reason being I knew he would scramble to reply to each of my points. He spent the night writing ridiculous excuses and stories to justify his actions. The level of contradictions made his strategy for the hostile takeover even clearer. It was exactly what I needed if this went to court.

The October Board meeting opened with the Catholic nun being self-righteous and asking how could I accuse Howard of wrongdoing. I asked if she read what I wrote and she said, *"I refuse to read this garbage. You should retire and leave peacefully and not stir things up"*. She was cold stern and accusing with no room to listen to anything other than what she was lead to believe by the person she referred to as *"Reverend Howard"*.

Then our deaf CFO being interpreted by Kathy said, *"You should leave now. Let someone else take over knowing you helped a lot of people. I can take care of the remaining business needs. You need to go."*

Then Howard went on to put me down. I just sat there. I knew that this part had to play out, I said nothing. The board majority had all made their decisions before the meeting; there was no receptivity for a transition plan. The board had decided to give Community ReStart to Howard. According to Howard it was check mate. He was gloating with a big smile. *"You are hereby removed from Community ReStart."*

Howard then demanded I take away all my belongings from my office immediately. I vacated my apartment in 30 days and received a severance pay of a beat up Saturn with 215,000 miles needing repair. Howard Fox knew I had given all my money and energy to the organization, and that my focus was selfless service. Howard wanted me on the street in 30 days, destitute. The joy he was exhibiting and big smile was very disturbing. It just affirmed I was dealing with a psychopath.

I unceremoniously removed my belonging from my office. I started talking with friends and was surprised to hear similar stories from organization builders who were ousted from their creation through devious means. This dilemma is reflected in our society as well.

Howard was not done. He then shut down the Food Net and took the $5,000 raised to start his own Food Hub. He wrote to my 68 participants telling them in an email that he was shutting down the Food Net and he had to fire Paul because of his incompetence. Then he promoted his newly formed Food Hub to the same group.

Next he shut down Work Force and transferred the operation with all our client info to develop their CR Work Force. There was Kevin Jones and Mark Christopher with Howard gloating at the impending demise of Community ReStart.

Two days later, on the front page of the Berkshire Eagle, read, *"Community ReStart's Executive Director has been removed from the organization and Howard Fox was asked by the Board to help remedy the distressed organization."* Things certainly appeared bleak.

These were difficult days to keep my heart open. I held my vision and I did not doubt this would turn around. I also believed that this was a test of sorts. If I held true to my heart and my connection, it would be a testament to the law of attraction when we succeeded. Yet not reacting in anger was tough. Some nights I would sit alone, cry, and let myself feel the hurt and let it pass through me. Then I could be more present with the joy that would await me after I accepted my hurt.

11) Communicate with Others

During the two months after my hospital stay. I received many calls from well-wishers. I was vague in my response of what was happening. I didn't want to disclose until I had plenty of data on Howard.

I needed to expose the truth of Howard's intentions. At first, no one would believe that the bible-quoting minister could possibly try to take this non-profit through devious means. Not many people were seeing the psychopath hiding behind charm, and a cross and collar. The present mind set when I brought up Howard's intention at the board meeting was, *"the disgraced incompetent executive director is trying to lash out at the kind minister trying to save the organization."* To change the mindset I needed clear evidence. My ten points and Howard's response was a good place to start.

The two most important people to inform of Howard Fox's plans were the two people who donated the organization's five buildings. Jim Conroy and his partner were dismayed by the financial and PR mess, but when we went through all the ten points they were convinced of Howard's evil intent. I reviewed Massachusetts law that gave a strong voice to donors who give to an organization and then have that donation taken by unethical means.

That is when they both agreed to stop Howard from transferring the major asset of the organization. They hired a lawyer to go through Attorney General's regulations and our Bylaws. We had a legal stand. Jim and his partner met with Howard and threatened a legal battle that would expose him if he tried to remove the properties to his corporation. With this threat of a battle he knew he could not win, he backed down. He wasn't taking the properties or shutting down Community ReStart. That was the first victory.

There were about 100 friends in the area that I had worked closely with over the years, starting with our local 9/11 truth activists. We had successfully undertaken the opening of an emergency cot shelter, a transportation access, Time Banks, and other projects. They felt like my brothers and sisters.

I established a core working-group of 14 trusted friends and former board members. Several of them helped form Community ReStart. I also had several core people who were working with me on existing initiatives in the organization. I met with them individually going over the ten points and discussing strategies. When I reviewed the facts, several of them got angry or upset. Then we would discuss utilizing the law of attraction. We would discuss using that energy being stirred up for positive action. It was a tremendous relief to have a bright team ready to do battle.

At our first meeting in my apartment, I felt excited and strengthened by the support of the people I had worked closely with. We were committed to keeping a positive and uplifting energy. It would have been easy to rant about Howard who they referred to as "Reverend Evil". Our group understood and wanted to apply the "Law of Attraction" as an integral part of our strategy. Joe Jackson, one of the core group members, kept on emphasizing not to engage in a pissing match because it will only bring our energy down and distract us from the task at hand.

The main task was enacting our organization's bylaws. We formed them to assure the power and the final say would rest with its members. The way we structured the organization in our Bylaws, the board is not the final arbitrator. . The board president does not have the final say to kick out the founder and executive director and try to take over or destroy Community ReStart's initiatives. The members are empowered to remove the board president. Members have the final say. Just as in the US, the citizens have the final say. The final say is not with deceptive people who hold office in high places.

To make this strategy work I needed to amass clear evidence. The group felt we had plenty to stand up in court if needed. The most important thing was to inform the 87 members who helped develop

Community ReStart. Let them know about the hostile take-over attempt and how dire the situation was. The membership needed to gather and vote on removing the Board President. We scheduled the event in three weeks

Our core group communicated to members. Some were arranging the meeting space. Others investigated Howard's past, with possible legal representation and help from the Attorney General's office.

This core group was a boost and uplifted me. As we divided tasks, and worked as a team and a community with a positive attitude, we were accessing a higher power.

When a group comes together holding truth and the sword of Light, no dark force can stand up to it. Light conquering darkness is more than a metaphor.

12) Have an Inspired Vision

Our core group saw Community ReStart continue to develop a sober supportive housing program based on community and personal growth. The Food Net and its gardens were thriving, and our new green-house providing nutrition to the most vulnerable. The vision included people having employment through our Work Force program and getting back on their feet. It was a wonderful vision we knew was possible because we had been doing it before.

Our core group was clear in what we stood for and the good we could do in our community. We could communicate a unified vision. This included repairing and furnishing our buildings, and developing sober housing focused on personal growth and community. Although smaller, our initiative would be focused on a key unmet need in our community.

The uplifting vision was one part; the other part was feeling good, no matter what the affront. Helping to manifest this vision means to be happy.

Keeping my heart open and connected to the Higher Vibration while in the middle of vicious attacks is not easy. It requires constant monitoring of thoughts and emotions. If I were to go to the dark side and hold anger or fear, I would attract what I didn't want. What type of energy field do I chose to hold in my aura? What type of information field do I want to create and project? My choice to hold a sword of Light meant I chose to hold a high vibration and a clear vision. That requires vigilance.

12) Grassroots Organizing

Our core team's weekly meetings and ongoing emails and phone calls brought us all closer together. When we discussed issues and strategies we listened to each other with respect, everyone was contributing as a team.

What was fueling our endeavor was this sense of positive collaborative engagement, a sense of community and justice. It was boosted by the gravity and timing of the possible destruction of what we had all helped to create in Community ReStart.

As the core group made phone calls to members they discussed what happened and if they wanted more info we sent them the ten main points showing Howard's deception, slander, and sabotage with back up proof. There was a growing circle of support that eventually encompassed the 84 members of Community ReStart.

When Howard got wind of our organizing, he did what he has done in the past, spreading slander and sabotage. He targeted Jim Conroy with legal action for trying to evict Howard's staff who were trashing the houses. The attacks were actually a galvanizing force for the core group, underscoring what we were dealing with.

As our solidarity grew, so did the ideas on how to get the organization back. Some wanted to go to the newspaper and lay it all out, some wanted to picket his church during his Sunday service, some wanted to put signs in the church widows declaring the devil resides there, some wanted to trash Howard using social media. They were strategies fueled by anger; instead, we kept on affirming a different resolution by taking a higher road.

The day came for us to organize on the next level. Our membership meeting was held on a cold dark December 15 night at the Pittsfield Library in a large conference room. Despite having many members in Florida and other warm places it was a good turnout. The large room was overflowing with chairs in the hallway to accommodate the 56 people.

We introduced our core team and then presented a power-point show of the many accomplishments we made in 7 years. I got to acknowledge the many people who helped the initiatives be successful. My main point was to show what the board president was tearing down. Our core group members spoke of our bylaws and our legal rights to stop this injustice. When we formed the organization in our bylaws, we made sure the members would have the final say, and they were about to have it.

When we started to discuss the attempted hostile takeover, the four representatives of Howard Fox who were in the meeting began by making ridiculous accusations that the members showed to be false. They even came with a list of attack points. That is when all the other people in the group came together and became a unified voice. One of the four was filming and refused to stop. She was escorted out and the other three followed.

We next held our vote of confidence of Howard Fox as board president. The tally came in as 49 votes of no confidence in the board president and removal. There were 0 votes of confidence in the Board President. The following day on the front page of the Berkshire Eagle the headline read, *"A Unanimous no Confidence Vote: Board President Gets no Support."*

Now it was our turn to use the legal system, so we thought. With a 100% no confidence vote and wanting his removal we thought Howard would willingly step down. Our core team next wrote a letter requesting his resignation so we could move on peacefully and continue to serve our community.

Instead, he began efforts to file bylaw changes with the MA Attorney General. His changes would disempower membership and the sole power would be with the board president and board majority. So the legal battle continued.

This played right into Howard's hands supporting his efforts to bankrupt the organization. If he could continue to hold the organization's control and delay any income, he would bankrupt the organization. Legal delays would do that. He thought it would be checkmate. He was encouraging his staff to break in the houses at night. We had to deal with puddles of piss on the floor and building damage. These same people during the day spent it with Howard.

14) No-co-operation

An important aspect of the law of attraction is holding a clear vision of a final goal, see it as if completed. We held our vision of our resident program, Food Net, and Work Force and felt uplifted and joyous about the services they would provide. We also began to act as if the vision was here. So we began planning to get the initiatives up and running.

We had confidence that Howard was losing his grip on Community ReStart. More and more people were finding out the truth. The entire take-over was based on sabotage, manipulation and slander, a stack of cards that we saw would fall.

Our volunteers and people aware of Howard's strategy unplugged. Our donors unplugged. Even those we served unplugged in large part due to shutting down the Pearl Street Center. I didn't respond to Howard's emails regarding my moving out of my apartment. No one engaged and refused to cooperate with Howard or the people he controlled. (Except for his resignation)

What Howard had was an empty shell and some manipulated legal claims. The heart of Community ReStart is its volunteers, its donors, members and those who receive its services. It is a community of mutual support that sustains its existence. The essence of the organization is the people who participate. That is the organization's lifeblood. The essence resided with our members who shared our vision. Likewise it is the citizens that are the lifeblood of society's systems. If enough people unplug what the elite have is an empty shell.

The slander and social media attacks by Howard continued. One core group member was targeted by Howard and she wrote a scathing letter to Howard's parishioners, which our core group decided not to send. Our communication was about restraint and moving forward toward our vision. Howard kept on writing emails attacking. We did not respond, and that only escalated his attacks. We proceeded, as if Howard was no longer a problem. We refused to drain our energy in discussing conflict or how evil Howard was. Instead, we moved forward to handle the issues needed for the organization's survival. We had our weekly core group meetings. We looked at the condition of our houses and the procedures to re-engage our membership.

We nominated nine new board members and five advisors to replace the existing board. We ratified the board at another membership meeting that we held on January 12. So a legal claim was that our membership voted in a new board and president, Jim Conroy. We didn't waste time taking action.

We had a crew who were able to get the buildings clear of the vagrants and begin maintenance on two empty buildings that could house ten people. We were able to get a donation for materials and began work on repair.

But the fact remained. Howard would not let go. We trusted that the Law of Attraction would bring the right solution.

15) Expose the Truth, the House of Cards Crumbles

Howard and his minions kept writing on social media a wide range of slander. In addition, Howard's emails to our core group and new board were vitriolic. We didn't want to distract our energy from the task at hand by engaging in stuff that Howard was making up. But that didn't prevent Howard's emails.

Here are some of the actual words Howard used: *"If you ever get the organization you will fail miserably. I regard your fake board as psychologically challenged to the point that you are becoming a danger. You are not the salvation of anything, and frequently you are the cause of great damage to people. You are deceptive to yourself and others. You are an autocrat. You belittle and badger your subordinates into obedience and compliance. You see the world as revolving around you. I do believe that you are mentally ill and need help, but I doubt you would seek that, you prefer to follow delusions of grandeur. You are miserable followers of a lost cause."*

These were just some parts of rants he sent our core group. Joe Jackson in particular would discuss restraint as Howard was trying to engage angry interactions. It was the strategy of a psychopath, so we didn't take it personally. We even checked among our group if any of Howard's claims held any truth and could find no substance.

The constant negative barrage did not deter us because we realized that these words reflected the energy swirling in Howard and could only attract negative scenarios for him. The information field he extended would only attract his end.

In late January, one of Howard's minions, a computer whiz, hacked our core team's email correspondence. He then posted it on several large social media sites using it to attack Community ReStart. He didn't realize that the long string of emails also contained Howard's emails. Our communication was about holding love and not reacting with anger or engaging in the hate Howard was extending. It actually made Howard look very bad.

That day I got emails saying: *"The truth has at last come out.".* *" Like a festering boil the gunk was finally being released."* *"I'm glad people following these posts get to see the negative crazy person who created this mess."*

Howard's two biggest fears, losing control and being exposed, were coming to reality. Some of his parishioners got hold of the communications. They confronted him. When you look at the energy he held while writing his emails. It was not surprising that he would attract failure.

The following day Howard wrote to us saying he was stepping down as board president as well as the board members that supported him.

I felt a dark energy lifted.

16) Community ReStart

On February 3, three of the newly elected board members signed papers with Howard and transitioned the legal control of Community ReStart to its members. After the meeting, we all adjourned to my apartment to celebrate. We took a collective deep breath and acknowledged how bleak it looked at times. We got through it. Everyone acknowledged how good it felt to keep a positive attitude and not operate at the same energy wave length as Howard.

We all realized we had a lot of work laid out in front of us. We moved our office to one of our buildings at 11 Faulkner. We had a crew move our files and desks with our furniture. It was our organization's new home.

Then we went over our books and talked to community leaders to assess the damage that Howard and his minions orchestrated. It was extensive. With the cancellation of the grant, Community ReStart's lost income was $95,000. Lost program fees and theft were included. And, on top of that, the PR damage was very significant

We knew we were taking on a big challenge. Howard wanted the organization to disappear so as to wipe out any evidence of his wrongdoing. His parting words to our board members were, *"You will never succeed."*

Despite these financial and reputation challenges we faced, our core team and members felt positive and enthusiastic to make our vision a reality. We focused our vision on a growing unmet need in our community: safe, affordable, clean, sober housing. There was the need for nutrition for our most vulnerable population.

Within six months all building repairs were completed; our program design, resident criteria, and agreements were in place. We had 18 residents and a growing wait list. Our organic gardens were once again producing.

Epilogue

Kevin Jones was convicted of stealing $6,300, spent time in jail for his crime and then put on probation for one year, with the stipulation of paying back $1,000 to Community ReStart. He still works for Howard Fox

Mark Christopher worked with Howard for another four months. Just as he did with Community ReStart he was taking money and his reputation spread as a very difficult person to work with. He was let go and lives alone unemployed with his parrots.

Eight months later, Howard Fox was described to me by a board member of his church in this way. *"Howard would always complain about you behind your back. The irony is that everything he accused you of he has done himself, but even worse."* He paused and gave his statement further consideration. Then said, *"Actually it's at least three times as worse than his accusations of you. The board has to rein him in and clean up his messes."*

The Real Battle is Energy and Consciousness

When you hold light and affirm love and joy ... you win the battle. You will attract a vibrational match for what brings love and joy. When you hold a vision with others, you help make it happen. If your informational field is held with others with a high vibration, you win. When you shine your light, you dispel darkness. These oppressive systems crafted by the .01% feed on darkness. They cannot exist in light ... and we will prevail.

Chapter 5

Global Solutions
with Local Strategies

In physics, the laws of gravity and electromagnetism repeat from the macro to the micro. Gravitational force applies from the dropping of an apple to the movement of the galaxies. From the electrical energy powering your lights to the electromagnetic radiation in the Universe, the same principles are at play.

Likewise, the laws of energy and consciousness apply to a non-profit organization facing a hostile takeover through devious means. The same principles apply to nations in the throes of a hostile takeover by devious means. Light dispels darkness regardless of the scale. This approach can free us from the societal trap, whose teeth are closing.

As an organizational development consultant, I look for processes and procedures to help assure a smooth transition. If I were to choose a process that would help us get out of this serious global situation, it would mirror the sixteen points described in the previous chapter.

The following takes each component to liberate Community ReStart and shows how it is a road map to liberate any nation from oppressive control. It is a direct way to rid ourselves of the exploitive systems that generate a low vibration of fear, divisiveness, and debt. It is a guide to peacefully transition to Common Good systems.

Just like the previous story, it begins on a personal level with the formation of beliefs that provide a blind trust. The first six points discusses how the corrupt systems were formed and the scope of their impact. Points seven and eight are about awakening and taking the stance of a warrior. Nine through sixteen are progressive actions to transform elite systems into ones that serve the common good.

1) Beliefs of Trust

Underneath all we perceive is all we believe. Our filter system of beliefs is always active. It affects all we take in from our environment, shaping our thoughts and actions. Our unconscious beliefs and collective unconscious are the primary framework of our life and what we perceive as real.

Inculcated for generations our reality is shaped since birth. The collective un-coconscious pieces together and reinforces perceptions. If we are brought up in an environment where the parents, siblings, friends all believe the same thing, it becomes part of your beliefs and perceptions. Beliefs include that the United States is the land of opportunity and freedom. The messages are repeated in the pledge of allegiance, one of the first things I memorized when I went to kindergarten. War movies portrayed the US as the good guys. I had many beliefs like most citizens that reinforced the general perception the United States was beyond reproach, an image that filtered stories to the contrary.

In Chapter 2 we explored how these beliefs are malleable. They can be revised by repeated images and messages. In many ways we are programmed to see the world a certain way. Repeated themes include: The United States stands for democracy and freedom, the terrorists are out to get us, pay your mortgage and taxes, the United States is the land of opportunity, strive for the American Dream ... blah, blah, blah!

But these are mere hollow slogans burned into our sub consciousness through repetition. There is a constant drumming of beliefs to reinforce the system through propaganda, deception and mixed with a wide variety of media platforms. The resulting subconscious implant shapes what we perceive as real. Behind that false perception is a planet ripe for the taking.

Marginalize the population by having them chase trinkets and possessions. Have advertisers paint ridiculous pictures of what it's like to own the latest thing. Believe that chasing after these things is what matters. A distraction is continuously being played by the surrounding media. Emphasize things like fashion, political and celebrity dramas, and the latest gadgets instead of awareness of what is truly going on.

We can hold beliefs that no one in our government could commit horrendous crimes like 9/11/2001 on its own people. It's incomprehensible. However, systems that are corrupt will encourage corrupt people rise to the top. A proportion of theses leaders are psychopaths, what the system requires suites their nature. The acts of psychopaths are often too horrific to believe. This further masks the perpetrator.

For myself, I didn't believe that an ordained minister would sabotage our social service programs, blame the failures on me, and then use slander to take the organization. Also, it was too outrageous at first to accept that 9/11 could be an inside job. Or even the wars instigated by the US are used to steal trillions and kill millions, all with US tax money, to enrich an elite few. I was naive to think people could be capable of such acts for personal gain, until I saw a psychopath up close.

Like my beliefs from the church, they were superimposed on Howard to provide a perception of trust. A veil can be a cross and collar, a police officer's badge or a politician's office. These beliefs become reinforced to create what is familiar. Individuals and societies will often choose to suffer instead of letting go of the "known" or the familiar. Even if the familiar is feudalism, or Wage Slavery, many would prefer that than growing into a new way of operating.

The systems are crafted to deceive, distract and extort wealth. The system even claims US citizens as their property if they get a social security number. It cascades into modern day enslavement and nearly everyone is unaware. But that is changing, and awareness is starting to grow. Still we are operating in systems that makes the 99% indentured servants with a modern monetary twist.

The constant shaping of our subconscious by the elite few provides a smoke screen for their nefarious acts. But now the repercussions from these systems are so blatant it can no longer be ignored. Take the growing wealth disparity as an example.

2) Exploring the Social System ... Follow the Money

An indicator of living in an exploitive system is unprecedented wealth disparity that continues to escalate. The decline of the middle class is not something that has happened all of a sudden. Rather, there has been a relentless grinding down of the middle class over the last several decades. Millions of our jobs have been shipped overseas, the rate of inflation has far outpaced the rate that our wages have grown, and overwhelming debt has choked the financial life out of millions of American families.

Every single day, more Americans fall out of the middle class and into poverty. More Americans fell into poverty recently than has ever been recorded in history. The number of middle class jobs and middle class neighborhoods continues to decline at a staggering pace. Look at these trends and determine for yourself if these Elite Systems are extracting our wealth and labor.

- In the United States today, the wealthiest one percent of all Americans have a greater net worth than the bottom 90% combined.

- The number of Americans that fell into poverty (2.6 million) set a new all-time record in 2012 and extreme poverty (6.7%) is at the highest level ever measured in the United States. In 2015 there were 43.1 million people in poverty according to the US Census Bureau.

- Most Americans are scratching and clawing and doing whatever they can to make a living these days. Half of all American workers now earn $505 or less per week.

- More than one out of every seven Americans uses food stamps as well as one out of every four American children.

- The poorest 50% of all Americans now collectively own just 2.5% of all the wealth in the United States.

Only FOUR out of 150 countries have more wealth inequality than the US. In a world listing compiled by a reputable research team [8] it was shown the U.S. has greater wealth inequality than every measured country in the world except for Namibia, Zimbabwe, Denmark, and Switzerland.

Despite our moral intuitive message, we have been seeing

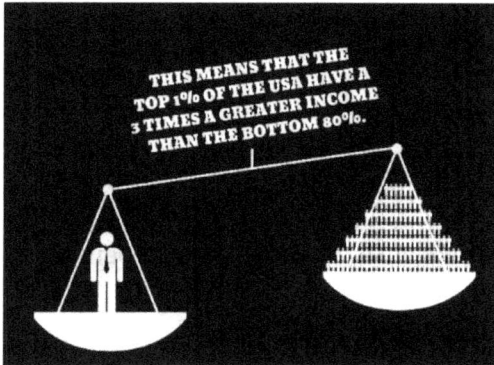

large corporations manifest the motto, *"greed is good,"* But that motto, belonging to Elite Systems, somehow justifies thievery, regulatory non-compliance, and misrepresentation in the name of profits. And those who suffer in such Elite Systems are the 99%.

This growing economic and well being divide between the elite and the rest of the population is a wakeup call. Its mechanism is to fleece the population through monetary and regulatory scams that need to be brought to light and transformed. The top 1% in the USA presently has three times the income of the bottom 80% combined. [9]

The pie graph shows .01% of the population control 81% of

Global Distribution of Wealth

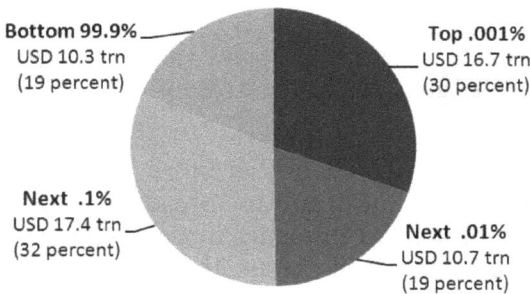

Bottom 99.9%
USD 10.3 trn
(19 percent)

Top .001%
USD 16.7 trn
(30 percent)

Next .1%
USD 17.4 trn
(32 percent)

Next .01%
USD 10.7 trn
(19 percent)

James S. Henry, 2012

the world's wealth. The distribution of total liquid net worth in the world per person in 2012 is depicted. The chart is divided into the top .001% (91 thousand people), the next .01% (800 thousand people), the next .1% (8 million people), and the bottom 99.9% (6 billion people). [10]

Elite Systems stretch globally and greatly impact the 99%. The more we can understand its nature the more effectively we are able to respond. They will do what they can to prevent organizing and to misinform the masses. Even getting factual information out will require creativity.

The Elite's ownership and influence over major media conglomerates result in a filtering, fabrication and spin of the message that we are being fed, increasing their ability to shroud their true activities. They oppose any form of government that does not adhere to their brand of 'globalization.' This globalization includes the Elite's plan to have a private Central Bank operating all nations' currencies. This empowers the "arbitrary authority" of the elite. It's a different type of global subjugation than the old British Empire, but still enslaves the population and feeds the coffers of the already fabulously wealthy.

Refer to the Appendix A to get a snap shot of the long history of battles with the banking elite. Appendix B and C show how vast the system is and how it impacts our health, wealth and well being.

3) Empowerment and Manipulation in the United States

Four characteristics are integral to Elite Systems: consolidated control, lack of transparency, disempowerment of the masses, and wealth and legal disparities between elite and the 99%. The goal of its engineers is to end democracy and have control through fear, debt, intimidation, and systems that make it all seem normal. Their purpose is to benefit the elite few who control monetary, media, commercial, and governance systems.

A huge shift of power occurred in 1913. Woodrow Wilson cut a deal with five banking families that essentially gave them the power over the monetary system. He gave them control of the Federal Reserve.

Wealth translates to power, which brings more wealth and even more power. From this foothold, it began to spread to a variety of institutions like a virus out of control infecting more and more of the systems and morphing into a horrible beast that preys on the masses.

Power and money provide the means to change legislation such as tax distribution, deregulation, and corporate governance. The architects of society rig it for themselves. But they went much further. They used the Office of Naval Intelligence early on and then developed the CIA and State Department. They have overthrown sixty-seven democratic nations, killing millions, displacing millions, putting citizens under brutal dictators, who took orders from the ultra rich. This was done using US tax payer money and military, all to provide more wealth and control for the elite few and their cronies.

In the '50s and '60s the United States' middle class blossomed with free education, good manufacturing jobs, and a wide variety of professions that paid well. One breadwinner could afford a family of 5 providing a good education for his children and a comfortable house, with retirement savings. The American Dream was real for many, it was for my family.

Then people began to wake up to the corrupt system. During that time the number of protests and demands for change was growing and the Elite felt they were losing control to democracy. Women's rights, civil rights protests, college demonstrations against the Vietnam War, unions gaining worker rights, and new forms of social systems made it appear their control was slipping through their fingers.

The backlash by the Elite has been devastating. It illustrates how they can manipulate our societal systems in a relatively short time to change the fortunes of the vast majority. They changed the systems to reduce democracy and reduce the challenge to their control and dominance.

The .01% attacked the wages. Between 1969 and 2009 the median wages earned by American men between the ages of 30 and 50 dropped by 27% after you account for inflation. Between 1973 and 2007 the average U.S. non supervisory wage adjusted for inflation dropped by 18 percent.[11] This has been during a time when automation has greatly increased worker productivity. An average worker needs to work a mere 11 hours per week to produce as much as one working 40 hours per week in 1950.[12]

They changed the playing field so laborers compete with world markets. This provided leverage to destroy unions, make the population fearful through job insecurity. Outsourcing of American jobs to foreign countries in the name of corporate profit has left blue collar workers struggling just to feed their families. Back in 1980, less than 30% of all jobs in the United States were low-income jobs. Today, more than 40% of all jobs in the United States are low income.

More than 40,000 US manufacturing plants closed in the past ten years. In 1970 the percent of wage and salary workers who were members of a union was 23%. By 2011 union membership was at 11.8%, now it is 10.7%. So labor representation declines and good paying jobs were removed.

Another part of their strategy was to change the economy from manufacturing to a financial paper economy. This is where the "banksters" have enormous control. They could create enslavement through debt. Since 1971, consumer debt in the United States has increased by a whopping 1,700 percent.[13] Inflate education cost and then enslave students to a life of debt. According to the Student Loan Debt Clock, total student loan debt in the United States surpassed the 1 trillion dollar mark in 2012. Most of that debt is owed by former members of the middle class.

They redesign the political and regulatory systems through corporate lobbyists. Regulation policy and enforcement is controlled by the businesses being regulated. Keep on empowering your political representative with money from travesties like the Citizens United decision. Make policy and spending to funnel money more directly to .01%. Keep the military industrial-complex profit machines humming by spreading war through the US contrived "War on Terror".

Push down the tax burden to the 90%. After paying an average tax of 22.5% from 1987 to 2008, corporations have paid an annual rate of 10% since. This represents a sudden $250 billion annual loss in taxes. Then bail out banks as if they are too big to fail, making it a double theft. Then they withhold wages from a single mom with three kids for filing the wrong papers.

They emphasize a middle man insurance scheme that transfers billioons to the elite. Under these systems our populations' health is deteriorating with diabetes, cancer and depression at an all-time high. The United States is ranked last in health among modern nations. Yet Canada, France have workable programs to model after.

Our education system has declined as students are given rote memory versus creative and critical thinking courses. College has become a mechanism of financial servitude with loans being paid many times over.

At first glance it's astounding how an elite few can impact so many. But from a systems engineering perspective, it is not surprising. Hierarchy is top down. When they gave these top dogs the Federal Reserve and access to all aspects of government, the shadow government was empowered. Help shed light on the shadow to dispel its darkness.

Just as the Elite puppet-masters restructured the systems that run our society so we too can restructure it for the common good. Community ReStart was empowered by its members and Bylaws when it acknowledged that they have the final say. Likewise, the US Constitution empowers the US citizens by giving them the final say. Now is the time to make a statement for change.

112

4) Divisiveness and Secrecy

The pyramid structure indicates how the control of the masses is vested into a few. In ancient Egypt the top of the societal structure was never questioned as the pharos was considered a god. The division of ministers and priests allowed the leader's orchestration of the nation's people and resources. The Pharos reign was in harmony with the people, nature, and a higher power. Their pyramid was all connected into a continuous whole. The Pharos was responsive to all their connections. Perhaps that is why they reigned for 2,800 years.

In our present ruling system the pyramid is disconnected at the top. There is a separation from the needs of the environment and citizens and a focus on their own self contained agenda. Their agenda is covert and the self proclaimed leaders based on family ties and nefarious confections make the all Seeing Eye. Like the eye on top of the pyramid in the movie and book "Lord of the Rings" it was bent on the destruction of mankind.

The goals of those who control this top pyramid are not the betterment of man or for the masses to reach their potential. It is about creating and reinforcing a system that furthers their agenda of control and domination. The signature of these systems is that they consolidate power at the top and are secretive. The entire system structure of the Elite is based on a wiring that allows the control by a few while unanswerable to the 99%.

In these Elite Systems there is a maze of hierarchy set in place to discourage dissent and change. The maze is a long path of requirements, approvals, and provisions that make any substantive change from the bottom of the pyramid impossible. When dissent about the imbalance in the system is expressed in peaceful ways, media distorts the protest; saboteurs are brought in so they incite violence among the peaceful protestors to justify crack-downs. Examples are in Appendix C and D.

Elite Systems provide the illusion of citizen participation and choice. In reality money controllers have power over deciding who will be the next political star to carry out their will. Politicians who oppose their plan find themselves struggling to stay in office.

On the Elite Road, secrecy and closed door operations are how the decisions are made and policy develops. A smoke screen of supposedly complicated negotiations, bi-partisan fighting, and deals becomes the excuse for the policies. Or they create a crisis so they can implement their plan as part of the imagined solution.

They create organizations they invest with power and privately elect who is in control. Some examples are the Federal Reserve, Tri Lateral Commission, Council on Foreign Relations, the North American treaty and the International Monetary Fund. All efforts are to create overarching mechanisms that consolidate military power, governance and currency. Steps of advancement translate into steps of allegiance in these organizations.

The ultra elite are well hidden from public view. They hire front people to create the illusion that their puppets are in control. A good example is JP Morgan considered one of the wealthiest Americans in the 1920s. When his will was publicly revealed it was shown that he was a mere front person for the Rothschild Empire.

Often layers of compartmentalization complicate a true picture of what is occurring. Operations are divided into tasks and functions so few can see the big picture. Layers of bureaucracy often cover the true perpetrators, and most importantly fracture the pieces of the plan so few get a true picture of what is going on. Each department controlling a single piece leaves only the executive team to see how it all works together. This reduces those who know the true strategy decreasing the probability of a leak. It also makes its source difficult to detect.

They are well organized in their secrecy. Realize that there has been, and most probably continues to be, significant efforts to prevent an organized opposing force from forming. I have seen the divisive strategy of their goons in the 9/11 truth movement. There are significant efforts to create divisiveness among the population. Paid saboteurs are brought in to incite incidents to fire up factions. Marginalize the population by having them go after each other, anything to divert attention, like unpredictable politicians. This is covered in chapter 10. It has been an effective mechanism: immigrants vs. citizens, black vs. white, racial unrest, gang wars, gay vs. straight, abortion vs. right to life, Republicans vs. Democrats. The propaganda machine engineers divisiveness among the masses.

A growing number see that the US government and the corporate world have secretly fused together, in a scheme to relegate the population to serfdom. Their collaboration provides a power that no individual can go up against. However, when the 99% come together, they generate a force that can eliminate this exploitation and install systems that benefit the community.

5) Painting False Perceptions .... Social Engineering

Social engineering can influence invisible control mechanisms in all of us. Experimenters began in earnest on humans with John B Watson. These scientists found they could employ a variety of techniques to get people to do what they want and stop people from doing what they didn't want them to do. It is the scientific reproducibility, the control, and the unawareness of the person being manipulated that makes it an important tool of the Elite.

Humans can then be seen as machines that can be manipulated by the 1% and create the illusion of a democracy. People can be programmed for certain actions; we are malleable and can be redesigned and shaped without our awareness or consent. You may not be aware of how pervasive social engineering is.

Virtually all law and governance has the effect of seeking to change behavior and could be considered "social engineering" to some extent. Proscription on murder, rape, theft, and littering are all policies aimed at discouraging undesirable behaviors. Governments also influence behavior more subtly through incentives and disincentives built into economic policy and tax policy, for instance, and have done so for centuries

Social engineering is often more apparent in countries with authoritarian governments. In the 1920s, the government of the Soviet Union embarked on a campaign to fundamentally alter the behavior and ideals of Soviet citizens, to replace the old social frameworks of Tsarist Russia with a new Soviet culture. A similar example is the Chinese "Great Leap Forward," an economic and social campaign of the Communist Party of China as reflected in their planning decisions from 1958 to 1961.

The Nazis themselves were masterful at influencing political attitudes and re-defining personal relationships with the state. The Nazi propaganda machine under Joseph Goebbels was a synchronized, sophisticated and effective tool for creating public opinion. *"If you tell a lie big enough and keep repeating it, people will eventually come to believe it. The lie can be maintained only for such time as the State can shield the people from the political, economic and/or military consequences of the lie. It thus becomes vitally important for the State to use all of its powers to repress dissent, for the truth is the mortal enemy of the lie, and thus by extension, the truth is the greatest enemy of the State,"* Joseph Goebbels.

Non-authoritarian regimes, in particular the United States, Great Britain, and Australia, tend to rely on more subtle social engineering campaigns that create more gradual, but ultimately far-reaching, change. On the Elite Road it is not the truth that counts but perception. The "War on Terror" has shaped much of our foreign policy and drained the United States' coffers. The manipulation of the media plays a large role in this deceit of creating an Elite/Banking/Corporate-run "false democracy" where power brokers can flourish.

Control of the media is essential to engineer consent. When I was a business consultant I worked closely with 28 TV broadcasting stations from 1987 to 1993. I dined with broadcasting executives who often expressed their concerns about the FCC regulation changes. There were an alarming number of mergers and buyouts, and they were seeing the repercussions in their industry. The only groups to win these merger bids were large corporate entities run by right wing extremists. These executives knew that when diversity is lost, and the group controlling the media has an extremist agenda, our ability to get to the truth will be greatly diminished.

In 1983, 50 corporations controlled the vast majority of all news media in the U.S. At the time, Ben Bagdikian was called "alarmist" for pointing this out in his book, *The Media Monopoly.*

These corporations owned and operated 90% of the mass media --
controlling almost all of America's newspapers, magazines, TV and

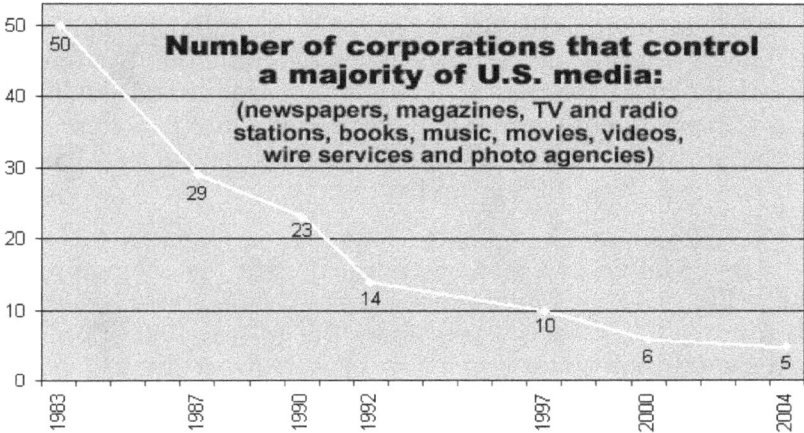

Number of corporations that control a majority of U.S. media:

(newspapers, magazines, TV and radio stations, books, music, movies, videos, wire services and photo agencies)

Year	Value
1983	50
1987	29
1990	23
1992	14
1997	10
2000	6
2004	5

radio stations, books, records, movies, videos, wire services and
photo agencies. In 2004, Bagdikian's revised and expanded book, *The
New Media Monopoly*, shows that only 5 huge corporations -- Time
Warner, Disney, Murdoch's News Corporation, Bertelsmann of
Germany, and Viacom (formerly CBS) -- now control most of the
media industry in the U.S. General Electric's NBC is a close sixth.

It is not only that the top down control of the news that make
up or distort stories, it is that journalists are being complicit. As the
vehicle through which information from the outside world is
captured, sorted, edited and transmitted into our homes, the mass
media has a huge responsibility. It shapes and informs our
understanding of events to which we don't have first-hand access.
The reporters, producers, and directors have a great responsibility to
report the most important news in the most objective way. Aside for a
few pockets of truth reporters, a major portion of main street media
is shaped by the Elite and their agenda. See Appendix C on Social
Engineering.

There are even more sinister uses of media control, the Elite's
most profitable venture, war. They get to charge the tax payer
exorbitant prices for the weapons they explode. They get to cause
great harm to a country and their people, steal their resources, charge
exorbitant prices for fixing the infrastructure they just destroyed, and
then the IMF charges interest to further enslave the remaining
population in debt. Then residents get to live in fear as drones fly
above with their deadly payloads.

6) False Flag Attacks

Nothing invigorates and empowers an authoritarian regime more than a spectacular act of violence. The Elite Systems use violence and fear as leverage for extracting freedom and wealth. The "War on Terror" has been a windfall for the Elite Few. From September 2001 to 2015 it has cost the US tax payers $1.7 trillion[14]. So you can see some of the motivation to orchestrate a "War on Terror".

Acts of terror and violence never benefit the average man or woman. They only benefit those in positions of power. There is a simple formula that always works under the guise of deception. It is a formula used by politicians and power brokers for centuries.

Nero fiddled while Rome burned from fires he set according to historians.[15] He had his scapegoats of Christians to blame, torture, and throw to the lions. Seventy percent of the capital of the Roman Empire was rebuilt in his own image and further restrictions were made to the freedoms of the citizens. The modern day process is: cause great harm, blame someone else who has what you want, attack the innocent victim for what you did, kill thousands, take what you want, and further enslave the masses. It's a formula that repeats itself.

This is why there are hundreds of documented examples of governments staging attacks in order to blame them on their political enemies.[16] In every civilization, in every culture, in every historical period, authoritarians have known that spectacular acts of violence help to further consolidate their own power and control. It is happening in countries throughout the world.

But when you look at recent false flag attacks, the United States has taken the most brazen and destructive path. Some of the greatest destruction of human life and property this world has ever seen has been perpetrated by the Oil/Banker Barons' covert strong arms. The CIA has sponsored terrorism in the 30 countries listed in Appendix B using this false flag strategy further illustrated in Appendix D. However, there are two false flag attacks that still have a profound impact on our US society today, and the world.

The first occurred in August 1964 when the public was told that the North Vietnamese had attacked a US Destroyer in the Gulf of Tonkin on two separate occasions. The attacks were portrayed as a clear example of "communist aggression" and a resolution was soon passed in Congress authorizing President Johnson to begin deploying US forces in Vietnam. The second attack was the primary reason cited to justify full involvement in the conflict.

`In 2005, an internal NSA study was released concluding that the second attack which provoked the war in fact never took place. The war hawks told a lie to plunge us into a war.

In effect, 60,000 American servicemen and as many as three million Vietnamese, let alone as many as 500,000 Cambodians and Laotians, lost their lives.[17] Now consider the tens of thousands of birth defects because of Agent Orange, the toxins left on the land and within the people who fought these wars. Let alone the mental toll on veterans and survivors.

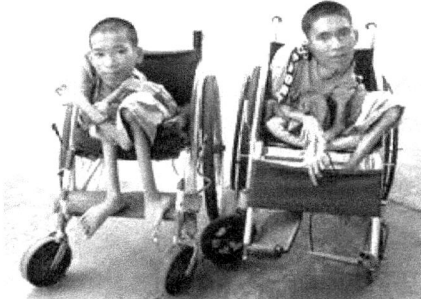

Their most brazen attempts to delude the population into a perpetual "War on Terror" is 9/11/2001. From the architects' points of view, they are a raging success. They have taken trillions of dollars in booty, caused the deaths of millions, displaced millions and further enslaved the US citizens and the rest of the world.

When you look at the facts and the content of the 9/11 Commission Report, the US government's "official story" it shows the cornerstone of the government's evidence of two planes bringing down three enormous skyscrapers (including Building 7), at free fall speed, is built on a fabricated story. It's a story repeated over and over to make it appear as true. Facts contradict the story, go to the Appendix D.

An investigation is needed. Irrefutable evidence pointing to the towers' collapse and the attack on the pentagon does not even come close to the fabrication that made the 9/11 Commission Report. The Commission failed with over 100 other questions, omissions, inconsistencies and implausible scenarios. All efforts to get a recognized independent investigation have been blocked.

These false flag attacks were used in Afghanistan, Iraq, but more recently in Libya. In 2011, shortly after Obama admitted the presence of covert operatives on the ground in Libya, (identified as CIA agents by the New York Times); he also admitted the goal of destabilizing the Gadhafi government. Foreign mercenaries were brought in to kill civilians and then the media blamed the Libyan government for killing its own citizens. They were able to use propaganda to justify an invasion by UN allies for "humanitarian reasons". Now the entire country is being ransacked, but that does not make the media. Syria is another country under US attack.

US Citizens can't even question these facts. Despotism now bears the mantle of "security." People are waking up and realizing that the questioning needs to go to the highest level and this delusional veil, shrouded as security, needs to be lifted.

An informed and engaged public is far less likely to go along with wars waged for power and profit for the Elite few at the taxpayers' expense and the greater expense for the countries invaded. And as the public becomes better informed about the very issues that the media has distorted for so long, they realize that the answer to all of the manipulation is to no longer support the distorted perception that they sell as news. Instead, get your news from independent reliable sources such as the Corbett Report (www.corbettreport.com) or Boiling Frog Post (www.boilingfrogpost.com). With spreading the truth more people can awaken.

7) Awakening

Awakening is the expansion of our consciousness to embrace a deeper truth. It is a breakthrough of limiting beliefs. A removal of the veil of delusion that hides what is truly going on and prevents seeing from a new perspective.

Waking up from this societal delusion can be as easy as turning on a light switch; but we may resist turning on the light because it may trigger fear. Sometimes the truth is horrifying; it brings up terror and despair. Especially if you are awakening to a corruption that seems so vast; the tentacles of the beast have spread far and wide (Appendix B). It may seem too vast and overwhelming and lead to despair, inaction or resignation.

When I awoke to the intention and trickery Howard had orchestrated, it shocked me to the point where it sent me to the hospital. I was literally blindsided. Awakening can be startling and overwhelming. It can bring up great fear as a nightmare appears to be true.

A poll was taken of the scariest movies of all time. On that list was a cheap B movie, "The Night of the Living Dead". What was horrifying was not its production, but its story line. Mothers, fathers, brothers, and neighbors suddenly turned into flesh eating zombies that want to kill you. The people you trust so deeply all of a sudden want to eat you alive. Finding out that the people we had elected and trusted are actually part of the force orchestrating global terror is a shock. It's a nightmare scenario.

Large portions of the population don't realize that their freedom is at stake. We are in danger of financial serfdom. The next wave approaches. Yet the vast majority doesn't realize that shackles are being forged. That is why the appendix is dedicated to lifting the delusional veil and exposing the true enemy and danger we are facing. We need to motivate beyond the propaganda, delusion, and beliefs that prevent action. True awakening, even to horror, brings strategic action that deals with reality.

Carlos Farer in "*Pedagogy of the Oppressed*" showed that true learning and change needs to be grounded in authentic rebellion. Action that liberates us from oppression is the key change agent in our society. It builds momentum based on expanding awareness. If you oppose an oppressor, you get backlash that often motivates people further to change the corrupt system. Our innate motivation for change, learning, and action is our deep desire for the freedom and well-being of ourselves and our children for generations to come.

Many recovered alcoholics have often shared with me how they had to hit rock bottom before they were ready to change. Running a center for the homeless and unemployed, I often hear stories of suffering, abuse, and disenfranchisement. But most times it is this very suffering that propels them forward to change their circumstances and awaken to a new approach to life.

Enough of today's population are feeling the backlash and strain of higher prices, lower wages, fewer work opportunities, and have outrage at seeing banking and corporate interest rule the US government. The vast majority of people is feeling the pain and wants to embrace change. They are ready to awaken.

The movie "Wizard of OZ" depicts an important lesson. Toto drew back the curtain to reveal the Wizard pulling an array of levers that put on a display to deceive the population. This tale gives a key strategy. Once the man behind the curtain was revealed, the wizard's mythical powers vanished and the travelers got all of their wishes fulfilled, realizing the answer was always there ... inside them.

The wizards I am referring to are far more sinister than the Wizard of Oz. They are hidden by the curtain of the media, layers of bureaucrat maze, and front people. They manipulate the levers that produce images that deceive and distract us from important topics affecting our lives.

This curtain of delusion is presently thick and opaque. The vast majority of the population goes on with their daily routines as if nothing is alarming, and yet an intuitive unease is telling many, "Something is deeply wrong." Instead of following this inner warning they push on with earning money for the mounting bills, watch mindless TV shows or receive irrelevance and partial propaganda draped as news. However, the impact of the wizard's levers can be seen and felt through the depressed housing market, rising health care costs, devaluation of the dollar, collusion of big business with government, escalating debt and run-away military spending. People are waking to the levers of the corrupt system.

Like the Wizard of Oz, once exposed, the mythical power disappears. We are pulling back the curtain exposing the .01% of the population, who are shifting the levers that are choking this nation and planet.

We could confront the Wizard, but he is really hard to find. We could dismantle the complicated levers and mechanisms on this road, but it is booby trapped. Another strategy is to turn off the Yellow Brick Road, to a road with new and improved systems. By changing roads these elite mechanisms have no control over you; the Wizard can only affect those who chose to drive on the Yellow Brick Road that leads to a false promise and enslavement.

A growing number are realizing that we do not need to subjugate ourselves to these systems. It is a catalyst for action. A catalyst to take a warrior's stand! Having knowledge of a strategy to get out of this mess can replace fear, concern, and disempowerment with hope, creativity, and empowerment.

We need to waken to a revolution! Not a revolution based on anger, anarchy and pitchforks. It is an evolution of awakening and empowering starting from within. It's an evolution to empower individuals, communities, and states, to reclaim their sovereignty and fight for the liberties of their sovereigns: We the People. Awake to the liberty that is possible through community and grassroots systems. The most powerful awakening for many, as it was for me, comes when you commit to holding a high vibration.

8) Hold the Sword of Light ......Be a Warrior

The warrior I refer to first does battle internally, breaking through limiting beliefs and unleashing the power of love. Gandhi, Martin Luther King, Jr., and Mother Teresa are warriors who held the sword of Light and dispelled darkness.

A sword of light is only held by the true of heart. A heart steeped in truth is vibrating in love. Truth and love vibrate at the highest spectrum, radiating a white light.

The power of the sword comes from our connection to a higher power. A warrior uses the laws of our deeper nature to do battle. A crucial peaceful weapon is the Law of Attraction and, as you will see, the very nature of energy. The sword bearer must be a vibration match of the sword, hold love in your heart to face opposition.

"Power is of two kinds. One is obtained by the fear of punishment and the other by acts of love. Power based on love is a thousand times more effective and permanent then the one derived from fear of punishment." Gandhi

Only love can empower a Sword of Light. A Warrior truly understands the nature of love: overcoming that which separates oneself from other life and instead compassionately embracing that which unites all. The energy of hate, fear, anger, and divisiveness wields its metal blade of brute force that people will avoid. Love is a thousand times more effective.

If you chose to hold the Sword of Light to change the corrupt systems, you are a Warrior. Nobody is born a Warrior in exactly the same way that nobody is born an average person. We make ourselves into one or the other.

However, it requires a tremendous commitment to love in the face of those that try to hurt us. This commitment will cause us to challenge our beliefs about our judgments and reactions. We must be committed to love beyond our own self-serving interests of what it will bring us. In time we become committed to love for the sheer enjoyment of expressing love. This becomes our commitment. Warriors that I am referring to nourish themselves with the love they express.

Warriors are forgiving of themselves and others. They recognize that all life's circumstances are created for learning purposes. Forgiveness helps unravel the distortions that people hold onto. We can let go of the low vibration stories, make love the final line.

Warriors recognize that they, and only they, create their reality. In other words, they fearlessly embrace every person, situation and circumstance that they have drawn to themselves. They proactively use the law of attraction to reach goals, practicing vigilance to the vibration they hold.

A warrior confronts and dissolves their limiting beliefs. To challenge our own beliefs requires courage because it means the end of our illusion of safety. Challenge your beliefs instead of defending them. In this way we are able to sort out the truth from illusions.

The words and deeds of a Warrior are aligned. There is no internal conflict of saying one thing and doing another. Honesty and integrity provide an internal alignment that does not dissipate energy.

Warriors must exercise their own will at the command of their heart, not an outside influence. Owning your own sovereignty and your own heart is claiming your highest vibration. A warrior who holds a Sword of Light must have the commitment to love humanity, even if you are attacked.

"It is quite proper to resist and attack a system, but to resist and attack its author is tantamount to resisting and attacking oneself, for we are all tarred with the same brush, and are children of one

and the same Creator, and as such the divine powers within us are infinite. To slight a single human being is to slight those divine powers, and thus to harm not only that Being, but with Him, the whole world." Gandhi

A Warrior realizes that 'fearlessness' is not to be without fear; rather it is to be continually confronting and breaking through fear the moment it arises by listening to its message and letting go of the messenger. A Warrior is not afraid of the truth. The true spiritual warrior is never afraid to look at what he doesn't want to see.

In my point of view, Jesus Christ was the greatest Warrior. He had the courage, discipline, and openness to Love unconditionally even as he was being rejected and physically persecuted. This is extraordinary impeccability. If he could love in his challenges, then we can learn to love unconditionally in our challenges.

9) Understand the Oppressor…. Be Strategic

In a hierarchy those who have and utilize the main powers, authority and influence, shape the organization and the systems that make up its functioning. If those in power use deception, secrecy, divisiveness, and the harming others, the resulting systems will reflect that behavior.

The personalities that thrive in these systems are psychopaths because of the many characteristics previously described through Howard Fox. Generations of psychopaths have filled the upper levels of power because power is the one thing they crave. These systems reflect the persona of those in charge.

So we are presently dealing with psychopathic systems. Just as this personality type consistently exhibits particular fears and concerns, the systems made in their image share the same vulnerabilities. The two biggest fears of a psychopath are being found out and losing power. This makes two strategies stand out. Inform the public of the deception and unplug from these evil systems.

Another key insight is not to be fooled by the psychopaths' masks. Charming and deceptive personalities take the stage to read story lines that paint false pictures. Often their personalities resemble Howard Fox. They are actors who play the game of deception. They can put on any mask to hide their personas. Under the façade of a cross and collar, or the garb of a politician or a corporate leader, may lay a malicious intent toward the 99%.

Psychopaths have "emotional deafness" — a biochemical inability to experience normal feelings of empathy for others. There is an insular focus on personal desires. This shark-like fixation on self-interest means that psychopaths often feel a clear detachment from other people, viewing them more as sheep to be preyed upon than fellow humans to relate to. They lack compassion and only think of themselves, "all for me and none for you."

They see themselves above others; the rules don't apply to them. *"I can do what I please."* According to them, they are the rulers of these lowly surfs. They see themselves as superior. However, the truth is very different. Psychopaths are dealing with a brain deformity that makes the reptilian part of their brain very active. These brains function in "survival of the fittest" mentality. They have not evolved to a collaborative and mutually supportive consciousness.

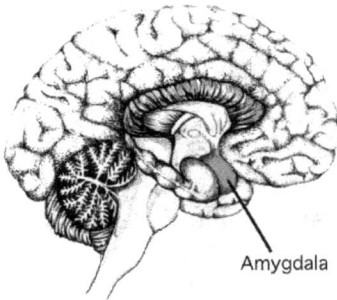

Studies on twins have revealed that psychopathy shows a strong genetic signature and there remains no effective treatment. Recent research has linked the condition to physical abnormalities in the Amygdala region of the brain.[18] It is like the reptilian part of the brain is dominating, like lizards who lack compassion eat their young. There are psychopaths who have a genetically inherited biochemical condition that prevents them from feeling normal human empathy.

A peer-reviewed theoretical paper titled "The Corporate Psychopaths Theory of the Global Financial Crisis" [19] details how highly placed psychopaths in the banking sector may have nearly brought down the world economy through their own inherent inability to care about the consequences to others from their actions.

We must realize that about 1% of the population is considered psychopaths. These are people who do prey on others. They are capable of great atrocities. With that in mind also consider that the Elite's most profitable venture is war and the pillage of countries. There are people who instigate war and tremendous human suffering for their personal profit. A major avenue for this aggressive approach to overtake democratically elected governments is through the

126

International Monetary Fund, United States CIA, the State Department, and multinational corporations under the guise of democracy and freedom.

One of the main protections of psychopaths is their ability to hide their true intentions through deceit and manipulation. They play people; just like Howard played and preyed on the board members to get control. Also most people can't imagine that someone would provoke such evil on others for their personal gain or amusement. The degree of evil can make some crimes incomprehensible as we have witnessed with genocide.

Sustained psychopathic systems breed sociopaths. The same lack of empathy can be seen through our social conditioning and what is required for great success in the corporate realm. It becomes the norm. Look who gets rewarded and rises to the top.

Here are a few key aspects of psychopath systems. First, their systems are based on divisiveness and opposing others, secrecy, lies and manipulation. It is the glue that binds this house of cards. If people were aware of their diabolical systems and deceptions, the house of cards would collapse. So, exposure of the truth is their biggest enemy and fear.

The other aspect is the psychopath's uncontrollable avarice for power. That also means emotional power by creating pain and suffering. Many feel pleasure from the turmoil and chaos they create. In their perverted senses, it gives them aliveness. If you encounter a psychopath, the top recommendation is to disengage. Don't communicate or give back energy. That is what I did with Howard. I unplugged and refused any more meetings, and stopped responding to his emails.

A simple strategy that is effective for psychopaths and the systems they create aligns with their two biggest fears: Exposure to Truth and unplugging from the systems ... non co-operation.

10) Gather the Facts ....Understand a Deeper Truth

The truth can set you free. However, truth can involve confronting beliefs and propaganda instilled since birth. Question the politicians, the bankers, the corporate leaders, and the media. It is our civic duty to question our officials if there is dishonesty, and, particularly, if treason is involved.

It is taking a warrior's stance of being a beacon of Light involving truth and love. To expose the truth may require you to first expose it to yourself. This means doing your homework on a topic you wish to discuss. When you discuss a topic there may be rebuttal that is based on propaganda and misinformation, which is why it is important to do your due diligence on the topic you want to expose.

False flag attacks can come into our monetary system, like creating booms and busts, and blaming it on the spending habits of the citizens. It can involve local mass shootings or bombings. As in past situations, they will create a catastrophe and somehow introduce solutions like more surveillance and austerity measures. Dig deeper than the mass media stories. (Appendix D)

We need to query why these Elite families control the Federal Reserve and their unquestioned power to create bubbles, busts, and inflation in our economy (Appendix A).

Question the CIA black ops and their overthrow of democratically elected governments to benefit US corporate interests. Question the "official" government data on joblessness, poverty, and inflation. Question, research by corporate interests and inform others. (Appendix B)

Question Fluoride in our drinking water and the Chemtrails left in our sky. Question our education and health care systems. Question the data on global warming, the impact of HAARP, and the safety of genetically modified foods. (Appendix C)

Being a truth seeker means accessing literature, videos, and the internet for the real news. Good places to start are podcasts and videos at (www.CorbettReport.com), and follow the links to other sources in the broadcast notes and weekly guides at

(www.LiberateGuide.com). You should question the main stream media and look for more reliable sources of information.

Become a truth seeker: third party supporters and libertarians, anti-war protestors and human rights campaigners, people who are upset with the government giving trillions to the banks that have engineered the financial crisis in the first place.

Everyone is now a potential terrorist, according to the governmental and media agencies that deign to limit our range of acceptable opinions and control dissent. However, that stance is powerless as more people become informed. So increase your circle of influence.

Only by exposing the myths can we produce a real democracy, not one dictated by special interests. A lasting peace will be possible, not one manipulated by the military/industrial complex. We can have an unbiased media, not one owned by the Elite few who script national consciousness. A true prosperity can be achieved, not a massive transfer of wealth to the elite few at the cost of the many.

11) Communicate to others ... Expose the Truth

To go it alone is futile. We need each other and we need to inform each other. Community is vital on the path in front of us. Community is needed to expose the full scope of the abuses and manipulations that are against our democracy and Constitution. Community is needed to embrace new systems that serve the common good. Community is needed to embrace the incredible potential that exists without parasite systems.

Spread the truth to your friends when you go out. Spread the truth through social media. Write articles and blogs. Start with people you know and notice the level of receptivity. Provide a lot of facts and put the right energy behind the words.

Studies[20] have shown that words impact interpersonal communication less than one may guess. One study went so far as to conclude that only 7% of what a person takes away from an interaction is attributed to the words used, while 57% of what is communicated is attributed to body language and 36% to voice tone. Body language and voice tone are expressions of the energy behind the words, which can account for 93% of the communication's impact.

We often spend time contemplating the words to choose while ignoring how we are feeling during our communication. A good communicator is conscious of the energy of their emotions and the impact it has.

Reflect on your own experience; how do you feel when someone is angry, ranting on about how bad someone or something is? They may get your attention, but do they get your listening and respect? When you take in someone's words you also take in their energy. Some people may want to empathize with the anger; however, this is usually a minority.

Think how it feels when someone communicates the facts in a compassionate way, with objectivity and clarity. What is your experience when someone enthusiastically gives a vision of hope and speaks of progress? Are you more receptive?

Simply put, emotion is energy in motion that vibrates in a range of frequencies. High vibrations are felt as love, compassion, and joy. All human beings either consciously or unconsciously want this expansive, healing and uplifting vibration in our lives. Words carried by that higher frequency are more readily received. There are two parts to exposing the truth to others, they are the facts and how you express them.

In the marketing realm, the idea is to engage a target audience with your message. Marketers found truth does not rule, perception does. Corporations spend billions to make images and words evoke certain emotions and shape perceptions. They look for the hooks that will get the attention of their target audience.

So the first question is who is your audience? Does your vision or solution align with the audience you are looking to engage? Are you supporting a movement that seems not relatable or perceived as being too unrealistic, or not credible? Most importantly does the movement oppose deep societal beliefs that people do not want to let go of? Are you exposing a "truth" that is too scary for many?

When a belief is in place within a society, even a false one, it limits your audience. When I was a coordinator of the 9/11 Truth grassroots groups we saw how effective the Elite's belief-forming mechanism worked. Our truth message opposed deep societal beliefs that people did not want to let go of. It was just too scary for people to realize that some people in power are terrorists. So it became easy to believe the media spin that there are conspiracy cooks walking around with tin hats who oppose the main stream story line and are not to be listened to.

In the Truth movement, it wasn't until a person was even slightly open to consider that someone within the US government could be complicit in this crime that they would listen to the facts. To cross that line and to realize that those who govern do not honor our constitution and laws, and then to realize that within parts of the US government there is the development of terrorists and the drug trade, is too big a leap for some.

Be aware of layers of listening and engagement that occurs on a mass scale. The more opposed your message is to societal beliefs, the smaller your circle of influence at first. Each topic listed below has an increasingly larger circle of listening.
1. 9/11/01 Truth Movement
2. Federal Reserve Reform
3. End the War and Pro Peace
4. Feeding the Hungry Locally
5. Local Environmental Concerns
6. Financial Stress (including housing market, health care)
7. Lack of trust in Government (government reform)

The first circle consists of approximately 24 percent of the population who suspect the government was involved with the 9/11/2001 event to create a catalyst for their "War on Terror." This last circle involves over 80 percent of the population who want government reform. The positioning of a movement involves the circle of listening you wish to engage.

Warriors can approach communicating truth in a variety of ways. Having a loving and kind disposition makes the truth more acceptable. Each time we provide a different perspective or opposing view, we are confronting the beliefs that our media, educational system, monetary system, and the war machine have implanted. When your opposing view evokes a reaction, remember the warriors' stance of love.

12) Have an Inspired Vision ... Be Inspired

When you communicate about our social systems, discuss the treason as a catalyst for change, and also the possibilities of what our society can become. There is abundance with the elimination of exploitive systems, banking scams, special subsidies, endless wars, draining of wealth from the masses to the Elite few. If a portion of that was given back to the communities, it would be a catalyst to provide prosperity for all.

Community is literally described as "joined in unity." But we must participate as community to define what we are unifying around. What do we hold in common, what is the community vision?

That definition of what is best for the community, what is the Common Good, is derived at by participation of community members. So the definition of what is good or what unifies a community is always different from one community to the next. It comes from the collective intelligence unique to each group.

Imagine if the trillions of dollars siphoned to the oil/banking families and their military/industrial complex were to be used for the common good. Imagine:

- Free education and health care for all.

- The repair of our infrastructure.

- Forgiveness of student loans.

- Locally produced clean energy to meet the community needs.

- Honest objective media coverage.

- A local food system where abundant, healthy, affordable organic food is available to all.

- A community response and support for the elderly and those in need.

- Productive, effective systems to care for our commons like our parks.

- Public banking institutions working for the people.

- *"Imagine all the people living life in peace... A brotherhood of man...Imagine all the people sharing all the world,"* John Lenon

Focus on what your community needs. Focus on what you have passion for. Our communities can recreate themselves with the enthusiastic energy of a few. Developing grassroots initiatives, as you will see in later chapters, can start with you. We can develop initiatives any way we want, so focus on co-creating what will serve the community through grassroots initiatives.

The vision has already begun. High-energy grassroots systems are developing all around us and are strengthening regional resources, exchanges, and investments. It consists of neighbors, municipalities, and counties working together to resolve issues impacting local residents. It can begin in a business, a family, community, or marriage. It is the next frontier. It is the revolution we are now living.

13) Grassroots Organizing

Regardless of the form or cause, grassroots groups have the potential to create great change. Grassroots organizing is the principal mechanism for changing societal systems that no longer work or that function poorly because they are corrupt or lack sustainability. History is filled with inspiring recounts about grassroots efforts around the world that have won freedom and justice from oppressive governments and corporations.

Just as the members of Community ReStart organized to face the tyranny, as a group we had a voice. We activated our collective legal rights as members. Our communities also have the constitutional right to organize and act collaboratively.

Developing grassroots groups is a way to empower people locally to take action for change and achieve common goals. Systems that support the Common Good are brought about through the participation of people like you. There are many ways to get involved as described in the next chapter. As you participate, you will witness the tremendous power that exists when we use community collaboration as a resource to accomplish great things.

There are three components to the foundation of any successful grassroots venture: Alignment, collaboration, and culture. These three components give power, resources, stability, and strength to group endeavors.

Alignment for grassroots development refers to the relation between a community's focus and need, with your personal and group's beliefs and intention. Take healthy, affordable, organic food as a community focus. I personally have a belief that healthy food is our right and that we should not consume foods that are genetically modified, irradiated, laden with man-made chemicals, and low nutrition. Personally, I have a passion to unplug from the corporate food system and plug into local healthy food systems. Several of my friends were aligned and we began the Food Net. The initiative has delivered up to 21,000 pounds of produce per year to local pantries and meal sites, all free.

An initiative can be on any topic serving the Common Good. Some communities may need clean water or air, affordable housing, ending gang violence, or job development. Needs will vary from one location to the next. It is through the grassroots venture that the alignment of our hearts connects with what the community needs and provides an avenue for effective action.

The alignment to change the Elite Systems must penetrate our hearts. The change starts from within, such as a belief in a cause. When there is alignment of a person's passion, words and deeds, it opens the doorway to potential that is beyond the material realm. The true asset that will bring about lasting reform lies within our hearts.

Collaboration ideally is integral to any grassroots venture. From the inception of any initiative, it is important to network. You want to form a community of support and respect before you launch an initiative. Avoid the mistake of not including those who have been proactively working on the same issue. The intention is cohesion and inclusion.

Development of a network of support allows access to another form of energy to fuel an initiative that is not dependent upon the private Federal Reserve Notes. This collaboration is crucial as it ends dependency on the key control mechanism of the elite system, such as private fiat currency. Through collaboration a new possibility and resource becomes available.

Culture is integral in the formation of community or initiatives. It is formed by integrating core values. It has the potential to develop and sustain the initiative, and nourish those who participate. Culture creates a unique cohesion among the group. The more this cohesive element is uplifting and supportive, the more attracting the group endeavor becomes. That is why integrating the six values, described in Chapter 7, is crucial to sustain and develop this uplifting group energy field.

Grassroots organizing is on the rise. There are many tools and insights gained that can help success; they are laid out in the remaining chapters. Dedicated individuals are uniting and participating in causes and initiatives around the world. Their coming together generates a focus and group energy, that when developed properly, holds the power to transform a corrupt system. The next chapter provides grassroots development tools.

14) Non-cooperation…Unplug

"You assist an evil system most effectively by obeying its orders and decrees. An evil system never deserves such allegiance. Allegiance to it means partaking of the evil. A good person will resist an evil system with his or her whole soul." Mahatma Gandhi

Mahatma Gandhi was the preeminent leader of the Indian independence movement in British-ruled India. Employing nonviolent civil disobedience, Gandhi led India to independence and inspired movements for civil rights and freedom across the world. Gandhi first employed nonviolent civil disobedience as an expatriate lawyer in South Africa, in the resident Indian community's struggle for civil rights. After his return to India in 1915, he set about organizing peasants, farmers, and urban laborers to protest against excessive land-tax and discrimination. Assuming leadership of the Indian National Congress in 1921, Gandhi led nationwide campaigns for easing poverty, expanding women's rights, building religious and ethnic amity, ending untouchability, but above all for achieving *Swaraj* or self-rule. Eventually, in August 1947, Britain granted independence.

"Non-cooperation is an attempt to awaken the masses, to a sense of their dignity and power. This can only be done by enabling them to realize that they need not fear brute force, if they would but know the soul within."

"I cooperate with all that is good. I desire to non-cooperate with all that is evil." Mahatma Gandhi

This needs to be a peaceful revolution; Gandhi has laid out a strategy that works. He brought the mighty .01% to their knees. One man sparked a blaze that freed an entire nation from oppression. There were many forces against him, but he had one Force that trumped them all. There is no stopping this Force that is not born from oppression, but from love. He was a bearer of the sword of Light. Here is some of the Gandhi's great wisdom to guide us:

"Non-cooperation is directed not against men but against measures. It is not directed against the Governors, but against the system they administer. The roots of non-cooperation lie not in hatred but in justice, if not in love."

"Non-cooperation is a protest against an unwitting and unwilling participation in evil....Non-cooperation with evil is as much a duty as cooperation with good."

"It is not that I harbor disloyalty towards anything whatsoever, but I do so against all untruth, all that is unjust, all that is evil.....I remain loyal to an institution so long as that institution conduces to my growth, to the growth of the nation. Immediately I find that the institution, instead of conducing to its growth, impedes it, I hold it to be my bounden duty to be disloyal to it." [21]

"There is no instrument so clean, so harmless and yet so effective as non-cooperation. Judiciously handled, it need not produce any evil consequences. And its intensity will depend purely on the capacity of the people for sacrifice."

"I consider non-cooperation to be such a powerful and pure instrument that, if it is enforced in an earnest spirit, it will be like seeking first the Kingdom of God and everything else following as a matter of course. People will then have realized their true power. They would have learnt that value of discipline, self-control, joint action, non-violence, organization and everything else that goes to make a nation great and good, and not merely great." Mahatma Gandhi

Non-cooperation is recommended by therapists when dealing with malignant narcissists, psychopaths, sociopaths, borderlines, drama queens, stalkers and other emotional vampires. It's commonly advised that no response is the best response to unwanted attention. They suggest No Contact (the avoidance of all communication) should be used whenever possible. When dealing with systems with a psychopathic construct, a similar approach of non-cooperation is appropriate.

It is a process of shedding an old skin. There is no need for perpetual war for the enrichment of the elite and the enslavement of the masses. There is no need for the corrupt politician game. No need to support too big to fail scams. No more needs for more advanced weapons to our police forces to fight against citizens. There is no more need for their delusion crafted through the media they own. There is no more need for the suffering and delusion they bring. It is time to unplug and end this abusive relationship and develop healthy ones.

We need a revolution to not support evil, which will make it an evolution. Furthermore, such an evolution would be constitutional, lawful, moral, and in compliance with the laws of Nature and of Nature's God. It is our duty to support and develop systems that support the Common Good and at the same time unplug from those that are harmful.

The Elite Systems lose their power when we refuse to participate in their scam. It is our participation that is the life blood of this corrupt system. We need to replace the beliefs that keep us participating in a system that fuels evil. We must first believe we can unplug from these systems.

Organizational development tools provided in the next chapter aid the formation of grassroots systems and once they begin to evolve with existing cooperative systems, we can further unplug from Elite Systems. If we utilize these tools wisely, we can transform and grow any organized group endeavor. In this way communities can become more self reliant while still participating in a revised global economy. Any community can transform corrupt systems to serve the common good.

The first and most important concept is to be the change you want to see. Utilize your ability as an antenna to broadcast what you want through your thoughts, feelings, and actions. Focus on vision and emotions, attract the change you want; use the Law of Attraction.

When you believe you can resolve community needs locally. When you believe you can be joyous, and partake in the abundance that surrounds us. When you believe there is hope. When you believe you can, you can. That is an important step to peacefully remove the oppression.

"First they ignore you, then they laugh at you, then they fight you, then you win." Mahatma Gandhi

15) Community Truth...The House of Cards Crumble

When the citizens who have awakened reach a critical level, the awareness will catch on in an accelerated way. A new behavior or idea is claimed to spread rapidly by unexplained means from one group to all related groups. It seems to register in the Collective Subconsciousness as a critical number of members exhibit the new behavior or acknowledge the new idea.

When a critical awareness occurs, the tyranny will be exposed, the public voice will become louder, and actions of non- cooperation will take hold. That tipping point for Community ReStart was through exposed emails. You never really know when it will occur, yet act as if the tipping point has arrived. Our society can experience a similar tipping point. Get the message out, be happy, have an inspired vision, and utilize the Law of Attraction.

16) Re-Start

Unplug from the corrupt systems and plug into Common Good Systems. Emerging spontaneously and without central leadership, this grassroots movement brings with it a very advantageous set of strategy characteristics. That is, it is non-violent, decentralized, self-propagating, liberating, inclusive, territory capturing, adaptive, flexible, minimally confrontational, and uplifting.

The Common Good spreads local empowerment to the many. It generates a greater ownership and participation in the local community. There will be many more resources to utilize as the massive scams are ended.

The existing government system is wired so that change will almost never occur from the bottom up. You are disempowered through trickery and illegal mazes. Just the legal system alone will have many cases shot down that tries to reform the system as it progresses to higher courts. The system assures the disempowerment of the citizens. This change needs to occur outside of existing systems. On the Common Good road we can re-start our societal systems.

Re-start new purchasing habits. Look at the behemoth corporations like Proctor and Gamble, Wall Mart, Monsanto ... if you support them then you support their agenda. Switch to local purchases, support grassroots systems. You don't even have to leave your home to switch your beliefs.

We can choose to be a conscious part of an uplifting evolution. We can choose to create an optimum environment for growth and development. We can choose greater fulfillment and community. We can choose to be uplifted in our group endeavors and by one another.

Because in reality, our Liberty is not a vague concept that we can reaffirm on occasion as it suits us. It is a choice that we make each and every day, to liberate. Our purchasing power, our group power, and individual creative power can light the torch of freedom. Even a choice of what we watch on TV or think about and how we feel can be a way to disengage from the Elite Systems. When we take action to unplug from this tyranny, and plug into Common Good Systems... every day is Independence Day; every day is an expression of Liberty.

Chapter 6

Grassroots Development

System change starts within communities, it is local and like the roots of grass, they connect and support each other. It is the mutual benefit found in evolved ecosystems. Grassroots organizing is on the rise, the evolution is among us. Dedicated individuals are uniting and participating in causes and initiatives around the world, independent from elite systems. Their coming together generates a focus and group energy that, when developed properly, holds great power and potential to nourish the common good.

Grassroots groups come together for a broad range of reasons. Through that connection they can resolve growing needs in the community or support community self-sufficiency. Grassroots communities have historically been the primary mechanism for social change, human rights, environmental regulations, and improving working conditions. The power of community has the potential to bring enrichment on all levels including personal and spiritual renewal.

Regardless of the form or cause, these groups have the potential to create great change. History is filled with inspiring recounts about grassroots efforts around the world that have won freedom and justice from oppressive governments and corporations. It begins with a belief and vision of change.

When we hold a vision with conviction that resonates with others in our community, we have a spark. It can inspire others to participate. This spark can ignite a powerful force. The power can raise a barn, find a missing child, respond to a natural disaster, or transform a nation

Community involvement does not necessarily require a big commitment of time or energy. Attending a meeting and following up on tasks for even a few hours a week can rid a neighborhood of crime, change repressive laws, and establish greater community self sufficiency.

All groups share fundamental commonalities that impact their success or failure. The laws of group dynamics, organizational development, and science pertain to all. The group energy field is governed by principles. These insights are covered in this chapter.

Community ... Our Deeper Nature

An integral part of Grassroots initiatives involves networking, participating with others toward common goals and building community around a common focus. Connecting and working in harmony with others feeds us, for this human connection reflects our deeper nature.

Interconnection is the foundation of existence. Look at life itself. All living things exchange energy. If this exchange ceases, life itself ceases.

You need air, water, and food. The very composition of your body is constantly exchanged with energy from our surroundings. This exchange generates new cells. Ninety-eight percent of the atoms in our body were not there a year ago. Our skeleton, which seems so solid, was essentially "not there" three months ago. The material world is fundamentally energy in constant relationship and exchange with itself.

All conceivable models of quantum reality must incorporate a relational connection. Irish physicist Jon Stewart Bell demonstrated that on a subatomic level, nature arranges instantaneous and ongoing connections between two photons. When subatomic particles contact, they create a link that physical distance doesn't break. Quantum energy creates relationships that occur faster than the speed of light across space and time. Scientists call such relationships "non-local." Einstein called them "spooky actions at a distance."

When we engage in relationships with others we are touching something inherent to all life and our deeper nature. When we network with others we are creating an interconnected field, which mimics how every particle is coming into existence. When we live, work, and participate in community, we align more closely with this characteristic of energy, particularly when our community becomes like family to foster intimacy that builds strong relationship. This alignment to energy's nature helps increase the group's energy vibration.

142

The impact of relationship can be measured on an energetic level. Dr. Valerie Hunt, a professor at the University of California, noticed this while monitoring people's electromagnetic fields. She found that if the human field does not interact with others, it loses its complexity and becomes narrow in vibration spectrums. The field weakens. When we become too isolated or withdrawn, we unplug our energy field from a source of renewal. However, as the nature of energy suggests, when we are active within a group field, we plug into energy much bigger than our own self-generated fields and if the connections are healthy and supportive, we become renewed.

Within a group field we want harmonious relations. Whenever a member is removed or added to the group, the change has a holistic impact. So it behooves us to look at who we bring into our relational fields. You may have experienced the power of one person to affect the whole. Perhaps your group was functioning very well; then someone new came in and the entire group began to spin down. Or one bright soul uplifted the entire organization. We will explore what brings a group's energy up or down.

When the higher vibration exists, we naturally feel connected to others around us; we feel energized and even become more attractive. When we connect with others in a good-hearted way we can't help but be uplifted. The increased vibration in our body connects more DNA nodes to energy and they become lit up. Grassroots communities help us access a power that not only results in great external accomplishments but also great internal accomplishments, such as our own personal and spiritual renewal.

Jesus said, *"Truly I say to you, to the extent that you did it to one of these brothers of mine, even the least of them, you did it to me.*[22]*"*

Beware of the False Life

The ultimate punishment in tribal society, a fate worse than death, was banishment. If a tribesman hurt the community, a similar wound was placed on the perpetrator—the ultimate wound being exclusion from the tribe. In ancient Hawaii, for example, the *kāhuna* would sever the *aka* cords, subtle energy that bound the individual to the community. They knew as did many ancient societies, how vital the community was for personal well-being. Yet in modern society we have lost much of this interconnectedness.

When I was in Hawaii in 1999, I spoke with a group of old-timers who had grown up on a sugar plantation in Paia, on the island of Maui. Their parents worked under harsh conditions. Yet they described the community of their childhood, now vanished, with a sense of reverence. That community had once consisted of six camps, located near the sugar-processing plant. Each camp had its own ethnic group: Hawaiian, Japanese, Portuguese, and Filipino among them. The community included a general store, barbershop, restaurant, post office, school, meeting hall, and ballpark. The kids from all camps went to the same school; they played together and roamed the community freely.

Harry Sondelon, a Filipino, remembered his experience of being an adolescent in the twenties on this lush northwest shore of the island. *"Everyone looked out for each other, regardless of the camp they were from. My friends were part of this ethnic mix. Our community was a cultural melting pot. The mothers of my friends took us in as part of their families. I can still remember the smell of fresh baking breads every Thursday in the Portuguese camp. They would give out hot pieces to us kids. It tasted great. 220 residents knew each other personally. There were many good-hearted people willing to share what they had. We would all get together for celebrations and games. We would gather to mourn the passing of someone from our community. If a neighbor needed help, we would all pitch in."*

The camps have long been disbanded. Harry's life in Paia today is very different. *"I don't know the people who live around me. We don't sit down and talk. When I need help, I don't feel I can go to my neighbors. I am scared to go out now."* His eyes filled with tears, and his voice began to quiver. *"Back then when I was growing up, that was the real life. Now I'm living a false life."*

In many ways modern society has dissolved community and the family unit. We have unconsciously banished ourselves from our deepest nature. We have created isolation, losing ourselves in our TV sets and cell phones or sequestering ourselves behind the closed

144

doors of our homes. As we have disconnected from relationship, we have disconnected from spirit. We are living the false life.

The elite societal systems have subtly and not so subtly divided us. How well do you know your neighbors? Most of us are so busy trying to make a living all day long and then are content watching the television at night; we don't even know who lives next door to us these days. These patterns need to shift if we are to access our true community power. That old saying *"Many hands make light work"* is an old adage I am reminded of constantly and this is so true. We must become real communities again, get to know each other and help each other out.

The Power for Societal Change

"When spider webs unite, they can tie up a lion." ~Ethiopian Proverb

By forming community, working with each other, we can tap into a power much greater than ourselves. By holding love and aspiration in our hearts we access a natural high vibrating power that can be used as a creative force. We can access the power to change peacefully. We can move into Common Good Systems where all basic needs such as medical and educational are paid by tax revenues. Rewire the deceptive flow of money to the elite few. Rewire it so revenues transparently serve communities. Through community, we access real sustainable wealth.

Non-violent grassroots community organizing is a well-proven and inspiring means of mass social change. Movements in India, the United States, and Poland demonstrate how grassroots initiatives can make monumental shifts, despite social and political environments that oppose grassroots organizing.

Mahatma Gandhi saw the results of more than a century of British rule and set about to reform that system. A strategy of civil disobedience on a mass scale began with home spun cloth and defying the British salt tax. The salt tax was a powerful symbol of engagement as salt is a necessity to sustain life. These tax laws placed a great burden on the poor. His protest began with a 240-mile march to the salt beaches, including dozens of journalists providing a world

stage. It was well planned with scheduled speeches at the villages along his journey, and each of the 24 days the march gained notice and momentum. By the time of Gandhi's arrest and the bloody protest at the salt works, India as a nation had changed.

Photo of Gandhi at Dandi gathering salt, April 5, 1930. Millions

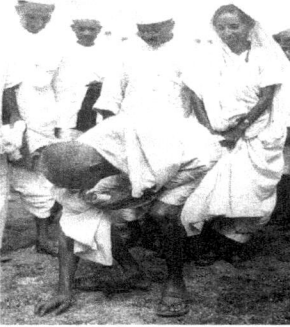

of citizens realized they did not have to subjugate themselves to a corrupt system and they could peacefully refuse to participate. The citizens can co-create a system that served the communities instead of an elite few. A powerful force was unleashed that eventually brought independence from the British Empire. The symbol of salt now represents India's independence like tea does for the United States.

Twenty-six years later students at Fisk University in Nashville, Tennessee, began attending a workshop given by James Lawson, a student of Gandhi. Lawson was a minister sent to that area by Martin Luther King, Jr. His objective was to desegregate this racially divided city.   He organized a grassroots group by introducing common disciplines, strategic planning, insight into non-violent philosophy, and a systematic approach addressing a wide range of scenarios and contingencies.

The first demonstrations started at "whites only" lunch counters.

Subsequent arrests galvanized the black community and encouraged a broader community involvement that expanded into a boycott of the downtown district. In a short time, the grassroots unity that developed was more powerful than their police force, attack dogs, prisons, repressive curfews, beatings, or threats. When the black community boycotted, downtown sales dropped 40%. Within six months of the initial workshops, an oppressive apartheid system that had been in place since the town was built, was changed. The movement spread throughout the US resulting in civil rights legislation that reformed the old system.

Another inspiring grassroots movement began in August of 1980. Workers at the Gdansk Shipyard in Poland organized a non-violent strike led by Lech Walesa. The strike was well orchestrated and included lines of communication throughout Europe. The strike quickly expanded to include forty additional factories. Workers demanded free trade unions and the right to strike, and increased wages and benefits. They became unified around their declaration of workers' rights and formed an organization they named, "Solidarity." They worked diligently and strategically, staging rallies and networking. Within four months, Solidarity grew to ten million strong. This grassroots movement was too powerful. Solidarity's constant pressure resulted in the fall of the corrupt communist regime that had its grip on the population for sixty years. Through Parliamentary Elections, Solidarity defeated the government in power by a vote of 10 to 1.

Our global history is filled with examples of this grassroots power at work.[23] These social shifts happened because people decided to unite around a cause, were well organized, utilized the public media to their advantage, and had an inspirational leader or a team who helped guide strategic action. The real power base is people coming together in community, taking action, and holding the belief that they will achieve their vision.

From the largest movements of social change to the smaller ones involving a town ordinance, it comes from the people. The power of community is a global change agent. Community provides something all of the ancient tribes new intuitively. It is where their strength lies.

This power is not a metaphor—it is experienced when group endeavors become a conduit for action that benefits their community. You can find it in a Volunteer Fire Department, among people who serve food assistance needs in the pantries and meal sites, within a community hit by a natural disaster, or a group searching for a missing child. But once we understand the ingredients that bring about this heightened sense of working together we can apply them in our groups' endeavors.

The Elite know that by breaking this community connection they break the only true power that can defeat them. The breaking up of clans, local family farms, the neighborhood stores, long-term jobs, and busting the middle class all contribute to the breaking of community. We need to renew our willingness to go back to community based systems. Become involved in a community initiative.

To become powerful, allow your community to be powered by All!

Civic Action

When I think of recent civic action within the United States, the first person that comes to my mind is Ralph Nader. His life exemplifies the difference one person can make with a relentless pursuit for justice. He has consistently stood up to big government and corporations with a primary weapon being his moral conviction. The results are safer cars, cleaner air and drinking water, and safer work environments for the entire country.

During a workshop I participated in, Ralph lamented the erosion of our sense of civic engagement and not taking responsibility for the Commons we share. Manipulation by design has nearly eliminated these topics from the media and our schools. In addition, the corrupt systems emphasize a different commercial/corporate value system that results in isolating and disenfranchising citizens. The present system discourages or even breaks up organizing and community. The erosion of our sense of civic responsibility goes deeper as beliefs are implanted that discourage civic engagement.

Increasing civic engagement involves renewed sets of beliefs. Let children understand early that their civic duty is needed to maintain freedom and justice. Projects that benefit our community should be an active part of each school year. Property tax payers should emphasize it to the school board. The rewiring of tax money allocation will allow all schools to be adequately funded for projects that benefit the community. Successful civics projects in schools throughout the country are plentiful on the web and there are also suggestions at the end of this section.

History is filled with examples of activists who maintained the strength to continue asserting their rights. It sometimes only takes a few people with the moral conviction that ignites a flame that can burn bright, even seventy years later. The change process requires patience as can be seen by the time lines of two system changes that affected human equality and air quality. Like today, they had to break deeply held beliefs that were being supported by the powerful elite at the time.

Women's Suffrage Movement

The women's suffrage movement began in 1848; six women with a strong moral conviction organized the first women's rights convention in Seneca Falls, New York. Woman suffrage supporters worked to educate the public about the validity of women's rights. Under the leadership of Susan B. Anthony, Elizabeth Cady Stanton, and other women's rights pioneers, suffragists circulated petitions and lobbied Congress to pass a Constitutional Amendment to enfranchise women.

At the turn of the century, women activists wanted to pass reform legislation. However, many politicians were unwilling to listen to a disenfranchised group. Thus, over time women began to realize that in order to achieve reform, they needed to win the right to vote. The woman suffrage movement then became a mass movement.

Congresswoman Jeannette Rankin speaks from the NAWSA headquarters, 1917[24]

In the 20th century leadership of the suffrage movement passed to two organizations. The first, the National American Woman Suffrage Association (NAWSA), under the leadership of Carrie Chapman Catt, was a moderate organization. The NAWSA undertook campaigns to enfranchise women in individual states, and simultaneously lobbied President Wilson and Congress to pass a woman suffrage Constitutional Amendment. In the 1910s, NAWSA's membership numbered in the millions.

The second group, the National Woman's Party (NWP), under the leadership of Alice Paul, was a more radical organization. The NWP undertook actions, including picketing the White House, to convince Wilson and Congress to pass a woman suffrage amendment.

Members of the National Woman's Party picket the White House[25]

In 1920, due to the combined efforts of the NAWSA and the NWP, the 19th Amendment, enfranchising women, was finally ratified. It was the single largest extension of democratic voting rights in our nation's history, and it was achieved through grassroots organizing.

The movement achieved a radical long lasting change after a 72-year process. It required a persistent pressure handed down through generations. This struggle for equality continues as we learn to embrace our community diversity and hold respect and compassion for all. When we work with others to uplift our community, the unity comes alive. The process will spread as change takes over our states. An example of how the change process can possibly move is the battle against the tobacco companies and our rights for clean air and truthful information.

Banning Cigarette Smoking in Common Areas

Back in 1960, smoke-filled rooms were a common and accepted practice. Joe Camel and the Marlboro Man were branded in my memory. In the 70s things began to change. The summary of "Milestones in Decreasing Indoor Tobacco Smoke in the United States "[26] illustrates the path that civic change can take, it often does not happen overnight and can be a winding, time consuming route.

1971   The surgeon general proposes a federal smoking ban in public places.

1972   The first report of the surgeon general to identify secondhand smoke as posing a health risk is released.

1973   Arizona becomes the first state to restrict smoking in several public places. The Civil Aeronautics Board requires no-smoking sections on all commercial airline flights.

1974   Connecticut passes the first state law to apply smoking restrictions in restaurants.

1975   Minnesota passes a statewide law restricting smoking in public places.

1977   Berkeley, California, becomes the first community to limit smoking in restaurants and other public places.

1983   San Francisco passes a law to place private workplaces under smoking restrictions.

1986   A report of the surgeon general focuses entirely on the health consequences of involuntary smoking, proclaiming secondhand smoke a cause of lung cancer in healthy nonsmokers.

1988   A congressionally mandated smoking ban takes effect on all domestic airline flights of 2 hours or less. New York City's ordinance for clean indoor air takes effect; the ordinance bans or severely limits smoking in various public places and affects 7 million people. California implements a statewide ban on smoking aboard all commercial intrastate airplanes, trains, and buses.

1991   The National Institute for Occupational Safety and Health issues a bulletin recommending that secondhand smoke be reduced to the lowest feasible concentration in the workplace.

1993   Los Angeles passes a ban on smoking in all restaurants. The U.S. Postal Service eliminates smoking in all facilities. A working group of 16 state attorneys general releases recommendations for establishing smoke-free policies in fast-food restaurants. Vermont bans smoking in all public buildings and in many private buildings open to the public.

1995   New York City passes a comprehensive ordinance effectively banning smoking in most workplaces. Maryland enacts a smoke-free policy. California passes comprehensive legislation that prohibits smoking in most enclosed workplaces. Vermont's smoking ban is extended to include restaurants, bars, hotels, and motels except establishments holding a cabaret license.

1998 California law takes effect banning smoking in bars that do not have a separately ventilated smoking area.

2002 New York (Public Health Law, Article 13-E), which took effect July 24, 2003, prohibits smoking in virtually all workplaces, including restaurants and bars. Florida voters approve a ballot measure that amends the state constitution to require most workplaces and public places—with some exceptions, such as bars—to be smoke-free.

2003 Dozens of U.S. airports—including airline clubs, passenger terminals, and nonpublic work areas—are designated as smoke-free. Connecticut and New York enact comprehensive smoke-free laws. Maine enacts a law requiring bars, pool halls, and bingo venues to be smoke-free. State supreme courts in Iowa and New Hampshire strike down local smoke-free ordinances, ruling that they are preempted by state law.

2004 Massachusetts and Rhode Island enact comprehensive smoke-free laws. The International Agency for Research on Cancer issues a new monograph identifying secondhand smoke as "carcinogenic to humans."

2005 North Dakota, Vermont, Montana, and Washington enact 100% smoke-free workplace and/or restaurant and/or bar regulations.

2006 New Jersey, Colorado, Hawaii, Ohio, and Nevada enact 100% smoke-free workplace and/or restaurant and/or bar regulations.

2007 Louisiana, Arizona, New Mexico, New Hampshire, and Minnesota enact 100% smoke-free workplace and/or restaurant and/or bar regulations.

2008 Illinois, Maryland, Iowa, and Pennsylvania enact 100% smoke-free workplace and/or restaurant and/or bar regulations.

When civic action proceeds through the system controlled by special interests opposed to the common good, it appears to be a timely and costly venture. This can shift when citizens demand change and rally around topics that can weed out political corruption so change is not blocked by elite cronies.

Some issues deeply affect us all and evoke a moral conviction to get involved. Get involved at a pace that keeps you engaged but not burnt out. Issues include:

- Educate others and help shift deeply held beliefs affecting system change.
- Elect government representatives who serve the common good.
- Have free health care, single payer with choice of doctor and facility.
- Audit and end the Federal Reserve.
- Require a living wage.
- End US military aggression and false flag attacks.

Let's take the top two. Throughout *Liberate* I have mentioned the primary battle is over our subconscious beliefs. The infusion of false beliefs deludes us into funding and supporting our own suffering and that of the entire planet. When more people are awakened, more are willing to engage in system change. It can snowball.

Civic engagement should not only educate others about the tyranny we face, it should also focus on the bright future ahead as we enact change. Once we stop the hemorrhaging of our resources to the military-industrial-government-banking complex there will be plenty for our community needs. The prosperity of the '70s will be like a candle compared to the sun-like bright future we face. This requires getting others engaged, and that means education and a positive vision as a catalyst for action.

Imagine if the population shed these false beliefs and the citizens took back control of the communication airways. Radio, internet and TV transmission is our Common asset. Have the communication and news provide a more honest perspective. This will in turn educate more people and get them involved which will accelerate system change.

The next civic action listed is electing government representatives who serve the Common Good. It requires getting involved with local elections, and screening and petitioning congress. Look at who is running for office and if they support the good-old-boy network. Does their past include shady business deals? Will they listen to the citizens and stand up for the rights of the people, or do the bidding of corporate cronies and war hawks. Are they willing to evoke system change? Vigorously support those who stand for the common good and remove those who do not.

One strategy Ralph Nader strongly suggests is to continually petition Congress; there are 535 to influence. Congress is a good focus as they have the authority over financial and budgetary matters, collect taxes, duties, and excises, to pay the debts and provide for the common defense and general welfare of the United States. They have the concentrated power to initiate system change. It requires a watch group being relentless like the NRA, who hound congressional representatives wherever they go. It takes organized long-term efforts to make a difference like the smoking change and women's rights. It requires finding out how the congressman or congresswoman votes and where their funding is from. See who supports subsidies to the rich and who does not. Party affiliation is not as important as the commitment to the Common Good.

Be aware of voting fraud, it is prevalent. Use exit polls to keep a pulse of electronic voting machines that can be easily rigged. The computerized systems can have voting numbers changed remotely. This requires local organizing. There are blogs like www.LiberateGuide.com or www.GreenAmerica.org. On the internet you can find *The Community Tool Box*. Utilize the resources provided by Ralph Nader at BreakingThroughPower.org. He has assembled relevant speakers to provide an important resource if you want to be exposed to a wide range of inspiring civic actions. Magazines like *Yes, Multinational Monitor, and Connections* are good resources for civic action.

Identify Your Community Initiative

If you are not involved with some community project, now is an important time to start. When you explore options start from looking within. Where does your interest lie? What are you passionate about? What brings you joy?

There are many local groups serving community needs, so take time to explore these volunteer programs and notice what resonates with your personal values and concerns. Are you searching for a faith-based community, programs to teach reading to children, ways to help food pantries, or involvement in town councils?

Analyze the situation. Who has the authority to change what you want changed? Is there a specific individual you can go to, or is your target dispersed? Who are your allies? Do you want to change one little thing or do you want to create an entirely new system? Is there a group already taking action on these concerns?

When we hold the intention of serving the common good and are willing to broaden our perspective of our community we can receptively listen. That is what we did at Community ReStart by having local experts at our potluck gathering. When we break away from the old assumptions and beliefs we can more clearly see the challenges, strengths, and opportunities in our community.

What are your community strengths such as residents, natural resources, common spaces, local co-operatives, successful local businesses, nonprofit organizations, or local farms? They are all part of the existing Common Good that we should nurture.

Research your communities' unmet needs. Sometimes that reality can be tough to look at or seem overwhelming as you see drug abuse, crime, unemployment, hunger and malnutrition, pollution, and housing needs. However, if you act locally, you can bring about real change. Through your example you can encourage other communities to do the same.

Exploring community needs can take several forms including available local statistics and reports, interviews, and surveys. If you have access to the internet it will make this initial exploration much easier. Find community wide statistics on overall needs comparing job development, food support, drug abuse, foreclosures, homelessness, environmental issues, public transportation, education, domestic violence, affordable housing, gang violence, teen pregnancy. . . the list can go on. Each town and city should have a planning department or education department where local data can be accessed. If there are no available sources that describe prioritized community needs, then find out by asking neighbors.

Identify where the highest community need intersects with your personal interests.

Nuts and Bolts of Grassroots Development

A grassroots community begins with inspired individuals. This inspiration can be a gradual process, or a motivational spark that suddenly awakens community involvement. That spark can ignite when someone feels overwhelming empathy for the plight of others, or becomes outraged by abuse. It can happen when one takes a stance for justice, takes action to uphold our constitution, or is moved by an inspirational speaker. For some it is a way to express their love that in turn feeds their soul. For many it's a way to support their survival in this economic climate. What moves *you* to participate in a grassroots group?

Practical tips are provided for getting started and recruiting, followed by tips on engagement, running meetings, group vision, and staging events that get noticed.

Getting Started

1.	Once you've chosen a group, you can start by going to a meeting or an event. Offer to help out with something small - there's always something to be done, and no amount of help is too little.
2.	If you see a community need that is not being addressed properly, get involved, start a group. See if there are national affiliations to your cause. Is it of value to associate with a group?
3.	One common way grassroots communities start is by having a dedicated individual inviting friends and neighbors to their home to support a political candidate, or watch a DVD about a topic affecting society. For some, it becomes a house party that stirs lively debate
4.	Don't know anyone in your area? Then start a search. You can place ads in papers, use computer networking tools like Facebook, post to newsgroups, make up and hand out flyers, put up posters, or anything else you can think of to find people. You can schedule a meeting and see what kind of response you get.
5.	Once you have even two or three people to back you up, you have a group. More people will show up as your visibility rises. There does not have to be a large group to form a grassroots community.
6.	Another way to start a group is to assemble people in your community who are already aware of a particular topic and decide to take a particular action, like the Food Net, which addresses community hunger needs or renovating abandoned homes for the homeless.
7.	Some groups may begin by sponsoring an event in their area, such as a speaker or a rally. The organizers and the expanded network attracted by the event then form a core group that continues providing beneficial actions and the formation of community.
8.	It may only take one person to make a difference and do things to educate the public. Joe from Connecticut shows movies at his local library, utilizes community access TV for showing relevant movies, and writes to newspapers. A one man force. That commitment creates momentum, and now he has an active support network.

9.	Be focused on what you are doing and be persistent. Just because one door has been slammed in your face, does not mean that another one won't open.
10.	When you realize you are not alone, that there are millions who are involved with their local communities, it inspires involvement. Talk to friends who volunteer and notice groups that are highly functional.
11.	When you are in a group share the material in this book, as it will help develop and energize your organization and cause.

Engagement Principles

1. Be committed to your deeper purpose. Do not allow unfavorable circumstances to blow the wind out of your sails. Know what you are for, not just what you are against. Focus on your goals and not your opposition.

2. When you lead or facilitate your personal energy is amplified in the group. Convey a sense of joy and love to the world. Bring happiness to what you are doing, whether it's an internal strategy session, a mail-stuffing party, or a news conference. Don't be all business and no fun when you run a meeting.

3. Build a structure that encourages and empowers people to step in and take responsibility. Committees are a good approach with other members leading them.

4. Delegate responsibility whenever you can. This allows others in the organization to assume some responsibility and splits the work load. Don't be afraid to delegate both large and small tasks while monitoring progress.

5. Never ask someone else to do something that you are not willing to do yourself. Don't communicate that you are dumping an unwanted or exceptionally onerous task onto volunteers just because you don't want to do it.

6. Explain things clearly. You may need to take some time to explain a particular task to a volunteer. At times, it may seem easier to do the task yourself than to explain it to a novice, but resist the temptation. This is training for you also. A volunteer will remember your attitude, and will remember the time you spent patiently explaining something.

7. Communicate to your volunteers/assistants that you trust them, and tactfully check on the completion of a delegated task. Ask people how things are going, and tell them that you appreciate their hard work and effort.

8. Take time to get to know your volunteers and invest in individuals. Find out who your volunteers are and why they are helping your organization. People often need to forge personal connections within organizations.

9. Focus on empowering people. Without individual ownership of the vision, you cannot build an organization with strong grass-roots based support. Focus on giving individuals ownership of the organization and its purpose.

10. Give individuals within your organization room to be different and understand that they are not all there for the same reasons. There might be multiple ways of doing things, and individuals might join your cause for different motives than your own.

158

11. Be willing to listen to people within your organization and be accessible to them. Maybe a volunteer just needs to check in with you and wants to update you on her/his progress. Is there a problem that someone needs to tell you about?

12. Watch for the good things. So often we tend to focus on the things that go wrong that we forget to notice the things that go well. Rejoice in the small victories that occur every day.

13. Formulate a rational point-by-point response to arguments. Don't just rely on your emotions for your response. Think before your speak. Do research and don't make charges without evidence to back them up.

14. Keep working toward your goals and keep things moving within your organization, even in the face of opposition or defeat. Believe in your vision and be persistent.

15. Word of mouth can be both a powerful and a detrimental public relations and recruitment tool. Talk to a lot of people about your ideas and encourage others in your organization to do the same.

Articulate Vision and Values

"If you don't know where you're going, how can you expect to get there?"   —Basil Walsh

You may be part of a group with clear vision and values that the participants own; if not begin the process. Initially a group might spend long hours hashing out what they're trying to create and figuring out how to collaborate. It is an important investment as these core values and vision lays the foundation for future action.

Values are the ideals set forth by the group. Vision is the image of what you want to co-create or where you want to go. Vision depicts the possibility.Vision cannot be dictated; it can only emerge from a coherent process of reflection and conversation. For that dialogue to occur requires an open environment, one that is safe, where differences can be accepted.

Developing Vision and Values

- Get everyone involved in the discussion for without involvement there is little commitment.

- Start with personal visions so the organization supports the self-realization of its participants.

- Encourage the dialogue and listen attentively to what the group participants value; listen to their visions of the ideal environment; create this together. Refer to Chapter 7 for information on values.

- The dialogue can occur one-on-one, within groups, or through writing. Have people speak only for themselves. An honest exchange is the objective.

- Objectively look at the data collected. Prioritize visions and values that are voiced the most. You can use visual images to help bring them into focus.

- The clearer, more specific and heartfelt your values and vision are, the more they will draw others into the co-created focus.

- State them in the present tense and state them positively. They should evoke strong positive feelings.

- Do something special to engage the group in the newly articulated vision and values.

- Integrate the vision and values into decision criteria, infrastructure design, policies, compensation, and rewards.

- It is vital that leaders "walk the talk" so they must be willing to adhere to and serve the agreed upon vision and values.

(**C**ommunity **O**rganized **T**emporary **S**helter)

An example of using these nuts and bolts of developing grassroots initiatives is from Community ReStart. After running the Pearl Street Center through our first cold winter in western Massachusetts, it made another community need apparent. When we opened in the morning, people came in cold and exhausted from being outside all night. They had to get up every few hours and walk to get some body heat. We got chastised by the health department for letting someone stay in the church and the church members would not allow it. We gathered some donations to purchase space blankets and foot and hand warmers.

The homeless of our community were sheltered under bridges, abandoned cars, the police station lobby, condemned buildings. Addressing a 25-year old unmet need was not an easy challenge. The mayor and his buddies from the housing department and a huge social service agency declared that there was no problem. That Pittsfield had two homeless people and they chose to live outside. I knew that wasn't true and that the agency was getting hundreds of thousands of dollars to deal with homelessness. Not finding problems was its most profitable stance.

There is a moral cost to our community for having people sleep outside in the winter months. There is also a financial loss to our community. There are currently uncoordinated community-based resources employed by unsheltered homeless people in their attempts to stay warm or even alive.

Barton's Crossing, the Pittsfield shelter, was full. At the time there was also a population who couldn't stay at this shelter because of some rule violation. So in desperation any avenue for warmth would do. Committing a minor crime to stay warm for the winter is an example. The yearly cost of housing an inmate at Berkshire House of Corrections is $44,000. Based upon 90 days, the avoidable incarceration of homeless people costs $11,000 per person per season.

Emergency room visits caused by the debilitating effects of sleeping out in the cold costs $500 for Emergency room visits. Some get admitted just to stay out of the cold. Admittance into McGhee Drug and Alcohol Rehabilitation Unit or the Jones Psychiatric Unit is sometimes precipitated by impending or actual homelessness. Homelessness plays a part in delays of discharges due to the hospitals honorable commitment not to discharge anyone to the street. A person could easily have $20,000 in hospital expenses.

These moral and financial costs could be easily mitigated. There were a lot of suitable unused heated buildings. There was a nonprofit community based organization ready to make it happen. But there was a lot of resistance from the people who were benefiting from having the housing system not change. They did not have the Common Good in mind. This provides a little window to resistance that can be faced from those who benefit from the status quo.

So I next put together a forum of the housing inspector, park ranger, some homeless people, social service agency directors serving this population, and the local paper. Eighteen of us pooled our knowledge, we estimated between 20 and 25 people would be out in the cold this coming winter. We got the media involved and searched for a temporary winter shelter space. I did not gain favor with the mayor and his good-old-boy network.

The Salvation Army collaborated with us in getting Berkshire COTS under way by offering their unused heated gym for the overnight shelter. Nine local churches supported a drive that enabled the purchase of forty-five high quality, foldable cots, insurance and a stipend for the nightly social service crew. The $6,800 raised also afforded some food and hot drinks. The Salvation Army provided breakfast.

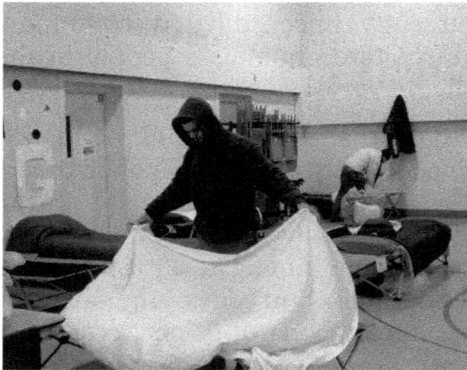

Berkshire Health Systems and Fox Hollow provided bedding. Berkshire County Jail provided weekly laundry service. Over twenty-five volunteers offered to take night shifts to staff the shelter and other operational needs. Several social service agencies volunteered case workers for morning coverage as needed.

People of all backgrounds used the shelter. Single adults, elderly individuals, veterans, and youth all experienced homelessness. Most came because they lost their job and then lost their living space. Many had part time jobs but couldn't afford the rent and there was no subsidized housing available. Persons struggling with substance dependence, disability, persistent mental illness, and with inadequately addressed physical health problems experienced homelessness. COTS was a safety net.

Berkshire COTS employed a behavior-based admissions policy that supports harm reduction: Men and women above the age of 18 who showed respect for the safety and well-being of our guests, volunteers, staff and facility, were welcomed. Berkshire COTS offered a warm, safe and respectful environment which included a nourishing hot breakfast, minor first aid, and access or referral to social services through nightly counselors.

COTS opened December 22, 2012, to April 30, 2013. During these cold months Berkshire COT's doors were open seven nights each week from 7:00 pm to 10:30 pm. After 10:30 pm guests were accompanied by a police officer.

We greatly underestimated the need and provided shelter for these individuals:
- Men 107   Women 24
- Age Range 18 – 69 Average = 36
- No Health Insurance = 48
- Met HUD Definition of Homeless = 110
- Veterans = 16

COTS's use was five times higher than what our local experts predicted. Some cold nights up to forty people were sheltered at our facility. It cost $2.72 to house, feed, and provide counseling per person, per night. This provided a lot of publicity. The following winter the local veteran's home, Soldier On, stepped up as well as the shelter to expand our community beds. We gave them our forty cots. They are still in use today.

Hold a strong belief that the outcome your team wants will occur even when there appears to be odds against you. Keep a vision of accomplishment, a positive attitude, and a sense of achievement. If you do not waver in your conviction, you put the right information field out, and you follow through on your intuition. You will make it happen.

Chapter 7

Group Energy Amplifiers

The previous chapter discussed the involvement and development of grassroots groups. Guidance was provided to create a framework for any grassroots venture. However, what the structure houses is even more important. There is a key element that reflects a group's essence, intentions, actions, and interpersonal dynamics; it is the group field.

This field is shaped by integrated group values. This gives the organization its persona. The sustained values of an organization are what gives it character and becomes its culture. When reinforced these values shape policy, structure, and interpersonal dynamics. They help shape the co-created energy field that is like the group's aura.

As a workshop facilitator and business consultant, I approached group dynamics as a powerful opportunity to work with participants to shift the group energy field so it functions at a high level. I never saw myself as a problem solver but one who brings in values so the group's energy and consciousness functions at a higher level. The group gets to create and own the strategy to develop the organization from a more expanded trusting and authentic place.

When I walked into an organization, I could feel the sustained group energy field. The frequency varied significantly. One downsizing ad agency I visited was filled with fear and backbiting; a constricted feeling when I walked through their doors. Another ad agency we restructured was an up; their office was filled with enthusiasm and creativity. Any sustained group has the potential to function in a high-energy group field.

Grassroots groups are valuable not only for what they can achieve but also for how people feel when working with others. A high energy emerges when people pull together and tap the power of community. In these moments, we feel buoyed and uplifted by our colleagues and companions; we're more creative, more responsive, more engaged and more at ease. In these moments of empowerment, communication and collaboration flow freely and easily, and celebration springs forth naturally and authentically.

People want to participate simply because they get much more than they give. The energy of every individual member of a group contributes to and merges into a collective energy, a synergistic force around which anything seems possible – and often is.

Group Energy Fields

Physical reality consists of fields created by interacting energies. For example, the moon and earth are not simply blocks of matter floating in empty space. The earth exerts a gravitational force on the moon as does the moon to the earth. The two fields push and pull each other in a way that creates a stable energy system or field. By Newton's third law of motion, gravitational forces are of equal strength and in opposite directions.

Energy fields are not phantasms. They have actual, measurable substance. The earth's gravitational field is all around us; it impacts the behavior of all material objects. The moon circling the earth generates ocean tides through a gravitational field. Electromagnetic fields, when harnessed, power computers and light bulbs. Fields are states of space filled with interconnected energy creating invisible structures that are often toroid shaped. There are also fundamental quantum fields that make up quantum energy. They are invisible, intangible, tasteless, and odorless and yet in quantum theory these fields are the substance of the universe.

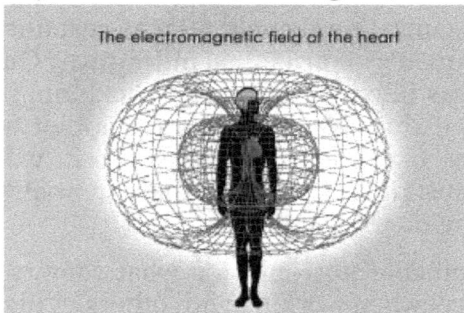
The electromagnetic field of the heart

We ourselves are fields of energy. Each atom of our being is charged with energy, and each cell has a field. This energy is constantly transmitted through our nerves and synapses. Layers of energy, called auras, surround our physical body

166

at all times. These energies combine to create a total energy field that is unique to each of us.

Your energy field may be invisible to the naked eye, but it is real and tangible. It can be measured and monitored, thanks to ultra sensitive equipment. But you don't need sophisticated equipment to experience it right now. Try the following:

Experiencing Your Personal Energy Field

1) Put on loose, comfortable clothing and find a quiet, undisturbed place where you can relax.

2) Sit with your spine straight and your hands placed palms up on your knees.

3) Close your eyes and begin to take long deep breaths, expanding your stomach with each inhalation. Allow your lungs to stretch, then exhale as completely as possible. Keep your mind focused on the breathing. Do this for several minutes.

4) Keeping your eyes closed; bring your internal attention to your hands.

As you inhale, visualize energy pouring into your lungs and then flowing down your arms, into your hands. Continue this visualization for several minutes as the energy pools into your hands.

5) Very, very slowly begin to raise your arms up from your lap. Keep the palms of your hands open. With almost imperceptible movement, bring your open palms closer to each other. When your hands are about three inches apart, stop.

6) Notice what's between your hands. Feel it. Play with it. Move one hand up slightly, the other down. Remember to keep your movements very slow, and continue to take long deep breaths.

7) When you're ready to end, come out slowly and gently. Slowly rub your energized hands over your face and neck.

Most people feel the energy field between their palms as elastic, vibrant, and full of substance. Some even sense color or shape. To explore this personal field, experiment with Tai Chi. However you perceive it, something is there.

Try this same exercise with a partner, playing with the energy co-created between your open palms. Become aware of the energy interplay. You have just experienced an important aspect of energy fields: They are always interacting with other fields.

Our relationships—in other words, our group energy fields— are real. They are experienced. We sense and feel the "vibes" of others. And this energy field can vibrate at different frequencies.

Energy Field Spectrum

Just as the variance of vibration gives colors their distinctions,

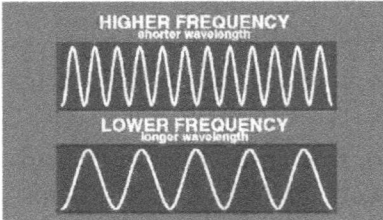

so too the energy we hold gives us distinction. We become aware of this unseen energy in motion through our feelings. Just as colors have a band width so do our emotions. The lowest vibration is fear and as the vibration increases the emotion is felt as anger then goes to sadness. As it increases further, energy's interconnected nature gets revealed and there is greater heartfelt relation and empathy for others around us. As the vibration increases we sense it in our feelings as hope, joy, and unconditional love.

All of these emotions communicate to us. I am not suggesting any emotion gets shut down. You don't want to shoot the messenger. However, overall we carry a vibrating tone. It is the frequency we most often reside in. What part on the spectrum do you normally reside?

The energy of group fields is also variable, just as personal frequencies are variable and an overall tone exists. It changes from one group field to the next. Certainly, you know what it's like to be with a group or person that invigorates you, and then with another that exhausts you. There are energy gainers and energy drainers. The same applies for systems and processes that define exchanges and relationships. This can uplift and enliven you, or it can leave you feeling drained and depleted.

Every system contains the potential to move its participants to a higher energy state. However, Elite Systems function at a low frequency or vibration because they hold a low consciousness of deceit, fear, control, and theft. Almost everything about the exploitive systems eventually dampens your vibration. It drains your energy and wealth. These systems are meant to create suppression, ignorance, and debt. They stir up emotions vibrating at a low level. When the political, corporate, and economic systems evoke anger or fear in you, it is a further indication of the frequency of these systems.

When you are functioning in a low vibration system, your thoughts are often about survival, or keeping what you have, and there is an element of fear. You will attract more of the same. Like frequencies attract.

In contrast, Common Good Systems function at a higher frequency. When groups adopt core values, like openness and interconnectedness, then the resulting system will be in the high part of the spectrum. The values we hold vibrate at distinct levels. These values are what develop and sustain a group's culture and the resulting group energy field.

The Power in Values

"Your beliefs become your thoughts, Your thoughts become your words, Your words become your actions, Your actions become your habits, Your habits become your values, Your values become your destiny."- Mahatma Gandhi

We have all had the exhilaration of meshing with others to create a synergistic experience, one where our spirits were uplifted. But all too often we've come away from these endeavors without the tools to sustain that energy collectively. Yet why is it that some groups and movements not only evoke this response from participants but also channel that energy into positive action? Are there common elements present in empowered groups?

After twenty-five years of working with hundreds of communities, organizations and teams, those that were empowered with impressive accomplishments had integrated six values into their culture.[27] Values are the ideals set forth by the group.

Values

- Values are the deepest and most powerful motivators of personal action. They prioritize our intentions.

- Values align the group field on an emotional level, helping to create a harmonious environment.

- Values can be energizing, motivating, and inspiring.

- Values replace rules.

- Values shape group dynamics and more tangible aspects such as: strategies, structures, policies, and compensation.

Values must be integrated and adhered to if you want to maintain the vibration of that value. This means enforcing the values you all agree to uphold as a group.

Chapter 4 described Community ReStart's supportive housing program where all residents look to maintain their sobriety. A core value of the program is sobriety. All residents agree to leave if they break their commitment. So we had to go around with random tests to see if anyone is using, if they test positive they need to leave. At first I was conflicted with another core value of the organization, compassion for everyone.

The solution to the conflict was collaboration. I worked with the director of the stabilization unit at the hospital, with the corrections facility, with social service agencies, and with the local half-way houses. A caseworker helped transition the residents from our houses to other housing, a detoxifying facility, stabilization program, half-way house, or any other appropriate plan. The exit plan was their next best step.

Values need to be owned and embraced by the participants; hollow values are nothing more than meaningless slogans. When groups own and integrate six core values, they tend to function in the spectrum I refer to as the High-Energy Zone.

170

Six Energy Amplifiers

While working with group energy fields, six characteristics or values came clearly into view. Leading workshops on yoga, personal growth, and relationships provided valuable insights. These programs created temporary group fields that typically involved sixty participants and lasted three to five days. I found that if the six characteristics were integrated into the group, the entire field functioned in the High-Energy Zone. Participants' consciousness expanded and they were able to break through dysfunctional beliefs at a much higher rate. They felt revitalized and transformed. What I witnessed in the group response was confirmed later by the participants' anonymous evaluations.

Eventually my partner, Christine Warren, and I went to work as organizational development consultants, working with permanent group fields in the diverse cultures of businesses and communities. This work offered constant proof of the effectiveness of these ideas. It allowed us to see the patterns that were spinning a group's energy up or down. We learned to identify the primary dysfunctional pattern—and the root of the dysfunction which acts as a "trigger." When the trigger is aligned with energy's characteristics, the entire group field became more vibrant. This happened consistently, time after time.

But why do high performing organizations have these values and what does this imply? The answer lies within the atoms that make up the universe. The very underpinning of our physical reality is a field of quantum energy and physicists have found this essence has six distinct behaviors. These six behaviors, along with the Law of Attraction, provide important strategic directions for any group endeavor. When we align with the nature of energy, and we attune to its frequency, we and the group access a power that amplifies our ability for success.

Thus, these six characteristics led me to the understanding that I had sought ever since a certain lightning bolt struck when I was seventeen. The awareness of these same six characteristics is not new. The science of Sankhya described these same characteristics 6,000 years ago, and they became a foundation of yoga and Ayurvedic medicine.

Six Energy Amplifiers

- Intention and Alignment
- Relational and Holistic
- Diversity and Balance
- Possibility and Uncertainty
- Open and Flowing
- Synergy and Love

These characteristics transcend form. When they are present in any group—whether it's composed of two people (a marriage, for example) or two hundred million (a nation)—that group operates in the high-energy zone. The six characteristics are also part of any healthy biological system. In fact, they are the underlying characteristics of every molecule that makes up our universe. They reflect the nature of potential energy, the essence of our being, the common thread that weaves the ever-changing tapestry of our physical universe.

Scientists, mystics, ecologists, and sociologists have all explored the nature of energy and its application to their disciplines. Now we'll see how their discoveries ring true with our own personal experiences. We'll see how to utilize these discoveries by applying them to intimate relationships, families, teams, grassroots initiatives, business organizations, communities, and nations.

It makes sense, everything is energy. Communities generate group energy fields, and when groups align with the nature of energy they vibrate at a higher level where love, trust, and collaboration flourish. A synergy with Universal Energy and Consciousness exists.

Each behavior is described from a scientific perspective and how it translates into a grassroots organization's or community's culture. This is followed by a personal introspection on how you align with these values. Symbols are used to represent the described behavior.

172

As previously discussed, what scientists recently re-discovered is what the ancient mystics knew, consciousness shapes energy. This emphasizes the importance of a clear vision and values. Intention and action are bound together and generate an information field. Intention comes first. Your intentions drive your actions and steer your behaviors. It also attracts what you are intending.

It is important that groups become clear about their intentions including values and beliefs. When a group integrates core values it aligns the energy of the group. If a group does not align its intentions and values, its energy becomes scattered as the field dissipates itself through opposing forces.

Dialogue and clarity about core values are vital for alignment. These values help channel the flow of energy just as the banks of a river channel the flow of water. When the group reinforces alignment of core values, it greatly increases the capacity of the group to flow in the same direction, even when challenges exist.

Intentions can be subconscious beyond our awareness. You may hold a subconscious intention to be in strict control of fear of imagined consequences. As you interact with others, you are oblivious to your behavior and the deeper intention driving it. But those around you see the demanding, tight behavior.

Your intentions are fueled by potential energy. There can be no action of any kind without intention combined with energy. Thus, intention shapes the information field and directs the energy of your actions. This conscious or unconscious intention makes us creators in our unfolding world.

Intention becomes a powerful attractor when it is focused. When intention is held with a high vibration, the Law of Attraction is given traction. When our thoughts align with our deeds, our values with our actions, we access a power. We dissipate that power when we say one thing and do another. Integrity strengthens intention and our ability to integrate values.

If we are able to sustain an intention we are dedicated to, we will probably be bathed in success. Earl Nightingale, a pioneer in business success theory, in the late '50s interviewed many of the top business entrepreneurs in the United States. He met with Carnegie, Edison and Ford, and many other industrial leaders. Out of all the parameters, skills, behaviors and attitudes he listed, he saw one that was integral to each person's success -- it was vision. It was a very active vision that focused intention into their undertakings. The intent can be good or evil, but holding a vision of the intention is essential for success.

"Where there is no vision, the people perish."[28]

The most successful business partnerships and executive teams have the same trait. They share core goals and values and intention. It doesn't matter if they are social friends or if they share the same outside interests. The important point is that they communicate openly about these shared values and goals particularly in light of personal behaviors and decisions that affect the organization. Initially it may take long hours together hashing out what the group is trying to create and how to collaborate. Refer to the previous tips on developing a vision.

Ongoing feedback mechanisms are essential in assuring that these values and visions are upheld and that there is alignment. Feedback provides great opportunities for us to grow and develop. If we see and transform the patterns that hold us back, our growth is unlimited. By soliciting feedback from supervisors and peers, we can receive gems of insight into our growth.

In electrical systems, feedback mechanisms are used to provide continuous data to an automatic control device so that course corrections can be made. In a similar way, we need feedback on the patterns that make up the major components of the group's circuitry.

When I was giving personal growth workshops, I could see that couples tended to integrate their insights from the workshop much more deeply and consistently than singles. Couples have each other. They can give each other clear and objective feedback. Like an ongoing feedback mechanism of a circuit they are able to make corrections to further align with the vision and values.

As a team, married or not, anyone can develop their potential by giving and receiving positive and constructive feedback. It's one of the most powerful tools for self-development. It takes some understanding, coaching, and practice to master the skills of feedback. See the end of Chapter 10 for tips on giving and receiving feedback. Give yourself honest feedback on how you have integrated the characteristics of intention and alignment.

Self-Test

- Do you set goals and intentions to start each day?

- Do your words, commitment, and intentions align with your actions?

- Do the groups you're involved in have active core values that guide their actions? Are the groups aligned to these values?

- Do the group intentions serve something beyond the actual groups themselves?

- Do your groups utilize feedback if someone does not adhere to the values of the group? Is there safety within these groups for this discussion to occur?

Relational and Holistic

Whatever affects one directly, affects all indirectly.
— Martin Luther King, Jr.

The nature of energy has forced scientists to pay attention to relationships. At the subatomic level, nothing exists unless it engages another energy source. This energy is part of a complex web of relations. Matter is the momentary manifestation of interconnected fields of quantum energy. These interactions appear as particles because the fields come together very abruptly in minute regions of space. We are made of these interacting particles. We are part of a relational field, all connected to each other and to the Source.

Irish physicist Jon Stewart Bell demonstrated that all conceivable models of quantum reality must incorporate a relational connection. On a subatomic level, nature arranges instantaneous and ongoing connections between two photons. When subatomic particles contact, they create a link that physical distance doesn't break. The webs of potential energy create relationships that occur faster than the speed of light across space and time. Scientists call such relationships "non-local." Einstein called them "spooky actions at a distance."

These links occur in your own energy field just as they do on the subatomic level. Information fields are non-local. When you are connected in a relational field, a bond of energy forms. You have probably noticed this when people have simultaneous thoughts as you. You think of them and the phone rings with them on the line. These "spooky actions at a distance" make us aware that connections are subtly present

Group field relationships create a holistic web where changes in one part of the field affect the whole. Energy is interconnected; each aspect of the field affects the whole. David Bohm described this wholeness: *"Relativity and quantum theory agreed, in that they both imply the need to look at the world as an undivided whole, in which all parts of the universe, including the observer and his instruments, merge and unite in one totality. The inseparable quantum interconnectedness of the whole universe is the fundamental reality."*[29]

This interconnectedness happens with all of us, and it becomes intensified where we live, work, and play. Whenever a member is removed or added to the group field, the change has a holistic impact. So it behooves us to look at whom we bring into our relational fields. You may have experienced the power of one person to affect the whole. Perhaps your group was maintaining itself in the high-energy zone; then someone new came in and the entire group began to spin down. Or one bright soul uplifted the entire organization.

This holistic web repeats itself with any micro- or macro-system that creates an energy field—our own biological energy fields, our families, organizations, communities, and nation. They are all interdependent, just as any evolved ecosystem. When they connect harmoniously they are all strengthened. When a relational field is connected, it generates a force that, if large enough, the .01% could never withstand.

The dark elite will always try methods to break up community, unions or any form of mass demonstration. In the mid-1950s, nearly 40 percent of American workers were either union members or "nonunion members who were nonetheless covered by union contracts." Today unions represent 11 percent of the work force. Our sense of community is a shadow of the 1960 landscape.

We need to empower community and our collective creativity instead of the Elite machine.

Be aware of outside influences to break organizing efforts. There are also internal challenges that affect how well a group relates with each other. I have seen these holistic effects throughout my business-consulting career. When you take an overview of an organization, including its personal, structural, and interpersonal patterns, you can see how the patterns reverberate throughout the entire organization and some fester divisiveness.

For example, ineffective policies that block creative exchanges will reduce productivity or bog down development. Two influential members who don't get along will trigger turf wars throughout the entire organization. All of these developments shut down interconnectedness and the group field has a lower vibration. Likewise we can create an environment where relations and creative exchange are nurtured.

Everything is connected. Wayne Dyer PhD, self-improvement author, calls us "environorganisms."[30] We are inseparable from our environment. The environment is our extended body.

So when we engage in relationships with others we are touching something sacred and inherent to all life. When we network with others we are creating an interconnected field that mimics how every particle is coming into existence. Just as synapses connect in the brain, the interconnected communication and exchange within a group creates a collective mind. This group intelligence has a profound impact on the way a grassroots initiative or organization emerges affecting success and profitability.

Self-Test

- Do you reach out to others? Are you an introvert or extrovert? Are you shy and withdrawn? Do you take risks by extending out to others?

- Do you actively participate in, and maintain webs of, relationships through family, play, and social group endeavors? At work are you involved in networks or teams? Do those networks feel like community?

- Is there active community in your life? Do you have pockets of friends that you periodically connect with? Do you feel a relational connection with them?

- At work and within sustained groups do you tap the power of the collective mind?

- Do you see that you are a part of a holistic web when you participate in a group? Are you aware of the repercussions of your actions?

Diversity and Balance

We must learn to live together as brothers or perish as fools.

—Martin Luther King, Jr

Within the seed of quantum energy lays the expression of the vast material realm—including our bodies and everything we encounter. Rocks, trees, oceans, and stars are all its expressions. This potential energy gives birth to everything in the universe, including the broad spectrum of vibrations. For example, some electromagnetic waves are just one-billionth of a centimeter in size; some of them arc over six miles. Energy's nature has a broad spectrum of vibrations and manifestations. If we are to be closer to energy nature we must embrace this vast expression.

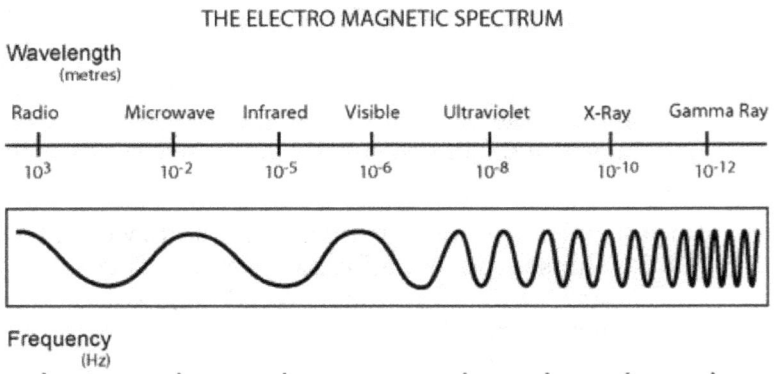

THE ELECTRO MAGNETIC SPECTRUM

Wavelength
(metres)

Radio	Microwave	Infrared	Visible	Ultraviolet	X-Ray	Gamma Ray
10^3	10^{-2}	10^{-5}	10^{-6}	10^{-8}	10^{-10}	10^{-12}

Frequency
(Hz)

When we accept the broad spectrum of expressions of humanity, we are embracing energy's nature. Intolerance of other religions, other paths, other cultures, other races takes you farther from our nature. For the same reason, the more we expand the range of acceptance of others—the more we tolerate differences and become less judgmental—the more we align ourselves with the nature of energy and the power of community. Diversity is nature's way; intolerance opposes our deeper nature.

In addition to diversity, the super string theory states that quantum energy in all its forms has symmetry and dynamic balance. Basically, opposing forces balance each other, just as the negatively charged electrons balance positrons. Physicists now realize that symmetry and balance are the keys to constructing accurate descriptions of nature.

Balance of work, play, family, community and rest mimic the nature of this higher energy. The optimal grassroots community structure involves this balance. To behave like energy's nature means to embrace diversity and be in dynamic balance in your life.

You demonstrate tolerance in your behavior. You communicate respect for others even if they are different from you – even if you disagree with some aspects of their thinking or their way of life. By accepting others beyond our differences, we become more aligned with the nature of energy. Energy's nature embraces all differences.

With a wide range of people frequenting the Pearl Street Center we practiced acceptance. One toothless, hunched, bag lady that wore a beat up vest with a fluorescent orange X, was a former college professor that I found to be very insightful. A long-term alcoholic who frequented the Center played beautiful piano pieces that he composed. I have learned not to judge others by their outward appearances or circumstances or disease.

Diversity involves a broad range of generations and cultural backgrounds. It means connecting with the different people who make up your local neighborhoods. A gay man once described for me what it was like to have to work with a fundamentalist religious couple. At first he dreaded their intolerant attitude to homosexuality. As he interacted with them, though, his attitude changed. That's not to say that he began to sympathize with their views. Rather, he began to see them as much more than their views. They worked hard. They were good team members. They were complete human beings with qualities he respected.

By accepting them beyond their differences, this man was becoming more aligned with the nature of energy. It's not an easy thing to accept and even respect others' differences. If teammates see beyond their differences and respect each others' contributions – that team is embracing energy's nature.

Families force us to go beyond our limited perceptions of what is acceptable and arrive at a place where our hearts remain open. Children adopt opposing views, preferences, and habits, and parents have to broaden their perspectives or shut down.

Bob and Bonnie Hunt raised thirteen children. I asked them what their biggest lesson was from taking on such a challenge. Bonnie responded without hesitation: *"Accept and love your kids even if you disagree with their choices."* Bob agreed.

Life opens up when we exercise our capacity to accept others in their diverse expressions of life. The United States was founded on diversity. The U.S. Constitution crystallized the acceptance of differences with the statement "all men are created equal." Cuban-Americans in Miami differ from Mormon-Americans in Utah who differ from Silicon Valley–Americans in California. We are diverse in our thinking patterns, points of view, and cultural differences. The principle of tolerance must be upheld in a society that embraces cultural differences and outlooks.

Tolerance allows individuals and groups the opportunity to express themselves. It encourages intellectual, artistic, scientific, religious, philosophical, and moral freedom. We set limits, of course, in order to protect the public good. But even while setting these limits we need to remember that the more tolerant a society is, the more likely it is to engender mutual trust and cooperation.

Self-Test

- What comments do you make or reactions do you have when your standards and beliefs are confronted?

- Do you have friends and acquaintances who are very different from each other? Do you participate in groups that are very different from each other?

- Do you function with a high level of tension, always putting out fires?

- How much balanced force do you have—when you are focused, centered, and at peace?

- Do you function primarily in a state of dynamic balance with work, play, family, and community?

Possibility and Uncertainty

In the quantum realm, energy has yet to take on a particle form. Thus, quantum energy exists outside of our dimensions of space and time. The quantum realm is not a world of actual physical events; instead, it is a world filled with numerous unrealized possibilities for actions. In other words, quantum energy is an omnipresent force that is pure possibility. We are literally surrounded by a vast ocean of possibilities.

When we act with possibility in mind, we see that we can be creative every moment. We believe in the fertile potential of others and ourselves. This is not blind optimism. When we act with possibility in mind, we see the glass half-full instead of half-empty. We see, encourage, and nurture the possibilities that can bear fruit.

Where there is possibility, there is also uncertainty. When physicists try to predict the behavior of quantum energy, they are forced to use a mathematical approach based on probability. Probability began as collaboration between mathematicians and gamblers to determine the odds in dice games. It is basically a systematic counting of the possibilities

Electron Cloud Model

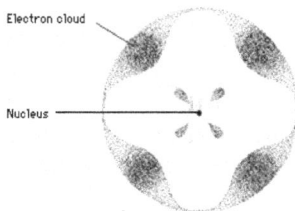

that a certain action can occur. Some events are more likely than others, and over an average of many events a given pattern of outcomes is predictable. Predicting the place of an electron is based on where the concentrated appearances are as depicted in the figure. So Schrodinger's equation, which mathematically describes all the possibilities of a quantum wave, is basically the same as a bookmaker's odds—it's an educated guess in an uncertain situation.

From the quantum perspective, each interaction is the unfolding of uncertain possibilities. The same holds true for any living system, for any group dynamic. Uncertainty and possibility is the way of life. You meet a person who creates a connection that opens a door, and your career takes off. You miss a train, and then meet the love of your life.

Each of us is a dynamic system. Our evolving future is uncertain. No matter how determined we are to increase probability, some degree of insecurity always exists. Look at the vast technology used to predict weather and how there is unpredictability. We all must be able to adapt to life's uncertainty. It is the deeper essence of our existence. Things that we take for granted as safe, secure, and permanent are illusions in the higher vibration field.

When we engage the Law of Attraction, we don't know how our vision will take form because we are attracting things that are outside of our conscious awareness. When we attract things in our life, it is uncertain how the events will unfold. Just as our Community ReStart team didn't realize that someone, hacking our email, would put an end to the hostile takeover attempt. Nothing in life is certain.

By integrating this deeper truth, we become less attached to possessions, less fearful of the unknown, and less resistant to change in this uncertain place. We put greater emphasis on family, friends, and relations. Actions become guided more by intuition as we sail through the waters of uncertainty to land on the shores of manifesting possibilities.

High-energy groups consciously develop possibilities by encouraging the development of individuals' talents and passions. For example: providing regular feedback on performance, entrusting members with initiatives, providing mentors, reporting to the group on other meetings, or leading a brief training or exercise during meetings. It means letting others take the lead on projects, give them space to learn. The idea is to support, not control, their leadership development, and at the same time provide honest feedback on performance. This value fosters a learning environment on all levels.

Letting Go of Fear

When we plunge into uncertainty, we merge with the present, which has ceaseless possibilities. We let go of old patterns of unconscious behavior that directed our energy and the energy of our groups. If we regard each moment as fresh and ripe with possibility, we are not being naive or flighty. We are acknowledging the true nature of our universe. When this happens, something new and different can be born from a group—what I call an emergence.

Whenever I facilitate a group, before the meeting begins I bring up a mental image. I visualize a pile of all the assessments, planning, and notes for this meeting, and I imagine throwing the pile out the window. I let go of my planning to allow the emergence of the group to dictate the flow.

I jump into the water, so to speak, and immerse myself in the group field. It requires letting go of fear that says I need to be in control. I still satisfy the agenda and get everything done, and yet I remind myself to respond organically to the unfolding of uncertain possibility. I relax my grip on my predetermined concepts, and I let the group dynamic determine the flow of the meeting. When that happens, the meeting itself creates moments that I never could have anticipated. When these unpredictable moments are held in the light of possibility, the energy of the group rises.

When there is room for uncertainty to blossom, the seed of a simple thought can take root and grow into remarkable results.

One of the major blocks that prevent people from immersing themselves in uncertain possibility is, of course, fear. It means working without the safety net of the familiar. If we give in to fear, we lose our capacity to integrate this characteristic of energy. Fear shuts down the group's capacity to embrace possibility and uncertainty.

There is an important distinction to be made in talking about fear. There is the appropriate jolt of fear that we experience when faced with danger—a visceral warning to stay alert and be responsive. For most people, this sort of fear occurs infrequently. The fear I mean is psychological. It causes people to dread what can be imagined around every corner. It immobilizes action and prevents change. It causes parents to resist their own children's expressions of independence. It makes employees undermine new company policies. It clouds a person's view of possibility. When sustained over time, this unnecessary fear spins down any person or group.

These exploitive systems are based on deception and suppression. The "War on Terror," accumulating debt, and the disempowerment of the many, all produce a low vibrating energy. These are meant to depress individual possibility and critical thinking, and to produce fear. It is the antithesis of energy's nature.

When I lead a workshop or facilitate organizational change, I make it paramount to develop a safe environment. It's the best weapon against fear. Confidentiality, communication tools, and objective nonjudgmental feedback are some of the elements. We must make it safe.

That safety within a group comes from trust, a connection that feels like family or a team. It is developing a sense of community. Integrating the values of relationship and diversity, we provide the safety for the uncertain possibility of the group to emerge.

Self-Test

- How do you view your own prospects and possibility?

- Do you speak positively of others and make light of your burdens?

- Do you see the advantages of an idea first, before pointing out the disadvantages? Instead of looking for reasons why something can't be done, do you search for ways in which it can?

- Does fear prevent you from taking occasional risks and experimenting with things outside your routine?

Open and Flowing

Werner Heisenberg, the German physicist who helped establish quantum mechanics and our ideas about elementary particles, called the nature of quantum energy *"the dissolution of the rigid frame."* The essence of all form is quantum energy which is formless at the higher frequency.

Energy is always associated with movement, activity—an ongoing flow in the moment of life. We do not exist in a static environment but in a dynamic, active world. This quantum truth applies to the behavior of ecosystems as well.

The most productive ecosystems are physically open, allowing a high-carrying capacity for nutrients. For example, the most productive marine ecosystem in the United States is the Bering Sea off the west coast of Alaska. It is a large open system where rich nutrients flow over a broad continental shelf. Currently this ecosystem provides over 56 percent of the nation's commercial catch of fish and shellfish.

An even more impressive example is the open upwelling off the coast of Peru. Currents there bring a rich flow of nutrients to the surface, making it the most productive marine habitat in the world. During some years the entire fish harvest of the United States equals just 20 percent of the catch taken in this area, which is about half the size of Pennsylvania.

A high-carrying capacity for nutrients—this is an important feature of high-energy systems. Systems with a low-carrying capacity tend to stagnate.

For any system to emerge requires openness to its surroundings. It must be open to what nurtures it.

Now let's look at human-made systems, such as grassroots communities. What are "nutrients" to these systems? Healthy, supportive relationships and great ideas are nutrients of development. Groups thrive when they develop and support the exchange of ideas through networks. These ideas nourish creativity, productivity, personal development, responsiveness, and effectiveness. These nutrients of relations and ideas feed the organization's growth.

These nutrients develop best in an open and fluid environment. To achieve such openness and flow, we need to dissolve the rigid judgments and structures we build in our lives, our relations, and our organizations.

There is a collective unconscious that opposes this value. We are a species of wall builders and space dividers. Walls give us security. We put up barriers for protection from all sorts of harm. But many of these barriers are unnecessary. Many of our protection devices actually harm us because they block the flow of energy and disconnect us from relationships and our source.

Think of people who live in self-imposed isolation, walled in the rigid framework of their own minds. We can stay walled-up in our homes, sedated by television and other habits. We can block ourselves from experiencing the wonder of life. Then we exist in a low-energy pattern—an unconscious trance.

Now think of people who are open to life, people who reach out to others, unguarded, with warmth and friendliness. When they listen, you feel heard. They have the capacity to flow with change. They seem to be more present. Perhaps you are one of those people.

Openness is feminine in nature; it is receptive. On a personal level, this openness becomes tested when we receive feedback. For many it is difficult to really listen and take in feedback that may contradict our own personal perceptions of who we think we are. When our personal egos are strong, it creates a barrier to reception and flexibility.

Groups and individuals who are open are flexible in their attitudes, behaviors, and actions. They aren't stuck in old habits that no longer serve the group's intentions. They tolerate change and the new ideas of the moment. The members exchange information openly. You rarely find pockets of withheld information. Leaders don't control information in order to hold power. In such a group the environment consists of co-creative exchanges. For a venture to sustain a high carrying capacity of information, it must keep its communication channels open. It must tap the group field for a higher wisdom.

In other words, the group acts like a brain with all its synapses firing. There is openness and receptivity. Its members listen even when there is disagreement. They can see the situation as others see it. In this organization, formality is far less important than the task at hand. Rules and regulations have given way to a spontaneity grounded in a common vision and shared values. They have fun. They laugh. Although high levels of stress occur in occasional peaks, the members don't feel long-term, ongoing distress. Such a group exemplifies what I mean by "open and flowing."

This may seem obvious, as business gurus have been preaching this idea for years. However, my assessments of over one hundred business organizations often showed bottlenecks of information at the top. Some managers and CEOs would hoard information. They saw this information and knowledge as power. But their grip on the channels of communication only choked the idea and relation exchange of the group. This choking is endemic of Elite Systems.

Arnold Toynbee studied twenty-six lost civilizations and found that they all perished for the same reason—they overprotected their tenants, the very ones that had first made them powerful. They eventually shattered because of their own rigidity, their closed views, and their refusal to yield to an evolving world.

Just as civilizations in the past have gone through transitions, it is our time to transition from the closed and suppressed Elite Systems to open and flowing Common Good Systems.

Heraclitus addressed the fluid nature of existence two thousand six hundred years ago, *"You cannot step twice into the same river, for fresh waters are ever flowing in upon you."* Within groups, as within life, there is a constant process of emergence—an everlasting becoming. The fresh waters of energy are ever flowing, making our world a constant flux.

Self-Test

- Do you tend to confine yourself to the four walls of your home? Do you often feel isolated and shut off from the world?

- Are you receptive to others? Are you a good listener?

- Do you listen to other's viewpoints even when you disagree?

- Does your internal dialogue begin to respond before the speaker finishes?

- Do you flow with unexpected occurrences or do you often shut down and react when things don't go your way?

- Are the groups you're involved with have open systems? Is there receptivity and exchange throughout the groups for ideas and information?

- Do you practice meditation, yoga, or a martial art that opens your being to Universal Energy?

Synergy and Love

Energy moves in waves. When two waves are in phase, the effect is greater than simply one-plus-one. With synergy, the energy waves are aligned. When a group produces more than the sum of its parts through the joint effort of its members, it is achieving synergy.

It is nature's way to be in synergy. Two cells out of sync will beat together when placed near each other. The power of synergy can be harnessed to create superconductivity and synchronous light emissions (lasers). A similar entrainment can occur for energy fields of individuals or groups.

Rowers can generate this synergy with their teammates. They call it "swing" when the boat seems to lift right out of the water.   One Olympic contender said, *"A boat does not have swing unless everyone is putting out in exact measure. And because of that, and only because of that, there is the possibility of trust among oarsmen. There is this trust and connection among all of*

them. All eight members truly function as one." Through that in-phase stroke they experience their highest level of performance.

When the whole is greater than the sum of its parts, synergy is amplifying the energy, whether in mergers, teamwork, symbiotic relationships or other cooperative ventures.

Synergy within relationships, families, teams, organizations and communities requires an energetic exchange that is coherent and aligned like a laser. For the energy to align, the participants must have a similar intention. They trust each other so that they are open and receptive to each other's contributions. They must respect their partners for the possibilities they bring to the co-creative process. When synergy is present, the characteristics of energy are present.

There is an emotional signature that resonates within any group; it is an indicator that synergy exists. This is something you can feel, as some meetings are caring, some confront tough issues, some are filled with anger, some with love. The emotion of a higher vibration— love, enthusiasm, and joy— occurs spontaneously when the group is in alignment with the nature of this higher vibration. When you feel that energy of love and excitement, you are feeling the vibration of energy's higher nature.

Like any reception device, our minds can resonate at a higher frequency. Radios receive their signal from the transmitting airwaves by aligning themselves to the signal being transmitted. When our behavior aligns with these energy characteristics, the body behaves like a tuning fork. It vibrates at a higher frequency and we likewise connect with a higher consciousness. The Law of Attraction is amplified with a more powerful information field.

This higher energy translates into exchanges that are uplifting, inspiring, and fulfilling. Love, respect, and a sense of brotherhood and sisterhood predominate. There is forgiveness, because the Light embraces the dark. Unconditional love is the predominant emotional exchange. In this way, the goal of all spiritual practices and laws are realized.

"'Love the Lord your God with all your heart and with all your soul and with all your mind." This is the first and greatest commandment. And the second is like it: "Love your neighbor as yourself. All the Law and the Prophets hang on these two commandments." Jesus, Matthew 22:37-40

Self-Test

- Are you sensitive to the energy you put behind your words when you communicate?

- How closely do you align with energy's nature in your own personal life?

- What is your most significant behavior that opposes energy's nature?

- How closely do the groups you are involved in align with energy's nature?

- Do you consciously practice holding love?

The High-Energy Zone

When we enter the high-energy zone we are engaging the essential characteristics of energy. But why does this foundational energy have those characteristics? Quantum physics suggests, and six-thousand-year-old yoga teachings assert, that energy is shaped by consciousness. So the universal quantum energy has a distinct behavior and shape that implies a Universal Consciousness shaping it.

When we align ourselves with the characteristics of energy's fundamental nature, that is, when we feel the exhilaration and connectedness I have been describing, we are tuning into a force that exists beneath the material realm and also beyond it. We transcend our normal "reality," which is limited by three dimensions of space and one dimension of time. In effect, we are plugging into an energy field that lights-up our spirit.

The rejuvenation of your spirit is not only accessible in the hallowed meeting places of churches, but any group has the potential to resonate in the high-energy zone and thus become a conduit to uplift.

Although we have discussed the six characteristics of energy separately, in fact they function simultaneously. Let's look at how the characteristics can be considered together.

We come together with others—whether for work or play, as family, community, school, business or a team—and co-create a group energy through relationships that act holistically. The cohesiveness of this field of energy relies on a common focus—that is, a group intention—and the alignment shared. This field of energy is not isolated. Its nature requires openness and transparency so that it can flow and emerge. This openness, naturally, results in exposure to diversity. Yet we stay balanced within that diversity through a deeper shared vision and values. This group energy is always evolving into possibility, and its outcome is uncertain. However, if synergy and love exists, the group will be a community and connected to weather any storm and able to creatively respond to opportunities.

If our lives and actions also have these characteristics of energy, we will harmonize with the fundamental patterns of creation.

Whether it's a grassroots group, a family, team, community or marriage, the high-energy zone is the next frontier. It is the evolution we are now living. By applying to our groups and relationships the same energizing characteristics that occur in nature, we can choose to be a conscious part of that evolution. We can choose to create an optimum environment for growth and development. We can choose greater fulfillment and community. We can choose to be uplifted in our group endeavors and by one another.

Chapter 8

Rewiring for Common Good Systems

This book has been about a rewiring of sorts. This rewiring is both internal and external. It began with the way our subconscious was unconsciously wired through social engineering, affecting our perception and behavior. Systems designed to subjugate the masses require covert means that involve manipulating beliefs. Consciousness is the primary battlefront; it is what sustains the delusion and what can end it. False beliefs act as filters, affecting capacity to listen to a deeper truth and to be aware of what is being done in the name of democracy. The rewiring involves removing false subconscious beliefs that disempower and delude.

The rewiring includes the way we create what we want in life. The Law of Attraction describes how information fields work. If we hold a high vibration with a vision, we attract what we want. This is how we are wired to potential energy and the quantum ocean we swim in. So why not acknowledge the wiring and act accordingly, use it properly. Training yourself to feel more joy and focusing on what you want is actually developing synapses; our neural pathways can be rewired.

As you take the rewiring externally, it requires connecting with others and being part of your community. This is the source of the resurgence, creating a force for change with others. Grassroots engagement is a way to connect locally and take on a more active part in this evolution. The power lies in the collective.

Within an organization, it is important to wire-in the nature of energy into the culture of the group. Integrating the six core values into the culture shifts the group field. By generating a group-energy field that vibrates at a high level, you help assure that participants become rejuvenated through their involvement. This rejuvenation is particularly important for volunteers, as it becomes a reward for their participation. These high-energy groups can fuel the needed system change.

Common Good systems are wired to spread local empowerment to the many. There is openness and collaboration. It can be a onetime event or a long term commitment to a cause. It generates a greater ownership and participation in local community development. A wide variety of organizational structures can be used to engage participation.

The distinctive wiring characteristic of the Elite system is its consolidation, centralization and control of power into the hands of the few. Rewiring government and corporate control involves moving away from consolidation and hierarchy. It means having resources more locally controlled with transparency. This local empowerment includes county seats, cities and local towns.

There are varieties of approaches; one is that the county seat is where funds are dispersed from state and federal taxes. These local and transparent systems would distribute funds to handle education, health care, infrastructure, enforcement, and emergency services. The strategy would greatly reduce money and power to the corrupt state and federal systems and instead transferring much more to a town, city and county level. For example, eighty percent of GDP is generated in cities. The cities have a level of control over income generated in their domain and can rewire allocation of tax revenue to not support evil and corruption. This can be done with citizen support.

Imagine trillions of dollars supporting our communities and environment instead of war, pollution, destruction and subjugation. It is a rewiring issue.

The Rewiring Process

When we deal with systems created through treachery, manipulation, deception, and psychopathic tendencies, there is a process that holds true on a local and as well as a global level. It bears repeating the strategies laid out in Chapters Four and Five for they show the important aspects to our rewiring process.

The first six points describe how we got into this situation and the way the present system is wired and functions. The next ten points describe the rewiring process to Common Good systems. These ten rewiring steps are summarized.

1) Awakening: It may be a shock for some to realize we are in the middle of a war we did not want or even see, yet it is upon us. The conquest by the .01% can result in servitude for you and your families, generations to come. The only ones that can really stop this hostile takeover are the people in danger, us. For some this is an exciting opportunity to bring lasting peace and prosperity while eliminating a scourge to our planet. It requires awakening from false beliefs and taking actions to spread a revolution that is really an evolution if carried out with a high vibration.

2) Hold a Sword of Light ... be a Warrior. You need a deep commitment and internal strength to hold a Sword of Light. It is vital not to hold onto low vibrating energy like fear, anger, and depression, but instead take control of your own emotional well being. Utilize these feelings as a catalyst for action which can transform them to hope. Prioritize holding love and enthusiasm; no dark force can overcome you if you persist holding a high vibration with your goal in mind. If you hold joy you will attract what brings more joy.

3) Understand the Oppressor, Be Strategic: The puppet masters are not like your next door neighbor or your kind uncle. The suffering they have been inflicting can only come from psychopaths, and the systems they create reflect their low vibrating consciousness. Psychopaths' greatest fears are being discovered and losing power. The masses can help them realize their fears.

4) Gather the Facts: There is a significant amount of credible documentation of actions taken by the corrupt oil/banker barons that shows their criminality. Learn about the Federal Reserve, 9/11/2001 truth, CIA Black Ops, HARP, GMOs, Fluoride, Chemtrails, education systems, and false flag attacks by keying in these topics to a reliable source such as CorbettReport.com which provides great references for further investigations. Let understanding be a catalyst for positive action.

5) Communicate with Others: Be prepared to debate topics as you confront peoples' well planted and groomed belief systems. Utilize the many approaches to communicate this information described in Chapter Six. There will be a range of receptivity based on held beliefs. With sharing facts it is also important to discuss the bright possibilities without these suppressive systems.

6) Have an Inspired Vision: Be inspirational. Utilize the Law of Attraction by being clear about the future you would like to co-create. We are surrounded by potential energy that responds to what we predominately think and feel. Keep your vision in mind and be happy

to generate the information field you want. Let others know what is possible as we redirect our taxes to improve free education, forgiveness of student loans, free health care, doubling the town's revenue, and lowering our tax cost by cutting out the theft by the power players.

7) Grassroots Organizing: Before we unplug from corrupt systems, it is important that grassroots systems are in place and functioning. We must come together if we are to be the power behind the change. Grassroots organizing can be about reform, resolving a community's unmet need, or educating others about system change. There is a wide range of organizing structures like co-operatives, non-profits, associations, clubs and religious based institutions.

8) No-cooperation with Evil: The only reason these corrupt systems exist is because we jointly agree to support them. It is our duty to not support evil, and many of these systems are. Without our participation, their systems become empty caverns walled by a deck of cards that will easily collapse.

9) Community of Truth--The house of Cards Crumble: Be patient and realize that media blowback and propaganda will most probably increase as more and more people become aware of the truth. Internet, social media, phone communications are being monitored to see how much of the population understands the truth. Most probably there will be counter moves, like a chess game. There could be an increase of false flag attacks. Widely dispersed grassroots groups, using nature's laws, will win the day through persistence. Neighbors educating neighbors will dissolve the glue of deceit that keeps this house of cards together, and it will crumble.

10) Community Restart: Pressing the re-start button on a computer can eliminate garbage that is slowing down the functioning of your device. As we unplug and re-start we will need to be more reliant on local systems. Decentralizing power to local communities, towns, cities, and counties, while greatly reducing funds and power to state and federal agencies, is empowering the community instead of the elite few. It is rewiring from a hierarchical to a community based framework.

To re-start community we must first find its power source.

Community as Source

Occupy Wall Street is a good example of a group of concerned activist coming together realizing that our monetary and government systems do not serve the 99%. Several hundred people were well organized within a little block of land called Zuccotti Park. It was only after this group began to experience cohesion and family that the crackdown occurred. Mayor Bloomberg forcibly began to break them up just as there was a semblance of community. He and the Elite knew that the protestors were tapping into a force they could never defeat.

The power from gathering and strategically acting in alignment can raise a barn, find a missing child, respond to a natural disaster, or transform a nation. Community can bring healing and a sense of being uplifted, and is the most powerful expression of celebration and worship.

Participation evokes a response from the heart and spirit of the participant, volunteer or worker. And it is heightened when it comes together in a common unity. If you develop community, you touch a generator of knowledge and co-creativity. When a company or any group acknowledges the power of community and provides a framework that allows community to emerge, it takes a giant step into tapping its core competence.

Grassroots initiatives have historically been the primary mechanism for social change, human rights, environmental regulations, and improving working conditions. It can be a way to rapidly create new systems that support community self-sufficiency.

The power of community has the potential to bring enrichment on all levels including personal and spiritual renewal.

Communities hold the real resources of our planet. It is the goods, services, environment, and relationships within a community that are the real resources. The claim of governments over the population through laws, often concocted from backdoor deals that serve the Elite, is a false claim. The true power is among us.

When we break through our beliefs about money and governance we see we are surrounded by wealth and abundance. We have tremendous resources to take care of all our needs. A community can raise a barn in a day. However, we need a different access and wiring mechanism from the one provided by the Elite. This requires strong community relationships, collaboration, and mutual exchange.

The solution is a networking and systems issue. It requires a turning from the large multinational banks, large corporations and the corrupt parts of our governing system. Turning to a Common Good road you become part of a system that relies on local exchanges and the worldwide connections through the internet to meet life's needs. We need to feed our community instead of the destructive beast. It involves choosing who we work with, who we purchase from or who we support.

You cannot compel the minds and spirits of people. Participants need to opt in, to join their colleagues in making voluntary commitments. Grassroots community relationships are connected by the heart and this connection is strengthened through a common focus and trust.

It is a community oriented approach to life that relies in part on the heart connection. It acknowledges the reality of why society chose to live in clans, tribes, or towns through history. Many have lived the "false life" long enough. Accessing abundance and resources through a community oriented approach brings a reward that uplifts your spirit.

With this approach money is not paramount in getting a local initiative underway. There is a different formula that will allow us to get things done by engaging the community through belief in the project and networking on a grassroots level. This opens up solutions and accesses to a wide variety of resources that are not dependent on the private debt based monetary system controlled by the elite few.

We can create grassroots projects to address community needs that require little or no money. The process uses unused or underutilized resources, volunteers, and creativity. It encourages barter exchange. It also acknowledges community needs, getting others enthusiastic about a solution and the possibilities and vision of the initiative.

Accessing the Collective Mind

Your brain is more creative when all its synapses are alive and connected throughout your gray matter. The same is true with organizational or group intelligence, which also relies on interconnected pathways. To increase the intelligence of a grassroots effort, or any group endeavor, you must nurture and encourage these connections.

Developing organizational intelligence is less about absorbing information than it is about forming a community. It is a social process built around information, participation, trust, and exchange. People need information to do their work, but it is only through working and interacting that they get the information they need. By sharing this data, the entire venture or organization raises its intelligence.

The genius of a collective mind is in the informal, impromptu, often inspired way that real people solve real problems. It is not about structure and not about formal processes, because these can restrict the exchange and possibility that can unfold in a community environment. Organizations are webs of participation and relationships. Especially when facing the challenge of developing common good systems with little or no Federal Reserve notes, the name of the game is community, networking, improvisation—not standardization and working in isolation. The benefits of a collective mind in a venture, group or community are invaluable.

Intelligent communities have a rich level of interconnectedness and networking. Barriers have been dropped. Communication flows openly and easily throughout its networks. Performance feedback is given on all important activities. The group is an inclusive environment that provides a solid web of information, strategic actions and relations.

Community ReStart illustrates a process for providing effective solutions starting with no more than the intention to work collaboratively to resolve the issue. We held 120 consecutive weekly meetings at my house. Participants even plowed my mile long road in a snow storm to have the meeting. We began with a pot luck meal. Over a weekly feast we connected on a personal level. Each meeting had a topic relevant to community issues and needs. We would often have presenters and local experts. Then we would be in a circle for brainstorming accessing our collective intelligence. This is how our strategies were born, as in Berkshire COTS, the Food Net, and Pearl Street Center.

Knowledge resides within the group. It resides on the front lines, where gems and insights surface. It resides in a flash of insight. Organizations that encourage a community spirit to emerge tap, not only the spirit of workers and volunteers, but also a powerful knowledge source. Developing this group intelligence requires meetings where ideas can flow freely, building and evolving with additional input. It requires trust and listening. Grassroots efforts that do not develop community have a lower probability of success.

Many businesses now encourage relationship building among co-workers with the goal of becoming "learning organizations." A learning organization taps the amazing mental capacity of all its members to create a process that will support its own improvement. Peter Senge, a business management teacher, describes the learning organization as a place *"where people continually expand their capacity to create the results they truly desire, where new and expansive patterns of thinking are nurtured, where collective aspirations are set free, and where people are continually learning to learn together."* [31]

The success of a grassroots venture is as much about the spirit and the relationships within each enterprise as it is about economics, marketing, and service. When the barriers between team members have dissolved, there arises one mind. It's actually a single intelligence that works collectively with people who are moving toward a common focus in relationships with one another.

Community meetings provide a social, psychological, and spiritual connection that nurtures us as we face many challenges. Community gatherings can help us overcome our fears. They empower and awaken us, and provide a forum to clarify strategies and assign tasks. There are a wide variety of meeting options available from town meetings to forums.

Throughout all grassroots initiatives, there is a need to collaborate and connect over the many opportunities to move the initiative. This level of collaboration and trust comes when the facilitator is open to and encourages participation. Allow the ideas to come from the evolution of group participation. A facilitator should leave idea generation to the group and the experts, don't push your little idea, and work with the group to develop their big idea.

Meeting Facilitation Tips

1. The most effective role of the group facilitator is not about teaching and lecturing, but about engaging the group and bringing out their wisdom, ownership and participation. Get the group energy behind your joint actions for a much livelier meeting.
2. Facilitate everyone joining in the meeting at the onset by people giving their names, and a brief check in. It brings everyone's energy into the circle.
3. Allow discussions to focus on topics agreed to and prioritized. One person speaks at a time. If many want to participate, have them raise their hand, let the moderator stack the names in order received or 'talking stick."
4. You may need to limit the time people can speak; a time-keeper should then be assigned. Make sure everyone gets to express their opinion. The facilitator should bring the speaker back on track if they go off on a tangent.

Meeting Set-Up to Aid Collective Intelligence

1. Structure meetings so that they are at a consistent time and location. This makes it easier to remember and generates momentum. Advertise these meetings in the promotional literature and for every event you have.
2. Some group meetings may be best to start with a pot luck meal. Everyone brings a little dish and it always seems to combine into a great feast with friendly personal conversations. It sets a good tone for the meeting. At Co-Act we begin our gathering at 6:30 PM and share our meal and social time until 7:30 when, with a cup of tea in hand, we begin our meeting that has a specific agenda.
3. Arrange the seating of the meeting in a circle if you are to have a group discussion.
4. Make your meetings interactive by asking for input on the agenda before the meeting, taking turns presenting.
5. Provide resources --books, handouts, posters, and flyers.
6. Bring in guest speakers on topics such as communication skills, understanding street action, fund raising, or developing talking points.
7. Bring in discussion topics that generate insights and actions. For example, discussions on the Federal Reserve and banking reform.
8. Bring in experts on the topics you are exploring. Use the internet and explore similar successful initiatives, adapt best practices.
9. Put together a draft agenda and ask for input prior to the meeting. Then, stick to the agenda so that the meetings are productive and attendees do not become frustrated by going off on tangents.
10. During brain storming sessions, do not send out heat-seeking missiles after new ideas are being expressed. Allow the ideas to flow and build, don't critique at first, let the ideas pile up.
11. Be sure you have someone taking notes and tracking the discussions.
12. The facilitator's energy is amplified in the group, so be aware of the energy behind the words. If you are tense or stressed, it will come out.

Meeting Set-Up to Aid Collective Intelligence

1. Be a cheerleader. You want to acknowledge people sincerely for their contributions. Do this every chance you get, but don't "toot your own horn".

2. At meetings encourage people to be involved; support their participation in committees. Empower individuals to take on tasks after they are well instructed. Delegate and follow up in a balanced way. You only need a few dedicated people to pull off a significant event.

3. Keep the group focused on a positive approach and bring it back to the strategy of a bright future and transformation. Don't go off track dwelling on how terrible this government is, how cruel people are . . . That focus generates a depressive energy that is draining.

4. Don't let individuals take over the meeting if they are not scheduled to. Welcome their input without letting aggressive people dominate.

5. After you have your ideas compiled, review them and ask the group to help prioritize the suggestions. Asking for a show of hands is one way, another is using little stick-ons so people can come up and register their vote.

6. You may want to have a committee more thoroughly review the ideas and make a presentation to the group about the options.

7. Once the group decides a direction, ask if anyone opposes it and why. If a person does speak up, let the debates continue applying listening skills. If the group is not convinced to change, then ask if this person is willing to support or be neutral to the strategy.

8. Once the issue, task, or strategy is identified, use the momentum of the meeting to assign tasks: who, what, when, where, why.

9. Ask for, and be receptive to, feedback on facilitating the group. After meetings, ask a few people, who will be honest with you, what worked well and what needs improvement. It helps the evolution of your meetings.

10. Encourage others to facilitate or co-facilitate a meeting, or parts of it.

There are initiatives springing up all over the planet that are based on the creativity and dedication of a few people who believe there is a better way. They look at the government and corporate expenditures and programs and say, "we can do better". With little or no Federal Reserve Notes, and a powerful vision of the future that engages others, people are uniting for the common good.

The Common Good

We all share life sustaining support from the air we breathe to the water we drink. There are many things we hold in common like our roads, parks, libraries, fire and police safety, and sewage disposal. Much of what we depend on lies outside of private ownership. The Common Good provides prosperity and abundance for all residents to share.

"Com" is derived from the Latin word together, or joined. When we come together to support what is good for "us" as community, we empower our ability to prosper and have a fulfilling life. Community is literally described as "joined in unity." But we must participate as community to define what we are unifying around. What do we hold in common and what is good?

Good is not a static definition when it involves what is the greatest possible good for the greatest number of people. That definition of what is best for the community, what is the Common Good, is derived at by participation of community members. So the definition of what is good or what unifies a community is always different from one community to the next. It comes from the collective intelligence unique to each group.

Common welfare is the purpose of government for and by the people. Its purpose is the protection of the individual rights of the citizens and the Common Good. Our constitution emphasizes this. Therefore, the government is to serve the Common Good, protect our inalienable rights and the Constitution that gave it birth. It is the citizen's responsibility to assure these high ideals are upheld when the systems of government have failed.

The existing systems are being set up where corporate profits outweigh citizens' concerns. Fracking pumps toxins into community water systems. Other activities include draining pure water from aquifers and selling it for short term profits of bottlers like Nestle and Coke. In Hawaii Monsanto is spraying toxic chemicals around schools, and citizens can't stop it. The result harms our common assets for the profiting by a few.

There are several structures that serve the Common Good. These include grassroots initiatives, non-profits, civic actions, co-operatives and political activism; each one has many structural options. When you participate in these options, they all can provide a sense of ownership. When we own the Commons, we take back a sense of duty and responsibility.

Owning the Commons

Common Wealth ... Common Unity ... Common Sense... Common Action

Common Wealth: When we, as a community, assume ownership and responsibility for the pooled wealth from our shared natural resources, taxes, and infrastructures supported by citizens, we become wealthy and empowered. Recognizing our rightful ownership gives us the freedom to stand up to any corruption that impacts our common wealth. It empowers us to be good stewards. This recognition provides a means to empower local people to trust in their own capabilities and spirit.

The commons comprises valuable assets that belong to all of us. This includes clean air and fresh water; national parks and roads; the Internet and scientific knowledge; the U.S. Weather Service and blood banks. Public services like libraries, schools, recreation centers and public transportation are there for us when we can no longer afford new books, health clubs or another car. So are Civic groups, non-profit organizations, community organizations, informal meeting places—indeed, any gathering of people for the common good is a crucial element of the commons. When you stop to think about it, most of the essential elements of our lives exist outside the realm of private property.

Many commons are now grossly neglected or mismanaged because in elite systems it's assumed that anything that does not make money is not worth caring about. That's why so many school buildings are in disrepair, and why a lot of public spaces are rundown and empty. As we support the common good, we evolve what we share in common, which at its essence is the Spirit of brother and sisterhood. Now is time for the community to reclaim our common wealth.

Common Unity: Grassroots systems are empowered and become alive through community engagement. Even the most solitary and independent individual must rely on community for some of his or her needs. We are not meant to divide into isolated pockets of "self". On the contrary, it requires collaboration and unified action. We need to acknowledge the role of family, local community, and towns. This is particularly true to accomplish the task at hand; together we can pull the plug on the Elite Systems.

That is why there has been such a history of destroying unions and breaking up organizations fighting against the corrupt system like the Occupy Wall Street movement. Hate groups thrive on dividing the population and having them fight among themselves. There is an us-against-them as seen in the election. Polarizing factions get pitted against each other, while the real enemy goes undetected.

The nature of energy is a unifying principle. It acknowledges our interconnectedness and the embrace of diversity. Those who seek divisiveness, oppose the nature of energy.

Common Sense: When we take ownership for our common wealth, and come together with others to create a new system, we tap a collective wisdom. It builds capacity and skills within the community. It emphasizes culturally and environmentally appropriate practices that develop relationships of trust and partnerships. When groups of informed citizens gather and group dynamics principles are applied, there is a sensibility that emerges. As a collaborative intelligence, your group amplifies your broadcasting transmission as you activate the Law of Attraction.

These collective gatherings are occurring nation-wide and form many other initiatives that become part of the Main Street solution. It is time to claim our independence from the Elite Systems and to stake out those rights that our forefathers and foremothers fought and died for.

Sustainability, productivity, good quality of life, peace, justice, and fairness are all simple common sense. These are the criteria we would all naturally use in making decisions when we keep the common good in mind.

Common sense means that we change our judicial system back to the "Common Law." Presently we operate in a system based on "Uniform Commercial Code." A system of law crafted by the banking industry to assure their form of extortion is "legal". As we claim our rights to make our governance based on the common good, this legal system must change from a system based on admiralty law and contracts to one based on common sense.

Common Actions:

- The Common Good is a community process, not an institution or a set of laws. It requires participation.

- The family that makes it a point to buy only local food involves the fate and well-being of local farmers and promotes the self-sufficiency of its community.

- The shopper, who chooses not to buy imported products from multi-national corporations, but instead uses local craftsman and resources even if it means paying a little more.

- Investing in local cooperatives or locally produced alternative energy.

- Identify community needs that align with your beliefs and passion. Get involved, help a neighbor.

- Network, collaborate, exchange, form community - they are all paths to develop systems that support the Common Good.

- Develop collective intelligence with others to resolve community needs.

- Put ideas into action through entrepreneurship, grassroots initiatives, or cooperatives businesses.

Cooperatives

While socialism has been cast by the Elite as a destroyer of our "free" enterprise system, the cooperative approach is not an -ism at all. It's a democratic structure that literally accesses and encourages enterprise— which is why the co-op movement is fast spreading throughout our country. The same initial process just described applies to the development of these cooperative enterprises as it does with any Common Good venture.

Cooperatives can be found in nearly every sector of the economy, including financial, health care, utilities, telecommunications, insurance, agriculture and consumer goods and services. Cooperatives allow consumers to be directly involved and to support local businesses that strengthen their communities.

While it's rarely mentioned by main stream media, there are 30,000 cooperatives in America (with 73,000 places of business). A 2009 survey by the University of Wisconsin's Center for Cooperatives (www.buck.wisc.edu) found that these energetic enterprises have 130 million members, registering $653 billion in sales and employing more than 2 million people.

There are several types of co-ops, including those owned by workers (there are 11,000 of these, with 13 million worker-owned). Also, there are cooperatives owned by consumers, producers, local businesses, artists and communities, as well as hybrids of those categories. They function in every sector of our economy — manufacturing, health care, transportation, banking, farming and food, media, interpreting and translating services, advertising, home building, high tech, and energy.

Co-op businesses do everything that a corporation can do, but with a democratic structure, an equitable sharing of income and a commitment to the common good of the community and future generations. Citizen co-ops are highly prized for their unique personalities, human scale, democratic values and community focus. Cooperatives often involve the following governing principles:

- Voluntary and open membership

- Democratic member control

- Member economic participation

- Autonomy and independence

- Education, training and information

- Cooperation among cooperatives

- Concern for community

Cooperatives are part of the Common Good Systems that ordinary Americans can implement right where they live. It gives small groups a pragmatic and effective way to be prosperous on this Common Good Road. Not only do co-ops work economically, they also make people important again, offering real democratic participation and putting more "unity" back in "community."

Cooperatives take a wide variety of forms and purposes. They are a way of structuring the community involvement in an enterprise. Other forms that work very well are grassroots initiatives.

Grassroots Initiatives

When you take ownership for our commons and our community you also become empowered with resources to improve the plight of yourself and your entire area. Responsibility gives the ability to respond and change our systems.

The framework of grassroots initiatives is also a spectrum based on formality and structure. On one end of the spectrum, the response is spontaneous for a single event. For example, a community responds to a flood threat and volunteers show up to help fill sand bags. It could be bringing over some soup to a sick neighbor or helping out a family who lost their home in a fire. The event could be neighbors getting together for a block party.

A little more formal is where people show up for regular volunteer duties. A good example is the nine pantries and meal sites in Central and Southern Berkshire County. Some volunteers pick up and distribute food, some cook at the meal sites. Their efforts account for over 1,200 volunteer hours a week, from over one hundred volunteers, to provide food for some 2,000 people.

It can expand to clubs and associations that put on events for fund raisers for community causes. As you increase the structure, you can include a town's volunteer fire department where they have a crew that receives regular training.

A more structured framework on this continuum involves organizations that provide sustain services. It requires no legal structure, but if you choose one having a non-profit status, it works best. This declares the organization a community asset as in Community ReStart. Its proceeds and donations serve a mission that donors and volunteers buy into. Non-profits make it much easier to retain volunteers and get local donations as it is dedicated to serve the community. It is also tax free so it does not support an evil system. When you utilize the commons and our community, it doesn't require hardly any fiat currency because you are accessing our natural abundance.

I cringe when I hear people say we can't do the initiative because we don't have enough upfront money. We don't have the Federal Reserve Notes to make it happen. That means those who control money must approve and support your project. The government, large corporations and foundations, often controlled by the Elite, dictate if you can do a program or not? This need for upfront money stems from the beliefs handed down through the Elite Systems. It prevents needed grassroots initiatives from taking root. What grassroots systems need is collaboration to feed it energy for development. Money does also represent energy into the system but collaboration and relationships are the primary drivers.

Elite systems and values are based on profitability, such as making money vs. the good it does for the community. This new system approach values community and its resources above fiat currency. This is an important aspect of the needed monetary reform later discussed.

The way we think about accomplishing community programs needs to shift. This requires the conviction that community is your primary resource and the primary driver to accomplish tasks, not money or government. Here is an example.

210

Berkshire Food Net

Berkshire County pantries and meal sites were running out of food at the end of every month because of a spike in use beginning in 2008. They also hardly received fresh produce. The diabetes rate in Pittsfield was the highest in Massachusetts. Yet we had abundant farms and gardens in our area. This made no common sense.

At one of our weekly Community ReStart meetings four of the Community Restart members got together to address this issue. In January of 2009, we held the first meeting of managers and directors of fourteen local meal sites and pantries in this area. Common needs and challenges of serving the charitable food demands surfaced, such as the shortage of food at the end of each month, the lack of fresh produce and protein, and the rising health issues associated with lack of proper nutrition.

The participants agreed that it was not the lack of food, nor the lack of physical facilities to handle the demand, nor the absence of willing personnel, or even insufficient creativity! Instead, it was found that the cause was lack of "systems," and that the solution would require collaboration and building new networks of access and distribution. It was a rewiring issue. This community born solution became the catalyst that inspired and launched The Berkshire "Food Net" under the umbrella of Community ReStart.

With $600 in donations, a small group of us got four high-profile locations with water and good soil. We wanted the gardens to convey a message to the community that no one should go hungry. We tested the soils, tilled and composted, fenced in the gardens and planted them with a wide variety of produce. With our four gardens being productive, we next focused on creating a community network. There were three additional components that greatly helped access additional produce into the Food Net system.

Farmers' "Second Harvest": The Food Net's "Second Harvest" program yielded approximately 4,000 pounds of produce a year. One "Food Net" participant explains what the "Food Net" has meant to her. According to Jen Salinetti of Woven Roots Farm in Lee: *"In the past, we used to compost our unsold vegetable starts and crops. It feels so good to know that people in need are able to plant community gardens and eat fresh produce thanks to the collaboration between our farm and the Food Net."*

"Grow an Extra Row": Private gardens in our program each donate about thirty pounds of fresh produce weekly. By simply working in their own backyards, gardeners got the additional satisfaction of serving a financially challenged population. Typically we had twenty gardeners participating.

Food Distributors: Connecting with food distributors was an important link. Some years we collected and distributed 10,000 pounds of produce. Restaurants, Resorts, and Grocery stores are also part of this food network through the "Buy One, Leave One" program, collecting 4,200 pounds of high protein foods.

The Berkshire Food Net's program encouraged and supported self-reliance and communal charity through gardens. The network of community and private gardens along with farms and produce distributors was a growing success.

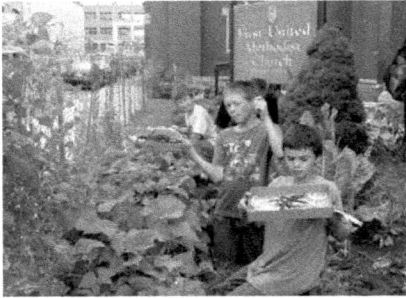

We delivered 6,000 pounds of fresh organic produce in the first year, 11,000 pounds in its second, and then 18,000 pounds. In its fourth year it leveled off at 21,000 pounds. The food was distributed to fourteen meal sites in central and southern Berkshire County. The Food Net contributed fresh produce and protein for 90,000 meals/year.

In purely monetary terms, we were growing and distributing fresh organic produce at about $.06 per pound plus the resource of community. The fresh organic produce that we supplied helped to reduce health disparities in our community and improved health issues such as obesity, diabetes, high blood pressure, and heart disease. There was a high return on investment.

The Food Net complements the present main supplier to our meal sites ensuring a much more comprehensive nutritional safety net. Whereas the Food Banks provide mostly processed, refined foods, with access and distribution relying on Federal Government networks, the Food Net provides a wide variety of nutritious, locally-grown produce that is not dependent on vulnerable federal grants or on expensive transportation networks. The local system can be expanded as the need arises.

With the transition to common good systems, it is important that every community prepares a similar food network as a secondary support to a government orchestrated programs like the Food Banks.

Emergency systems need backups, especially with basic food needs. It's a great way to engage the community.

Once we lift the veil of delusion imposed by our monetary and governance system, as a society we begin to access our true abundance without the enormous transfer to the Elite. With resources going back to the community, grassroots initiatives will have more than enough resources to be effective.

It is a false myth that you need the pieces of paper that control so much of our society. The resource of community working together is the exchange from the heart versus fee for service. This exchange to be sustained requires a culture that supports group energy fields and collaboration.

The culture you create is a key piece in making this community approach work. There needs to be an environment created where people get more than money. You may have experienced a job where an important benefit was the relations, the camaraderie, the excitement, the satisfaction of helping others. Culture is the framework for developing an organizational environment where that is a "payment" for participating. It is working for the common good that is heart -warming and fulfilling.

With an understanding of our community ownership of the Commons and how helping each other as community holds great potential, we can develop initiatives that will change these exploitive systems. Being able to be self sufficient, without government intervention, with minimal need for the elites' currency, provides a freedom. This allows us to take on a key challenge, the monetary system.

Chapter 9

Monetary Reform

Our culture, government and work are dominated by economics. Those who control great wealth and the monetary system are able to manipulate systems that further enhance their power. Rather than being a co-creative force, the majority of the population is degraded to consumerism and a feudal form of slavery. What has allowed such control of our monetary system was a major US battle that the citizens lost in 1913.

A war has been raging for centuries by elite bankers against the 99%. Their mechanism of enslavement is the privately owned debt-based monetary system. See Appendix A for an historical perspective. The most significant lost battle affecting US society today was the formation of the Federal Reserve. It is also the trigger that can rapidly bring about positive change.

The fraudulent and counterfeit monopoly on issuing money by an elite few, with no basis in real value, must end. The borrowers provide real value not the lenders. The control of this debt-based system by the power hungry few has paved the way to debt and wage slavery. If we are to end this increasing tyranny and subjugation, we must pull out this corruption by its roots.

Moving the control of fiat debt-based currency from the hands of private interests to public control is an important step. End and audit the Federal Reserve replacing it with a transparent government run Central Bank for the people. The reform can go further by changing the exchange mechanisms for goods and services. Money is simply a tool making trade easy and efficient; it makes the division of labor possible and is a means of exchange.

The control of monetary exchange can be viewed as a continuum. On one end is the private control of a fiat currency by a few. The other end of the spectrum is the control by individuals or communities through local currencies or barter systems. This end of the spectrum eliminates the burden of a debt based monetary system. Local monetary systems are being developed to bring wealth and development to local communities.

The rewiring of these exchanges requires rewiring our habits of purchasing to focus on local exchanges and greatly reduce purchases from large corporations. It may mean using something different than a Federal Reserve note in an exchange. Rely more on local banks, co-operatives and other similar organizations that serve the community. With the internet, we don't need large corporations. Even global market outreach is possible for even a small family business through the internet and phone. We have the tools and leadership for the needed reform.

Primary Dysfunctional Patterns and Triggers

Shift a single key element and an entire system can rapidly change to serve the common good. One of the most effective ways to transform any system are triggers that are so pivotal to change and success that it can cascade into improvement on many fronts.

The kinds of key domino transformative triggers I refer to can be found in an individual, a team, structure, or system. For virtually all organized systems there is a key, a primary pattern that sets the dysfunctional tone throughout the group. You can change symptoms of a primary dysfunctional pattern—but unless the primary pattern is transformed at its roots or disempowered, the dysfunction and its repercussions will remain. This taproot of the primary dysfunctional pattern, when changed, can trigger a lasting transformation.

Personal growth therapies all focus on behavioral patterns, and they all approach change by trying to get to its root. They may not agree on methodology, they may not agree on whether that root is mental, physical, chemical, or emotional, but they all agree that transforming the root is the direct route to change. Most of our behavioral patterns are rooted in our beliefs. Our beliefs feed our behaviors just as roots feed plants. The roots are invisible just as our beliefs are often unconscious and directly impact the system or

216

organization. This main dysfunctional pattern has a profound impact on the systems with repercussions that create secondary dysfunctional patterns. These repercussions can mask the primary dysfunctional pattern.

For example, I encountered the behavioral pattern of a leader who had difficulty trusting others. This resulted in holding onto too much control and bottlenecking operations. His need for control was rooted in a decision he had made after being ripped off by his first business partner and the resulting belief of mistrust. His control bottlenecked the work flow at the top; this pattern was amplified in a cascade of secondary dysfunctions that included poor communications, teamwork, and responsiveness throughout the company. But the trigger of the dysfunctional pattern stemmed from the leader's belief in mistrust of everyone.

You can do some training with staff but, until the primary dysfunction is handled, the dynamics will remain. The trigger for the organization was the leader learning to trust. When he realized the repercussions of his behavior, he immediately got counseling and worked with his executive group to develop trust. Within a short time, all those secondary repercussions were gone. Very similar to what happened to me in my Alaska consulting firm.

Another example is one striking structural pattern: a virtual void of connection among the executive team. A company that I worked with rarely held meetings among themselves. This was further reinforced by departments that were structured and functioned as independent entities. Each department manager had his own little fiefdom. It greatly affected workflow and customer service. The roots of this pattern went back to an antiquated approach set up by the founder of the business. When that pattern changed, the entire organization prospered.

In a case of dysfunctional interpersonal patterns, two department heads in an ad agency were embattled. Their root was miscommunication that occurred while serving several clients. This escalated to a point where they enlisted their staff in the battle. The secondary repercussions were poor client service, lack of interdepartmental cooperation, and cost overruns. The trigger was resolving some miscommunications.

In business organizations poor morale, stagnant growth, and lack of creativity can all be symptoms of an uncorrected primary dysfunctional pattern. That is why well-intentioned efforts can sometimes produce very little improvement in the group. Worse, they can even do harm. You have to transform the root of a primary dysfunctional pattern. This root can be trigger rapid and uplifting change.

Dysfunctional patterns can become reassuringly familiar, like background noise. We can be blind to alternatives that are more suitable and productive. We let opportunities pass us by. Unconsciousness locks us into cultural patterns that reduce the group's potential to thrive. Then they become difficult to discern through our own personal filters and the group-induced cultural trance. Within this culture lies the tap root of the primary dysfunction and often a belief is holding the root in place. Pull the tap root and it triggers a holistic shift.

The concept of triggers applies to any system. When we expand this perspective to include the systems in the United States, we can see that the root of our societal woes stems from an elite group who have gained monetary control and who see themselves separate and above the 99% of humanity. What gave a select few, five banking families; tremendous power was the creation and control of the Federal Reserve. That gave this elite class unprecedented power. It was powerful enough to break down the immune system of our nation and allowed this virus to spread throughout our societal body. This infection has extended through our other systems. It has turned the US into a beast that is feared by nations with resources. In Appendix B and C is a description of how this has shaped media, education, medical and military systems and the head of the beast is the monetary system.

The societal taproot of our primary dysfunction is the privately owned Federal Reserve monetary system that the .01% control and dominate. A change from private to government or state control can be a trigger. One of the founders and board members of Community ReStart would often state that the foundational issue for societal system change is our monetary system. Ironically his name is John Root and he has been very active in the local currency movement discussed later.

Our debt-based monetary system and its control by private interests through the Federal Reserve ... is the taproot of the elite systems. Control of the monetary system feeds the elite's plans for global domination through systems like the Bank of International Settlements. The trigger is to end the private control of the Federal Reserve and take on monetary reform.

It is a community awakening where we end the private fiat currency of the Federal Reserve and replace it with a currency system that serves the Common Good. Many grassroots groups are promoting legislation to make it happen. If enough citizens unite and see the change, it will happen despite the challenges that seem to lie ahead.

Pulling this Federal Reserve trigger requires a strength that can only come from people like you and me uniting to take action to change our monetary system. When we connect around a common purpose, we are interconnecting like energy's nature and become a source of power. To change the monetary and other exploitive systems requires a united strength. Realizing what is at stake will aid our unification.

The Money Scam and Debt

Rising prices, lower wages and increasing debt continues to bring distress, foreclosures, divorces, and missed opportunities. It keeps us in a job we hate just to make ends meet. Debt is a slayer of creativity and entrepreneurship. Look at how interest affects so much of our society. Yet it is a simple scam that has brought great suffering, a scam that can be easily remedied.

Money is a social construct that represents value of goods and services. Money makes things comparable. It allows the division of labor and the exchange mechanism required in a complex society. The US fiat currency has no precious metals or anything backing it except our social agreement. Money is an accounting system that brings a consistent measure. In actuality, money is nothing more than a receipt for goods or services. We provide things to each other that we value and give each other receipts that represent that value.

Circulating currency needs to balance inflation and deflation, while providing enough to represent goods and services. The Federal Reserve can easily be manipulated for personal gain. The bankers can generate bubbles and depressions at will, taking a huge bounty at every turn. The result is a plunder over the past one hundred years that sets a new standard on Earth.

Interest is paying tribute to those who lend the money. When we utilize private, debt-based, interest-bearing money, the nation gives away one it's most valuable Common Good assets to the .01%. We are basically paying tribute through interest to an elite few, because of shady back door deals made over 100 years ago. The Federal Government to a large extent has become a branch of the Federal Reserve. Look at the 2009 banking bailout swindle. It illustrates how the banking elite benefit at every turn; they rigged the system.

When the government borrows more money, the U.S. government borrows U.S. Treasury bonds for "Private Federal Reserve notes," thus creating more government debt with each transaction. Usually the money isn't even printed up; most of the time it is just electronically credited to the government. These Federal Reserve notes are backed by no precious metals and have no intrinsic value of their own. Yet the citizens pay interest to these bankers through our taxes for borrowing money instead of the Federal Government issuing it. Realize there is a hidden sovereign who issues the money that we pay tribute to.

When each new Federal Reserve Note is created, the interest owed by the federal government on that new Federal Reserve Note is not created at the same time. So the amount of government debt that is created actually exceeds the amount of money that is created. The result is that there is too little credit in circulation to support the needed exchanges. A mechanism of perpetual debt is set up.

Back in 1910, a couple years prior to the passage of the Federal Reserve Act, the national debt was only about $2.6 billion.[32] A little over 100 years later, our national debt is now more than 5,000 times larger. When the US Government borrows money at interest, it slowly transfers wealth from the American people to those that lent it.

At the end of FY 2017, the gross US federal government debt is estimated to be **$19.5 trillion**, according to the FY18 Federal Budget. U.S. taxpayers now pay half a trillion dollars annually to finance our federal debt. Why is this privately run for the profit of a few? Isn't it our common asset?

This servitude of debt is primarily because of deception and backdoor deals that the citizens had no part in creating. It is a false yoke placed on the backs of the citizens with a mounting burden. We can end this madness.

The overwhelming sense of fear created by debt is leading to a state of paralysis. Only 51% of last year's college graduates have fulltime jobs. And their average wage is $12.27 an hour before taxes. I would not expect that trillion dollars in student debt to ever be paid. [33] However, the debt cannot be discharged and students are condemned to a life of servitude.

This Federal Reserve debt and money-supply fluctuation scam bankrupted the United States in1929. Then the Fed seized all the gold in the US as payment. They replaced it with worthless paper. Then asserts that were not enough, claiming all of its citizens as their assets in 1933. The banking interest shaped the US courts to run under Uniform Commercial Code, which empowered the corporations and their bankers. This allowed other wealth transfer mechanism through false contracts, like home mortgages.

"Who controls money controls the world". – Henry Kissinger, Counsel on Foreign Relations

According to the ideology that Rothschild and Kissinger promote, this statement is true, but only has merit in elite systems and seen by this consciousness of enslaving others. However, on the Common Good Road the private banking tender of the Elite can be transitioned out and replaced by federal, state, community or personal tender. Other methods like mutual credit and barter are available exchange mechanisms. So that statement is not true on the road to prosperity and the common good. In fact there is a spectrum of monetary exchange options.

The Exchange Continuum

Our monetary systems over history can be looked at as a spectrum of control. On one end of this range is the private, secret, independent Central Bank modeled by the US Federal Reserve. As you expand participation, the next is a government controlled Central Bank, and then we go to the model of North Dakota and state run banking systems which disperse the power to the states. We can have a debt, interest-free system run by the Federal or State government. On the far end of the spectrum, this monetary exchange can occur through local currency systems and mutual credit. The community can bring money into circulation through projects that enhance the Common Good. Or it can be a simple barter. We can choose on this spectrum how we want our transactions to occur. Presently the US and much of the planet resides in the most controlled and dysfunctional part of this spectrum.

Spectrum of Monetary Control

Control by few--- --Control by many

Private_Government Bank_State Bank_Crypto Currency_Local Currency _Barter

Private Central Bank

To regulate credit creation, some countries have created a currency board and granted independence to their central bank. The US Federal Reserve, the Reserve Bank of New Zealand, the Reserve Bank of Austria, and the Bank of England are examples where the central bank is explicitly given the power to set interest rates and conduct monetary policy independent of any direct political interference or direction from the central government. We let the fox manage the hen house in the United States.

In order to maintain the money scam they must maintain the secrecy of the ruse. The Federal Reserve has never been audited by an objective third party, not once in one hundred years.[34]

The thievery through monetary control continues today. Presently, the Federal Reserve pays banks not to loan money to small businesses so there will be no hyperinflation. But they are loaning as much as 7 billion dollars at 0.01% so big banks can buy commodities like corn, soy, wheat and oil to drive up the prices you pay at the store and at the gas pump.[35] It does allow a steady transfer of wealth from you to the bankers. But that is what the system is designed to do.

The first two private Central Banks lasted their initial 20-year charters before being eliminated. The current private Federal Reserve Bank Central Bank has lasted over 100 years. Isn't it time to eliminate it? Ron Paul introduced a bill to eliminate the Federal Reserve Bank (see GovTrack.us.H.R. 2755--110th Congress (2007)) and to abolish the Board of Governors of the Federal Reserve System and the Federal Reserve.

Government Central Bank

This system empowers government to direct the economy toward sustainable solutions, which are not possible if government spending is financed with more government debt from the private banking system. In particular, a number of monetary reformers, such as Michael Rowbotham, Stephen Zarlenga and Ellen Brown, support the restriction or banning of fractional-reserve banking (characterizing it as an illegitimate banking practice akin to embezzlement) and advocate for the replacement of fractional-reserve banking with government-issued fiat currency, which is issued directly from the Treasury rather than from the private/fake quasi-government Federal Reserve. It is a direct path to stop paying private bankers and ruining our country for something that our government can easily oversee.

Government Issued Debt-Free Money

Some governments have experimented in the past with debt-free government-created money independent of a bank. The American Colonies used the "Colonial Scrip" system prior to the Revolution much to the praise of Benjamin Franklin. In 1757, the King of England and Parliament made Colonial Scrip illegal. Franklin believed it was these efforts of revoking this government-issued money that caused the Revolution. Abraham Lincoln used interest-free money, called "Greenbacks", created by the government to help the Union win the American Civil War. Remember, money is nothing more than a receipt for goods and services. Imagine you receive a receipt and the banking powers proclaim you have to also pay them interest for your receipt.

State Run Banks

North Dakota is a state with a sizable budget surplus, and the only state that is adding jobs when other states are losing them particularly in 2010 when economic woes were high. A poll reported in February ranked that weather-challenged state first in the country for citizen satisfaction with their standard of living. North Dakota's affluence has been attributed to oil, but other states with oil are in

223

deep financial trouble. The big drop in oil and natural gas prices propelled Oklahoma into a budget gap that is 18.5 percent of its general-fund budget. California is also resource-rich, with a $2 trillion economy; yet it has a worse credit rating than Greece. So what is so special about North Dakota? The answer seems to be that it is the only state in the union that owns its own bank. It doesn't have to rely on a recalcitrant Wall Street for credit. It makes its own.

The state bank would not replace private banking institutions, but would partner with them, particularly with community banks. This connection would provide them with new customers and help them provide new services. The benefits would support states instead of the .01%.

Commodity money

Some proponents of monetary reform desire a move away from fiat money towards a hard currency or asset-backed currency, which is often argued to be an antidote to inflation. This may involve using commodity money such as money backed by gold, silver, or both, which supporters argue possesses unique properties. They are extraordinarily malleable, strongly resistant to forgery, their characters are stable and impervious to decay, and they are inherently limited in supply.

Crypto Currency

It is a digital asset designed to work as a medium of exchange using cryptography to secure the transactions and to control the creation of additional units of the currency. Crypto currencies are a subset of alternative currencies, or specifically of digital currencies. Bitcoin became the first decentralized crypto currency in 2009. Since then, numerous crypto currencies have been created. Bitcoin and its derivatives use decentralized control as opposed to centralized electronic money and centralized banking systems. The decentralized control is related to the use of Bitcoin's transaction database in the role of a distributed ledger.

Local Currency

There are many creative local currency options available that work. They allow a way to unplug from the monetary system and build your local community. The Common Good financial system (CG) is a good example of a locally created currency system that is gaining traction. www.commongoodbank.com

At first glance, the CG system looks like a simple payment system. You put US Dollars into your CG account and spend them using your Card. Then come the incentive rewards ("CG") — electronic community credits issued to you whenever you buy or sell something through the CG system. You get $20 for signing up and a 10% reward on whatever you buy or sell (decreasing gradually). Spend these rewards at any participating business.

The CG concept evolved over the course of a decade and has been thoroughly tested for over two years in Greenfield, Massachusetts. In April 2015, Ann Arbor, Michigan, became the second CG community.

The Greenfield MA system has handled over $1,000,000 in transactions. It has grown from 3 participating businesses and a dozen members to more than 30 businesses — including many popular restaurants and food markets — and hundreds of individual members.

You can help make it happen, by signing up and inviting your friends to join you. All it takes to launch a CG community is a few dozen members and a few food-related businesses such as grocers, restaurants, and farms. It could start with you.

Local currency systems can operate within small communities, outside of government systems, and use specially printed notes or tokens called scrips for exchange.

Exchange Trading Systems

The furthest on the spectrum is personal barter exchange. It is estimated that over 450,000 businesses in the United States were involved in barter exchange activities in 2010. There are approximately 400 commercial and corporate barter companies serving all parts of the world. There are many opportunities for entrepreneurs to start a barter exchange. There are two industry groups in the United States, the National Association of Trade Exchanges (NATE) and the International Reciprocal Trade Association (IRTA).

Bunz - built as a network of Facebook groups that went on to become a stand-alone bartering based app in January 2016. Within the first year, Bunz accumulated over 75,000 users[36] in over 200 cities worldwide.

In Spain there is a growing number of exchange markets. These barter markets or swap meets work without money. Participants bring things they do not need and exchange them for the unwanted goods of another participant. Swapping among three parties often helps satisfy tastes when trying to get around the rule that money is not allowed.[37]

TimeBanks exchanges needed resources without a cash transfer. People can both receive needed work services and give services to others thereby gaining the satisfaction of providing for the community's well being. TimeBanks helps to create abundance, extends a person's community network, generates possibilities, and provides stimulating social connections.

For every hour a person spends providing a service for someone in their community, they earn one Time Dollar, a liquid currency, which is electronically placed into the TimeBank. Then one has a Time Dollar to spend on receiving personal services from others. With families no longer staying in close proximity, many older citizens find themselves without the family network to help them with many needed tasks, and often find they are isolated and lonely. This helps the reconnection with community.

Timebanks USA was founded by Dr. Edgar S. Cahn in 1987 www.timebanks.org. Timebanks USA is a simple idea, but it has powerful ripple effects in building community connections. TimeBanking is a growing social change movement, with over two hundred and eighty six chapters in seven countries and on six continents.

Berkshire TimeBank

Michael Costerisan and Karen Andrews founded Berkshire Timebank in 2009 under the auspices of TimeBank USA and Community ReStart. We noted how important it was during times of high unemployment. A pot luck dinner started the community collaboration.

Many Berkshire County residents were suffering from a reduced standard of living due in part to reduced income. In December 2009, the United States unemployment rate was 9.8% and the underemployment rate was 17%. There is an incalculable loss of personal esteem for those who cannot find suitable work or who are underemployed and not able to exchange the fruit of their labor. A sense of isolation is often associated with such situations and TimeBanks provides a solution.

One of the most revolutionary components of TimeBank is its egalitarianism. Everyone's hour is equal. TimeBanks nourishes the best aspects in its members and creates a system that connects unmet needs with local resources. The more members and services that Berkshire TimeBank accrued, the more functional it became. Berkshire TimeBank in a short time had one hundred and eighty one different service offerings and ninety-four different service requests posted by the members on its website. Some examples of service offerings include a physician's and psychiatrist's office visit, handyman services, gardening, yard work, companionship, baking, sewing, cat and dog sitting, rides and errands, web design, computer hardware and software assistance, music lessons, healing therapies, fitness sessions, and language lessons.

In the Berkshire, a core group of members met at least once per month, and communicate several times per week to plan ahead and to report on activities. All core group decisions have occurred by consensus and by design, there is no leadership hierarchy. This core group has been involved in all of the various types of activities of Berkshire TimeBank and is therefore cross-trained.

Berkshire TimeBank attracted people of all backgrounds, ages, ethnicities and income levels with a variety of skills, interests and hobbies. It was a virtual organization without an office, a community gathering space or a membership fee. Berkshire TimeBank membership grew after two years to one hundred and twenty three members as of January 28, 2011. Translating these member exchanges of services into dollars since its inception in 2009, results in a valuation of $37,695 based on 1077 community hours of membership activity at $35/hour.

Here are some examples of how Berkshire TimeBank has directly affected the local economy already:

- *"There's something really happening here,"* said TimeBank member Jeanne Bassis of Alford. *"It's so creatively out of the box from the way commerce happens in the world. I love that it's not about money; it's about value and time. It's an equal hour. I've benefited from cat sitters, body workers and computer help. No question, this is an amazingly radical and timely notion in our society of growing gaping discrepancies between the rich and the rest of us".*

- *"I went to do some yard work for a TimeBank member and after I did my labor she gave me many plants and much gardening advice. Furthermore, unbeknownst to me, she hosts a web-based dating service that had brought my girlfriend and me together! Small world, closer connections, that is what TimeBank is all about!"* - Robert Connors

We found that when jobs are plentiful the use of TimeBanks declined. When there was unemployment, it became a more viable system of exchange. This was true for ride share programs like Ride Buzz. When the gas prices skyrocketed, there was very high use, and use declined when gas prices dropped. It is a valuable tool to utilize when regular currency is tight.

Actions

The fact is, we do need a revolution! Not a revolution based on anger, anarchy and pitchforks. It is a revolution of awakening and empowering our communities. We need a revolution of the individual states: to reclaim their sovereignty and fight for the liberties of their sovereigns (We the People).

A sound strategic approach is to unplug from the Central private bank and transition from private to public currency. The state bank is a proven mechanism. There are movements within several states to use the North Dakota model.

Furthermore, such a revolution would be constitutional, lawful, moral, and in compliance with the laws of Nature and of Nature's God.

- We must put an end to private Central Banks' ability to create private money. Restore money production to the public through a phased transition from private to public money. Developing government or state run banks would aid the transition.

- Audit and end the Federal Reserve by an objective commission.

- Elect government representatives who will insist on phasing out the Federal Reserve and revising tax collection and distribution.

- The U.S. Congress votes to take back all of the functions that it has delegated to the Federal Reserve and begin to issue debt-free United States Notes.

- Educate others. Help expand the number of well informed people capable of critical thinking.

Chapter 10

Bumps, Roadblocks, and Detours

Any initiative, regardless what phase of development it is in, encounters challenges. A vital tactic will determine your success or failure. It is not about an external strategy or action steps. It is not about money, personnel, physical resources, or some missing component. The vital tactic is within you.

The most important challenge you will face is your mental and emotional state. The real challenge is your ability to be positive and hold a clear vision of success despite a bump in the road or even a road block. Realize that even the most monumental tasks seem to get resolved when you hold to your vision, take action, and feel positive in accomplishments. This encourages you to further pay attention to and empower this natural ability. Being aware of the information field you hold, and what you are broadcasting from within you, is vital.

In addition, understanding case histories, preventive techniques and having response tools provide valuable insights for learning from and moving past obstacles. These bumps and blocks can take many forms. The four categories discussed are based on my experience working with over five hundred organizations and grassroots groups. The following case studies include internal development, external competition, government blocks, and saboteurs. Provided at the end of the chapter are important preventive and response measures that can avoid potential challenges or reduce their impact.

Grassroots Bumps and Blocks

Discussing the bumps and blocks is not meant to empower them by creating fear and anticipation. It is to help you be aware of types of challenges and ways to avoid or respond. Utilizing preventative techniques and best practices can avoid problems from occurring. There are tools available for effective responses. The best response is to stay positive, to use the situation as an opportunity to learn, and to be open and creative.

Four Categories of Grassroots Challenges

1.   Internal Development: Personal, Structural, and Interpersonal dynamics within a grassroots group is the most common challenge; it is a result of ego, poor communication, structural deficiencies, or lack of teamwork. Positive and constructive feedback tools are provided at the end of this chapter. Help resolve issues before they become a block. A challenge brings opportunities.

2.   External Competition: These can be a reflection of success, attracting imitators. Another organization may provide more effective alternatives than you and it could fuel innovation. Some organizational threats are government sponsored groups funded to replace grassroots initiatives. Some may use strong arm tactics to get what they want.

3.   Government Blocks: Regulations, ordinances, and local laws that prevent grassroots organizations to carry out their plans. Examples include stopping protests, preventing Freedom of Information, blocking funding, and allowing corporations to write legislations that further their gain.

4.   Saboteurs: They are hired by the CIA and other agencies to stop grassroots organizing that threaten the dominance of the Elite Systems. The attacks are especially evident against successful ventures that take on national organizing. As a former grassroots coordinator for over three hundred 911/Truth groups, I became very aware of their tactics. These strategies are also discussed.

Out of this listing the most prevalent is the first. The personal, structural, and interpersonal dynamics impact an organization and the initiative. The remaining three are often used by the elite few to squash organizing.

Any social order based on inequality of wealth or power depends on repression and deception to control the disadvantaged majority. It is valuable to look at these oppressive tactics and remove the fear they try to associate with them. Realize the Elite System is mostly smoke and mirrors filled with false promises. They oppose truth and organizing.

Next are true stories of grassroots participants responding to challenges. The names have been changed in the stories, but all other developments occurred.

Case Study 1: Internal Development

The Community ReStart clean/sober, affordable and supportive housing program previously described, was born from a community need. After one year the program had been running well. Our five houses were full with a growing wait list. Our collaboration with the local hospital's substance abuse program, the corrections facility, the Crane Center and Community Support Options allowed us to develop an aftercare support for the residents, all accomplished without money. Members of these organizations were part of our board and advisors meetings.

In the beginning we worked with four organizations involved with recovery to develop a handbook with guidelines for those who came into our residency program. We also developed residency agreement forms and an aftercare program. All residents signed off on each with a witness present. The agreements included not using drugs and alcohol, random drug tests, attending weekly mandatory meetings, paying their affordable monthly fee, and getting along with the other residents.

After one year, we had to remove six residents; they left without incident as they acknowledged they broke our program rules. We provided a wide range of options for their safe transition. This included detoxification and admittance in the hospital program. We had a path that included jobs, housing or other treatments more suitable for them than our program.

Despite our success our entire program was in jeopardy from one program participant, who made a flaw very visible. June Pratt signed a contract prior to moving in agreeing to leave immediately if the contract was violated. After four months of residency, the problems began. She did not pay her program fees, she refused to attend the house meetings, she abused drugs on the premises, she refused a drug test and she refused our request to leave. Additionally, her numerous disruptive behaviors were stressing the other residents in recovery who also wanted her removed. We served her verbal and written notices to vacate which escalated her disruptive behavior.

With our lawyer's involvement, police were called to remove her, only to inform us that we had no rights to remove her, nor any rights to enforce the agreements she had signed. Further, the police informed me that if I tried to remove her, I could go to jail and I would get sued. The state provided her with an attorney who argued that her tenant rights required that we go through the normal eviction process, and supported her case to stay.

To remove June took a 6-month process while the court allowed her to stay there for free. The lost income to our program and court and sheriff costs reached over $4,000 (without lawyer fees). We had another resident that took 9 months to remove and cost $8,000. This "legal" system assures that people can "use" in the house and that the residents and organization must endure their presence. In short, a single person, who we all agreed needed *help* far more than removal, was jeopardizing the support service for 19 others. Any of our participants could have done this to our organization.

To keep Community ReStart's low program fees, no one on our volunteer team receives payment for their work. We have a tight budget and receive no government funding. We are taking a risk when we accept people referred to our program from the hospital's recovery unit. We are dealing with a population that would be homeless; many have issues and are dual diagnosed. We needed to be able to uphold the rules they agree to that assure the safety of the house.

We understand the position of our court and enforcement systems. The irony is that these institutions are the very bodies most in need of relief from the deleterious social consequences of the opiate epidemic. Yet the system they operate under prevents clean/sober housing needed to reduce recidivism. Pittsfield has a big recovery community. Safe, supportive housing is a big need. Yet the system, the courts, and police enforcement say you have no rights to make agreements among yourselves; only the police and judges have that right. You are disenfranchised.

Our volunteers who worked so hard were crushed that *system* obstacles, not the already difficult recovery obstacles our residents face, made it impossible for us to continue providing a sober, supportive, and safe environment for them.

By preventing us from removing tenants, word gets on the street that you can go in and use. We lose our sober residents. Our program is particularly vulnerable as we receive marginal people often dual diagnosed. If any of them chose to follow June's path there is nothing we can do as local police and laws encourage and protect this approach under the present system.

This was definitely a road block. This forced to more fully examine our process and the way we were running the program. The first thing was to go through a certification program so we would be registered to handle residents with mental illness. That is what happens to addicts, especially opiate addiction. There is mental illness that sets with addiction as neural pathways are changed and they need to be supported to stabilize. With that certification we could work with Department of Public Health. This would allow us to remove people who relapse.

It also became clear that we needed a project director who could better screen potential program participants and be on top of issues before they became problems. So we hired an addiction counselor who had been serving the community for 26 years. The end result was that the program continued much better able to handle the population we were supporting.

Case Study 2: External Competition

The Food Net, described in Chapter 8, began to resolve food shortage and the nutritional disparities for people on food support. One garden in particular stood out, a community garden which raised 200 pounds of produce per week for distribution. It was also an educational program for 23 neighborhood kids, ranging in age from four to twelve years old. The success and notoriety of the program included radio, newspaper and TV coverage. Many people considered it the best thing to happen to the West Side neighborhood in a long time.

The community garden located on Robbins Avenue was started by Thom Pecoraro. It received the most funding of the gardens. In 2010 that garden received a total of $15,000, which went primarily to the kids' program. There was $3,000 from the City of Pittsfield that was administered by Berkshire Directors Council (BDC), the largest non-profit in the county [38]. We relied on these monies to pay our garden manager for the last month of the season. BDC did not transfer the monies from the city to us and refused calls and emails for two months.

I was concerned when Becky, the garden manager, alerted me that Dan Bywater, BDC's Director wanted to meet with her privately. Becky responded saying she would only meet if our three board members present, Thom, a local lawyer and I. When we met, Dan came with Donna Woffer, the City's program director. They then hit us with something we did not expect, that in order to receive the $3,000 we would have to give the garden over to Dan Bywater. We were shocked by this demand and the three board members and the manager refused.

They then tried to justify their taking the garden accusing us of not having a contract with our garden manager and our tax filings were improper. It helped that our third board member was a lawyer, and showed them all of the contracts and accounting with everything in very good order. Dan and Donna's frustration built and they left in a huff proclaiming we would not keep the garden.

The following day Donna took away the bench at the garden site donated by the mayor. She next removed the AmeriCorps sign and our computer with our files. Dan Bywater had no gardening interest, had never had a garden; he was a massive 300-pound-plus cigar smoker who couldn't bend down to pick up a piece of paper. Also, he had no staff with garden experience. Yet this City representative demanded he take the garden because it was on city land.

Donna next proclaimed to the community that she had to take the Robbins Street garden away from us. The city took away our lease. Donna announced she was saving the garden program because Thom Pecoraro, the founder and director of the garden, was pilfering money. This was far from the truth, as I knew that Thom put in over $500 of his own money into the program that year. He donated

236

countless hours, and never received a penny in return. It was made-up slander.

Imagine the message it gave to all grassroots groups in the region. If you develop a great program worthy of funding, the "government controlled behemoth," BDC, as well as the "good-old-boy network," will try to take it from you. In addition, they will also trash your reputation in the community for serving community needs. It did not end there.

When it came time to submit a proposal to the United Fund, which is by far the largest funding source for local grassroots organizations in Berkshire County, the Food Net submitted one. Despite the loss of one garden, we had four additional community gardens, twenty one private gardens, and an association with nine farms and several produce distributors. We had a network of fourteen meal sites, distributing 11,000 pounds that year. We were the main source of local fresh produce and we were expanding the learning program to the 90 kids who had summer lunch at the Pearl Street Center in a different part of the city. We felt confident in funding.

BDC also submitted a proposal based on no experience with gardening and only having the one garden that they had taken from us. They claimed in their proposal that the two years of sweat equity that we put into the garden program as theirs.

The president of the United Fund, Cindy Ham, pulled the Food Net's proposal, not allowing it to even be considered along with the other applicants. BDC became the only applicant for a garden program and received full funding. The city of Pittsfield, under Donna Woffer, provided more funding, and when you include the Federal grant that BDC also received, their budget for this little garden program reached nearly $40,000.

The Food Net had put three years of sweat equity into this grassroots initiative that had been highly successful based on the recipients responses. The Food Net was not able to receive funding through conventional means because of these strategies by the "good-old-boy network" and the back door deals of the two major funding groups for the area. This was a big bump.

Yet the Food Net team all believed in the program and saw the good it was doing. The appreciation from participants and recipients filled our hearts. We kept on delivering produce, spreading the word and encouraging local food sustainability and organic production. We kept on joyously doing the weeding and harvesting.

The following year BDC took over the Robbins Street garden program and it became a mere weak shadow of the program that we had originally run. Hardly any money made it to the project. The neighborhood mourns its passing. We also had our "Poster Child" from this incident to show the impact of the Good-Old-Boy network.

We were not silent. We had people submit articles in the local newspaper. This, in turn, had people asking questions. Because I work with many churches and synagogues in the area, I was asked by many ministers and rabbis what happened to the Robbins garden. I laid out what had occurred.

The ministers were shocked by what they referred to as Mafia type tactics. The people behind the tactics were empowered. BDC was the largest non-profit organization and Donna was the director of the city programs. Each had a big say in how our social service monies were used. Many of the ministers were activated knowing how much the Food Net had supported the pantries and meal sites. They saw the links supporting the good-old-boy network and how it was crippling our social services.

I did not encourage the ministers' silence and they talked to members of their faith communities about what happened. The result was that the message got to a number of the Board of Directors of BDC. This and the accumulation of other issues resulted in Dan Bywater being fired. He had been director for fourteen years. Board Members of BDC then tried to get financial information and the CFO refused and he was fired. An audit showed significant discrepancies in how the funds were actually used versus their intending purpose of serving the public needs. After lawsuits and accusations of millions stolen, -the organization shrunk to 40% of its previous size.

Donna Woffer suddenly left her city post and moved out of the area. It was interesting to hear the joy that resulted from her departure. In fact the Good-Old-Boy Network was getting more exposure and their vice grip on health and human services was being released. It also allowed more effective management of community programs that BDC once ran, as others are doing it better. This restructuring of the social service landscape was in part due to one little community garden and the power of truth.

During this entire time we just kept on planting, weeding, harvesting, and delivering beautiful organic produce knowing the good it provided. We kept on providing a positive message for local subsistence and supported local organic farms and distributors. The Food Net received funding from a wide base of community organizations like Project Bread, Civitan, the Rotary Club, several Churches, and small grants from a variety of sources. The Food Net was stronger than ever and served the growing needs of the community.

The moral of the story is to be positive, feel good about what you are doing. Speak the truth and expose corruption while providing a solution. There are forces that seem to take care of things beyond what we are consciously aware of.

Case Study 3: Government Blocks: Low Impact Hydroelectric in Berkshire County

During one of our Community ReStart's meeting the founder of the Center for Environment Technology, CET presented to our group of 40 interested local residents and discussed alternative energy options for this region. We came to the conclusion that Berkshire County can become self sufficient in electrical energy. We also realized we would need to create a different approach than offered by the existing systems. There seemed to be no better place to start than the mechanism that started supplying electricity in our region.

Hydropower supplied energy to most of Massachusetts's industry well into the early 1900s, a major reason why most Massachusetts towns are located along rivers' rapids. A romantic notion during this time of unprecedented need for clean energy is to refurbish our region's "initial power grid." Utilizing existing dams in the Housatonic Watershed will yield cost effective reductions in Hydrocarbon emissions and generate over one hundred million dollars of revenue to local municipalities over the life of the project. To access this common wealth for our community requires a local collaborative approach.

Housatonic River

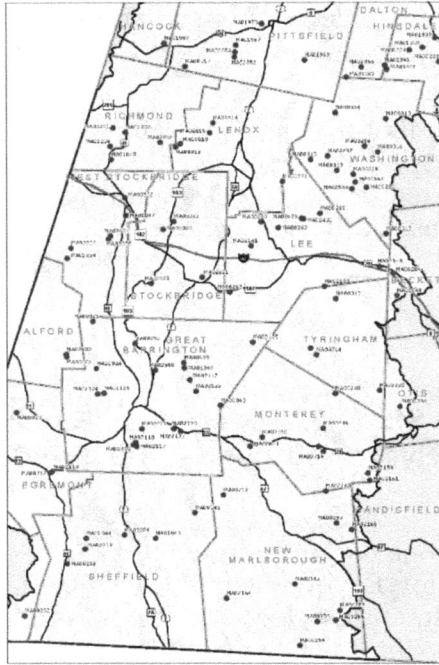

Dots are dams.

An initial analysis showed the major block to access low impact hydro electric in the US is the Federal Energy Regulatory Commission, FERC. We began by interviewing 32 hydro engineers in Massachusetts and Vermont. I asked each one the following question: *"If a regional group got together with all of the regulatory agencies that report to FERC, and if they were to agree on the proper management and development of the river ecosystem is there any purpose for FERC?"* Thirty two said it serves no positive purpose. It seems the only purpose they serve is to prevent municipalities and other groups from effectively using this natural resource. The purpose is to add cost, delays, and discouragement from pursuing this.

Community ReStart then pioneered a new strategy to make low impact hydro a reality for our region. In November of 2009, focusing on Southern and Central Berkshire County, I facilitated the first hydroelectric symposium of its kind in our region. This meeting of environmental, regulatory, engineering, and funding professionals, along with owners and managers of facilities, made for an informative exchange. By the conclusion of the panel discussion the group had identified a cost effective, efficient approach to put dams in our region back "online" and generate hydroelectric power.

Community ReStart first applied its collaborative strategy by conducting a preliminary assessment of eleven low impact hydro projects in the Housatonic Basin of Berkshire County. Since that first inquiry, another eight dams in Pioneer Valley were being investigated. In all, these nineteen dams are capable of generating $1.6 million yearly in returns. Presently, this resource is being wasted, as it is for most of the dams in the region.

Revitalization of existing dams and tapping appropriate runs of the river sites requires a process of collaboration and due diligence. Our team included Essex Partnership, an engineering firm specializing in low impact hydro. Licensing and approval for small hydroelectric plants typically costs several hundred thousand dollars and takes four years or more. This new approach can cut the time required to less than two years and greatly reduce costs. Our goal was a 50% reduction in time and pre-installation costs, compared to existing standards. This would make small hydro power feasible throughout Massachusetts while opening up the model for a clean energy economy throughout the United States.

Typical < 500 kW Hydro Project Timeline

Task	2009	2010	2011	2012	2013	2014	Cost ($1,000)
Screening	▄						$25 - 100
FERC – Stage I		▄					
FERC – Stage II			▄▄▄	▄▄			$100 - 250
FERC – Stage IIII				▄	▄		
FERC Order					●		
Design and Permitting				▄▄	▄		$25 - 50
Equipment Procurement and Manufacturing					▄▄	▄	$2 - $6/kW
Construction					▄▄	▄	
ARRA Deadlines			●		●		

The development model can be applied state wide. Part of this process involves the stakeholders identifying criteria for dam selection and "smart development". For example, the criteria we gathered from our meetings for the Housatonic include: minimal water diversion, structural integrity, potential improvements to the fish and wildlife habitat, and recreational use development.

The advantages of using this approach add up. Compared to photovoltaic panels that last for twenty years, hydro generators are built to last for one hundred years. This process allows access to dam "barriers" on a stretch of river to improve portage, recreational use, and safety. It also provides the benefit of an improved power transmission from distributed generation which will support the power grid at many points.

Rising Dam

The process we utilized also results in channeling the generated proceeds back into the municipalities in which the dams are located. Revitalizing appropriate, established hydroelectric facilities will provide energy and income for generations to come. This is a form of economic development for underserved communities while increasing our energy independence.

At this time there were Federal Stimulus Funds to develop alternative energy in Massachusetts. Hundreds of millions of dollars was set aside to make MA the leader in alternative energy use. We sought this collaboration with the Commonwealth of Massachusetts. State and local officials were needed to support this watershed development for municipal power generation as it involves contiguous municipalities.

I made a presentation with several of our Community ReStart board members to a panel in Boston illustrating the financial benefits and the positive image it sends for self sufficiently. Five panelists verbally gave their enthusiastic support, none opposed. They stated out of all the proposals presented in Massachusetts this made the most sense.

We left giving the panel a detailed proposal. Their promise was that they would get back for us to make a presentation to the decision makers. So we waited and waited. We then called the members who initially supported us who now refused to return our calls. We tried our inside contacts who said there were administrators blocking its progress.

We next received the notice that the stimulus monies from the state were distributed. The majority went to creating an electrical transmission corridor from MA to several hydro facilities in Canada. Not one penny went for local dams. In the Berkshires it would have cost under $8 million. The citizens lost out on receiving over a $100 million boon over the life of the project and making our region a model for natural resources serving the common good. Instead the governor allowed more cash to the good-old-boy network who built the corridor at exorbitant costs and we still have to pay for the power.

Like we did before, we continued to expose the truth and the corruption and injustice. The absurdity of their decisions to support the Good-Old-Boy network and the ridiculous costs illustrated how these Elite Systems tried to prevent our Common Good initiatives from happening. But like the Robins Garden they may initially appear to win, but we have truth and the common good on our side.

Recently legislation was passed to bring about FERC change to make it closer to what we proposed. Small, low impact hydroelectric can once again be a feasible, attractive, and reliable source of renewable energy where it is compatible with ecosystems. It is the time to reclaim our region's original power grid for the common good and expose the government/corporate blocks through bogus regulations and diversion of funds to the Good-Old-Boy network.

Case Study 4: Government Saboteurs

There is a more sinister presence that exists if your group is for government or corporate reform. The primary power in a democracy lies with the people; however to access that power the populace must organize. Busting up organizations and creating chaos is another strategy of suppression.

Thanks to the "Freedom of Information Act," documents revealed FBI infiltration of activist groups throughout the 60s, 70s and 80s. (Documents from the 90s to date are currently not available). Government Agents eliminated leaders and busted up mass movements without undermining the image of "US democracy."

Don't be naïve or paranoid; realize there are efforts by the CIA, FBI, and private contractors to prevent organizing. There is nothing ethical about their strategies; lies, deceit, or fear was used to disrupt and divide. Examples abound, such as programs to destroy Students for a Democratic Society (SDS), the Peace and Freedom Party, Vietnam Veterans against the War, and the many other groups standing for social reform, labor organizing, and Native American rights. We can learn from past attacks and strategies they employed[39], and use this knowledge to develop sound counter measures.

9/11/truth is the Achilles Heel of the corrupt military/industrial/government/media complex. The Elite System's survival is dependent on stopping the truth from coming out. My personal experience came as the grassroots coordinator for 911/truth.org that involved groups throughout Europe, United States, and Asia.

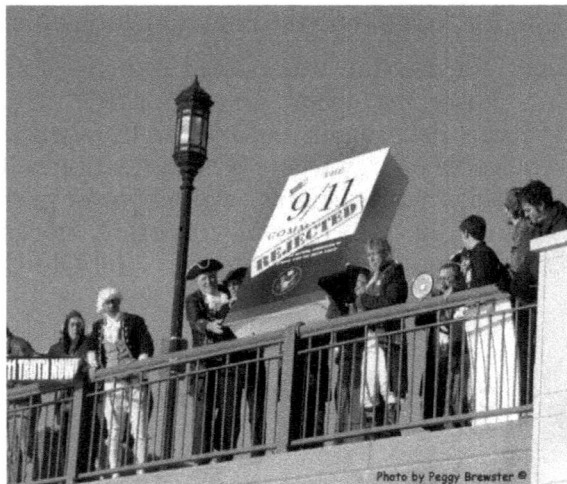

Photo by Peggy Brewster ©

There were 281 grassroots organizations in the US and 62 international. Through these communities, we invoked a collective power and authority. However, to access that power for change we had to act collectively and strategically focus our energies. The community collaborative bond is what attracts saboteurs. Their efforts were to primarily disrupt collaboration and bust up community, particularly organizing efforts over large geographical areas. Like this protest staged on the anniversary of the Boston Tea Party. We threw a replica of the 9/11 Commission Report and all the passed laws into the Boston Harbor at the very spot the tea was dumped. After our third year it began to get national recognition as the "Tea Party." Then the Republicans suddenly claimed the name through endless media coverage.

As groups grew, government agents infiltrated them and orchestrated disruptive activities. Infiltration mostly occurred in cities where there were a lot of new faces. Infiltration doesn't work well when you have a group that knows each other. These connected grassroots groups provided and array of data that painted a picture. For the 9/11 truth movement there were not many saboteurs involved. In New England I personally knew of six government-sponsored saboteurs focused on the 911 truth movement. The tactics were similar.

Typically, they would enthusiastically volunteer for an important project and not follow through. Back biting others, continually being negative. They would provoke shouting matches and create factions. There is a list of disruptive patterns provided.

If you find yourself in a situation where you need to deal with a disruptive person, there are useful tips listed. To deal effectively with divisiveness and disruption, whether it stems from inside your group or covert operation, involves prevention, awareness, and a skillful response. These three lists can be very valuable as you grow and develop your initiative.

Preventive Measures

- Get on the same page. Identify your group's values, like non-violence. Clarify a common focus or a mission statement that the group aspires to. If members excel at supporting these agreements give them positive feedback and if they stray offer constructive feedback. (Feedback tools are at end of chapter).

- Establish a reporting process: Anyone can bring up concerns about divisive behavior without upsetting or engaging the entire group. Assigning an experienced person or someone with good interpersonal skills is recommended.

- Establish meeting decorum: Mutually agree on how your meetings are to be conducted. Here are some suggestions:

  o Prior to meetings all members can provide agenda suggestions, but during meetings stick to the agenda. If you go off track, bring the group back to your focus.

  o One person speaks at a time. Listen to others' opinions and input with respect, even if you disagree.

  o Make suggestions that are solution-oriented instead of just undermining ideas and strategies.

- Support each other: Speak well of your group members. A very important agreement is to not talk negatively behind someone's back. Go to them directly if you have an issue, and if you need to give constructive feedback refer to the end of this chapter. Don't gossip about rivalries, disagreements, or tensions. If you hear these types of gossip, remind them not to speak demeaning about your group members.

- Be a collaborative team: Expertise and leadership should be spread among the group, and different group functions should be headed by several people. If your group is run like a hierarchy, your leader is an easy target for disruptors. If you function as a collaborative, group attacks target the entire group. This usually results in greater unity and the elimination of the disruption.

- Develop communication skills: Conflict resolution, as well as listening and feedback are vital tools in a collaborative environment; it is a different skill set from the old hierarchical way of operating. Review communication tools at end of chapter.

- Become a community: Your group bond is one of the most important preventions to divisive attacks. Be a community where you come together to help each other, have parties to celebrate, and gatherings to mourn the passing of loved ones.

It is that sense of being brothers and sisters that help face challenges together.

- <u>Form coalitions:</u> Work with other activist and social reform groups. Attend their rallies, share truth information, and table at their events. Establish relations with other activist leaders. Your network is a safety net.

- <u>Cultivate local relations</u>: Reach out to the media, first responders, and legal systems. Connect with sympathetic journalists who are willing to publicize covert operations. Get to know your local police and develop a relation with a concerned lawyer.

- <u>Protect your email addresses</u>. Do not send out your email addresses in bulk so anyone can access your list. Keep your list private, use mailing features that do not display other recipients. Disruptors sending poison pen emails, using easily taken email lists, have caused chaos and hurt feelings among several grassroots groups.

Awareness of Disruptive Patterns

Follow a person's actions and notice what is left in their wake. Regardless if their actions are of a saboteur or unconscious disruptive behavior, the effect is the same. This is not meant to accuse someone but to heighten awareness of what often drains the group's energy. Here are some of the more common divisive patterns I have encountered:

- Makes accusations behind someone's back and will not discuss issues personally and privately with the one they are accusing. In general, doesn't have good things to say about others and will degrade people when their backs are turned.

- Enthusiastically volunteers to do a task and then does not follow through on assignments. Or aggressively takes control of a project ignoring the input from the responsible committee. Also, can consistently derail or slow down projects.

- Opposes plans and actions of the group on a consistent basis without providing alternatives to meet the group's objectives.

- Can publicly attack leadership using ridicule, divisive labels, accusations, insults which are all broadcasted for the purpose of a divisive battle. Avoids civil and polite debate.

- Repeats the same claims over and over even when people have proven that such claims are contrary to the evidence causing dedicated activists to waste time rebutting claims and theories.

- Spends more energy causing in-fighting and disruptions then helping with projects.

- Attempts to start a splinter group or wants to radicalize the group. If successful these splinter groups are positioned to compete against the original group.

- Alienates large sections of the population by attacking certain religious, ethnic, or political groups often as emotional rants, with no reason. The attacks also extend to other well meaning activist groups. Such attacks have often been showcased by the major media as representative of the group's views.

- During street action they confront passersby and exhibit or encourage non-peaceful involvement. They are eager to break the law and jeopardize the safety of members.

- Calls leaders in the movement names and attacks their personal life. Falsely accuses affiliations with the military/industrial complex. Publishes degrading cartoons of respected members in the movement.

- Disruptively acts out in meetings such as ranting on and on about topics not on the agenda or attacking others in the meeting.

Skillful Responses

- The power of attraction. Keep the positive vision and feeling of accomplishment. Feel good about what you want.

- Deal with issues before they escalate. Sweeping things under the rug does not work. Often you will find the issue of contention was based on a miscommunication or misperception. During my years in organizational development I estimate 80% of the contentious issues were based on a miscommunication. Meet with those involved and check out perceptions and interpretations verses the facts. If an issue involves two people, they should try to handle it by themselves or with a facilitator; avoid engaging the entire group unless necessary.

- Be aware of the verbal attacks. It is a primary communication tactic used by covert operatives. When they speak to you, they send an endless stream of accusations and insults, questioning your ethics, and spreading rumors. If you don't engage, they fail their task.

- Don't Accuse Suspected Provocateurs. If you suspect someone is a paid provocateur, be cautious. Accusations without significant irrefutable evidence tend to only fuel the controversy and divisiveness. Admissions by provocateurs are rare.

- Maintain a High Vibration. Be aware of angry reactions, and divisive communications and actions. It doesn't matter if the person is an agent, has emotional problems, or is uneducated. You can hold a loving energy even while others attack. Try to see if truth exists in this feedback.

- Don't feed negative gossip. Avoid forwarding emails that degrade others, avoid discussions that are negative, confusing or harmful. Disruptors aim to flood the grassroots communication web with negative propaganda and falsehoods; you can cut off that flow by not passing it on.

- Alert others. If someone admits to consciously trying to break up a group or if there is significant irrefutable evidence, let other activist know; often provocateurs go from one group to the next using similar tactics.

- <u>Check out authenticity.</u> Research disturbing letters, phone calls, or rumors before acting on them. Contact the source of the accusation. Fabricated communication has been a common tactic to divide a group.

- <u>Avoid one-on-one confrontations.</u> They will try to confront in public, don't get drawn in. It is meant to engage and waste your energy. It is best for the group to expose this divisive behavior instead of the leader going one-on-one with the attacker.

- <u>Make harassment known to the public.</u> Turn an attack into a publicity campaign; for example, how government sponsored covert actions threaten fundamental human rights.

- <u>Give Feedback.</u> When you observe divisive or disruptive behavior affecting the entire group, it is important to check out if others had a similar observation. If so, several of you should provide constructive feedback to the person in question. Use the Communication Tools provided next.

Group intelligence is heightened using the mechanism of feedback. Like the feedback units in electrical mechanical systems that allow adjustments and response to a changing environment or situation - groups need similar mechanisms. But for these mechanisms to be present in groups there needs to be a safe environment. A grassroots community needs agreements about giving and receiving both positive and constructive feedback and the knowledge and skill to do it.

Positive Feedback

Positive feedback is one of the greatest gifts you can give to another person. It lets someone know that what they do has a positive effect on you and others. It inspires them to continue doing this, and makes them feel appreciated. Positive feedback lets another see their own worth through your eyes.

Since many people dwell more on their faults and shortcomings, positive feedback builds up their confidence and self-esteem. As a direct result they feel esteemed, appreciated, and therefore more enthusiastic and creative in what they do. Don't make the mistake of assuming someone knows what you appreciate about them. Tell them!

Positive Feedback Steps

1. Be specific, not general
   Not helpful: *"You're a nice person to work with."*
   Helpful: *"Whenever there's a need, you always pitch in to help resolve it. Yesterday, when you helped me distribute the flyers, I really appreciated your support."*
2. Be immediate
   Send a brief note, email, or tell the receiver as soon as possible.
3. Note any significant change or improvement
   When someone makes a sincere effort to change something about their work or performance, let them know you see their effort and express your appreciation.
4. State it positively, not negatively
   Not helpful: *"Your flyer isn't nearly as messy as your last one. It's almost as good as the one I did last year."*
   Helpful: *"The flyer is improved; your new layout makes it much easier to read."*

Constructive Feedback

Constructive feedback, given consciously, helps another person consider changing their behavior in positive ways. Feedback communicates useful information about how they affect others, how they can support an individual to grow, and how they can achieve their own personal and group goals.

Ineffective feedback has an intention to blame, find error, or make them feel they have done something wrong. And, it will insure that you emerge the winner, the one who's right. Blaming and judgmental feedback, given emotionally, usually results in alienation, conflict, and a weakened relationship. Their ability to hear the content is almost nothing.

How Receptive Are You to Feedback?

- In the face of feedback, do you shut down, deny, or blame?

- Does your mind automatically go on the defensive, creating rationales when you violate your agreements? For example, when late for a meeting do you make up little stories about why?

- Do you find yourself making excuses for your behavior instead of really listening to feedback and seeing another perspective?

- Do you feel grateful for supportive feedback?

- When you receive feedback, how do you digest it? Do you put a negative spin on the message, laying waste to your self-esteem?

- Do you openly inquire about your contribution to the group, asking for perspectives and exploring for insight?

- Do the most influential people of your organization receive feedback?

- Is there an agreement among your group to give and receive feedback?

Constructive Feedback Steps

1. <u>It is well timed</u>. Be certain both you and the listener have adequate time to discuss the feedback and complete your conversation.
2. <u>It is usually given in a private setting</u>. Avoid giving individual feedback in front of others, which could make the listener defensive. If there is an issue affecting the entire group, and they are all aware of it, it may be appropriate for the group to confront that person.
3. <u>Declare your intention</u>. Before giving feedback, tell the other person the positive reasons why you want to give them feedback.
   Example: *"Our relationship is important to me. I don't want anything to get in the way of our working well together. Because of this, I'd like to clear up something that happened between us."*
4. <u>Be descriptive, not evaluative</u>. Describe only the facts of what took place. Do not make evaluative comments which label the other person or their behavior. Not Helpful: *"You are so rude and offensive with people."* Helpful: *"During our street action you confronted the construction workers and the veteran in a way that made me uncomfortable as the yelling persisted."*
5. <u>Be specific, rather than general</u>. Address one or two specific incidents, rather than telling someone they *"always"* or *"never"* do something, which shuts down their receptivity. Avoid generalizations about their behavior.
6. <u>Describe how you are personally affected by the behavior</u>. Use "I statements" ("I feel...", not "You make me feel...") to describe how you are personally affected. Avoid "band-wagoning."
   Not Helpful: *"Other people feel this way too"* or *"I'm not the only person who thinks this about you,"* which creates defensiveness for the listener. Helpful: *"I feel upset when you behave like this."*
7. <u>Address changeable behavior</u>. Do not address situations or behaviors over which the individual has no control. Not Helpful: *"You're too intense and outspoken. You need to be more relaxed."* Helpful: *"I'd like you not to raise your voice and pound the desk around me."*
8. <u>Check to insure the other understands clearly</u>. You might ask the receiver to paraphrase the feedback they have received from you to insure they have clearly understood what you are saying.
9. <u>Make a specific request</u>. The other may not understand what you are asking for and may mentally exaggerate your feedback to be a monumental judgment or request. Make specific requests of what you would like changed.
10. <u>Listen Carefully</u>. Listen carefully to the other's response, be willing to learn about yourself, and be willing to admit your own errors.

Implementing Feedback

- As a group, have you agreed to implement a feedback mechanism?

- After an event, does your group meet to debrief on performance?

- In your life, as head of household, supervisor, manager— in whatever way you are a leader—do you give positive and constructive feedback to those you oversee?

- Have you worked to develop feedback communication skills?

- Is your group wired so there is a clear and direct reception of what is happening within the field and on the front lines?

- If potential conflict arises, do you have a mechanism to support a harmonious resolution, such as a third party mediator if needed?

- In your workplace, do you have performance reviews that are utilized as a professional development plan? Can you apply it to community development?

- Do you feel that you could go to members of your group and give them feedback? Would they be receptive?

- Do those people with the most authority, power, and influence encourage this type of ongoing reflection and feedback throughout the group?

Chapter 11

A New Social Awareness

Physics and astronomy involve observing behaviors and capturing them in formulas that predict movement and outcome of the tiniest particle to the largest galaxy. These sciences shape perspectives about our universe and can harden into beliefs to help shape societal consciousness. Sciences can go through transformative shifts, where their formulas change as well as the associated beliefs and consciousness. The fundamental shift from Newtonian to Quantum Physics or the shift to a Copernican perspective from the Ptolemaic model of the heavens, which postulated the Earth at the center of the galaxy, illustrates how significant the change can be. We are ready for a similar social shift.

The shift for all sciences occurs when there is the realization that their thinking and framework was based on an erroneous premise or there is a deeper truth to grasp. Our social order is going through a similar shift, realizing this framework is based on a false premise. Those who control these societal systems are mostly Eugenicists, believing that a self-selected group of elite must rule and subjugate the masses. It is a separatist, controlling, hierarchical approach and promotes a consciousness that is against nature's way.

Our present reality it is very sobering. Present systems and even our perceptions are a construct to serve a hegemony that spews deception. The Elite have crafted systems that have put us in an erroneous, low vibrating consciousness. Society has embraced this false framework. The monetary system provides the parasitic elite the mechanism to control the masses and suppress their potential. It is our erroneous consciousness that keeps us asleep to the mechanisms that entrap us. It is time to awaken and liberate ourselves by embracing a new social awareness.

We need another social framework to operate from. The essence of energy provides a deeper truth to guide our societal framework. We are made of energy. We are affected by its laws, we are not separate. Collaboration, love, balance, openness, and unlimited possibilities are our higher potential. Out of this framework, the systems we develop will embrace our true nature.

A Systems Issue

As a planet we have the capacity to feed everyone with nutritious food. Provide clean abundant water. Breathe fresh unpolluted air. Develop our potential that will in turn benefit society. Pursue fulfilling work and earn a fair wage. We all have the potential to benefit from that which we hold in common.

We are surrounded by abundance. Every person should live well and have ample opportunity to prosper. There is more than enough. There is no real reason why we cannot have this through our labor. It is our moral right.

We are evolving beings, it is our nature to grow and develop. Our mental, physical, emotional, and spiritual evolution is influenced by environmental surroundings and societal systems. What are the optimized systems for our potential to blossom?

Aristotle and St. Thomas of Aquinas expounded that the purpose of a political order is to help people develop those moral and intellectual qualities that make them distinctively human. We cannot be fully human without the kind of environment offered by the right kind of political order, they argued. The best political order is not one that simply provides its citizens with security. It is the one that makes them morally and intellectually better and truly supports them in developing their potential.

I have diligently explored that question as an organizational development consultant. I have witnessed the enthusiasm, joy, camaraderie, and creativity that occur when an organization's structure changes from a disconnected hierarchy to a collaborative transparent system. Once people experience the freedom and support to develop their potential, they tend to flourish.

That same camaraderie and creativity can be released within our communities by shifting to transparent, collaborative systems. These are systems and approaches that serve our potential and the Common Good. The Food Net demonstrates how by rewiring access and distribution of local food we were able to meet a growing nutrition need in our community. We can rewire our societal systems to be an evolved ecosystem.

A revitalized local economy will blossom with the rewiring of how collected taxes are spent. Tax investments into grassroots initiatives instead of bloated military budgets would create a boon of prosperity. Local development would support the unique character and culture of that area.

In an evolved ecosystem, there is a greater level of participation. Citizens will no longer be disenfranchised and will be encouraged to participate in local governance. Citizens can prioritize the Common Good over personal profit in legislation. For example, corporate charters could be revoked if they do harm to the Common Good.

Community groups and the systems they create are valuable not only for what they can achieve but also for how people feel when working with others on community initiatives. A high energy emerges when people pull together and tap the power of community by aligning with nature's way.

In these evolved systems we feel buoyed and uplifted by our colleagues and companions; we're more creative, more responsive, more engaged and more at ease. In these moments of empowerment, communication and collaboration flow freely and easily, and celebration springs forth naturally and authentically. The energy of an individual member of a group contributes to and merges into a collective energy, a synergistic force around which anything seems possible – and often is.

Liberate

Liberation is freedom, open-mindedness, unconditional love, and unencumbered will to express our higher selves. It is lifting the shackles from oppression and control that can either come from internal restraining beliefs or the external unjust economic, political, and social conditions that plague so much of the planet. Liberation is both an internal and external process.

Internal liberation is a self-awareness of our true nature. Regardless how imprisoned we may be externally, the flame of liberty can still burn bright in our hearts. That Light can be lit any time we chose by accessing the infinite energy that is part of who we are. The emotional frequency of energy's higher vibration is love, peace, and joy. We can access this higher frequency without external events triggering it. Love is our deeper nature; it is the frequency of connection to a higher power. It is a connection that grows stronger with practice.

Hebb's Law states *"neurons that fire together wire together."* It is something you can see plainly in everyday life: If you're forging a new path through the woods, the first trip is the most challenging and you have to be deliberate. But the more times the path is traveled, the more defined it becomes and the easier it is to follow it. Your brain works the same way: The more times a certain neural pathway is activated (neurons firing together), the less effort it takes to stimulate the pathway the next time (neurons wiring together).

The internal access can be further strengthened by non-attachment. In other words, connection to your joy is stronger than your attachment to earthly things or emotional upset should things not go your way. Your stance in love gets easier with practice and it allows bigger challenges to be absorbed and dispelled through love.

It is our human ability to access that higher vibration through our God given connection to this Universal Energy; this is where our internal liberation stems from. By holding the higher vibration of joy and love in our hearts regardless of our external circumstances, we have found Liberation. We are able to soar like an eagle even if we are physically shackled.

This brings us to our external liberation. The existing shackles placed by the elite are against our fundamental laws. There is no man, government, or cabal above us, only the Creator, a justification for the US Declaration of Independence. The existing international banking and corporate cartel have no true claim to rule over us without our informed consent. It was the primary rational for the liberation from the clutches of the King and his Bank of England in 1776. This same truth is still relevant. The *"Laws of Nature and of Nature's God"* entitle us our Liberty.

"When in the Course of human Events, it becomes necessary for one

People to dissolve the Political Bands which have connected them with another, and to assume among the Powers of the Earth, the separate and equal Station to which the Laws of Nature and of Nature's God entitle them, a decent Respect to the Opinions of Mankind requires that they should declare the causes which impel them to the Separation."

"We hold these Truths to be self evident, that all men are created equal, that all are endowed by their Creator with certain inalienable Rights, that among these are Life, Liberty, and the Pursuit of Happiness That to secure these Rights."

"Governments are instituted among Men, deriving their just powers from the consent of the Governed, that whenever any Form of Government becomes destructive of these Ends, it is the Right of the People to alter or to abolish it, and to institute new Government...." The US Declaration of Independence.

The constitution preserves and defends our rights for external liberty and if the existing governance system does not obey, it is the citizens' duty to change it. However, we cannot change it from within the Elite System. However, we can make the Elite Road obsolete by simply not driving on it. Peacefully stop participating in the corrupt elite system. Simply do not feed and support those businesses and systems that are doing harm to our society and help develop grassroots initiatives to support the Common Good.

To bring this liberation to our social systems, it is ideal to be liberated within. From that place of freedom and freed energy, we can co-create a common good way. In a liberated external environment, it becomes easier to nurture our internal Liberation. There is no better technique to develop both the internal and external liberation than using nature's way.

Think and Grow Common Good Systems

During the 1930s Andrew Carnegie, the steel baron, commissioned Napoleon Hill to reveal the elite's most important strategy and mechanism for creating wealth and power. He exposed the secret in *"Think and Grow Rich"* published in 1937[40]. The book's premise was that whatever you think about most of the time with the greatest emotion and duration, you will attract it. His title was not "work hard" or "strategies for wealth", but merely "think" and grow rich. If you think you can or if you think you can't, you are right either way. At the time of Hill's death in 1970, *Think and Grow Rich* had sold more than 70 million copies worldwide.

There are many societies and organizations that promote, teach, and reinforce these concepts we have referred to as the Law of Attraction. These more subtle teachings are part of the highest order of the Free Masons, a group of trained practitioners who support a collaborative project with a shared vision, greatly increasing their probability of success.

Regardless of the individual, the premise is consistent. Think about what you want while feeling good with frequency and duration. You become a broadcast tower for your vision. Through group endeavors we are able to create a collective intelligence. Through the group's consciousness you create a more powerful broadcast tower.

Hinduism, Buddhism, and Taoism all claim that consciousness, rather than matter, is the ground of all being. Consciousness, with its inherent intention, ultimately helps shape reality. And we become co-creators with others in this emergent reality.

The theme is consistent from the greatest secret the elite hold, to recent scientific discoveries, to ancient mystics. We are a broadcast tower sending and attracting what we want. The signal strength relies on our emotions, beliefs, and duration.

When our personal energy feels good, we fuel the transmission of what we want. If we are in a state of fear, we are fueling what we don't want to happen, or attracting what we fear. So feeling good is part of the challenge to Liberate. That is being countered by the Elite system's design to evoke fear, suppression, debt, and divisiveness. Attracting what you don't want is what the Elite system designers want.

The development of grassroots initiative expands with this understanding. Our thinking and emotions when properly used can be a powerful building tool. The battle ground shifts from armaments, money and politics to consciousness and emotional energy. Spreading the truth and peacefully unplugging from corrupt systems puts us in the driver's seat.

It is realizing that life may not be what it seems. There is a deeper law that actually shapes our circumstances. It is a law that empowers you as a human being. When we acknowledge that truth and enact these laws for the good of others we empower our community and the potential for Common Good systems.

If we don't come together as community, and utilize this tremendous power, we become "sheeple," people with the mind set of sheep, being herded to the whims of those who control the Elite Systems. We hold much greater power than the fake elite system that is based on deception and theft. We need to wake up to our Liberation, come together, and take action to claim this power.

Focus on what your community needs. Focus on what you have passion for. Focus on being happy. Our communities can recreate themselves with the enthusiastic energy of a few. Get involved with:

- Locally produced clean energy to meet the community needs.

- Honest objective media coverage.

- Education and health care paid for by taxes.

- The end of wars.

- A local food system where abundant, healthy, affordable organic food is available to all.

- A community response and support for the elderly and those in need.

- Productive, effective systems to care for our commons like our roads and parks.

- Public banking institutions working for the people.

- Taxes to go directly to support the Common Good through a different collection, accounting and distribution system, such as concentrating on county level vs. the national level.

- *"Imagine all the people living life in peace... A brotherhood of man...Imagine all the people sharing all the world,"* John Lennon.

If you believe you can, you will succeed; if you believe you can't, you will fail. You are right either way.

Tune into a Higher Vibration

We know what it feels like to be in an energy field that resonates at the level of love, joy, and even bliss. We look for it everywhere: in our relationships, in our work, in our play, in religion or spirituality, in every arena where we hope for fulfillment. We may call it by different names: spirit, passion, enthusiasm, or life force. We may desire it in different forms: joy, love, health, abundance, well-being, and connectedness. But it is all energy. Everything consists of energy, and we seek this high vibrating energy.

Just as the variance of wave length gives color its distinctions or sound its scales, so too the energy we hold gives us distinction. We become aware of this unseen energy in motion through our feelings. Just as color has a band width so does our emotions. The emotions vary in strength or amplitude, like the radio frequency and volume control.

The lowest vibration on the dial is fear and as the vibration increases with turning up the dial, the emotion is felt as anger then goes to sadness. As it increases further, energy's interconnected nature gets revealed; there is greater heartfelt relation to others around us. As the vibration increases, we sense it in our feelings, from hope and joy, to unconditional love and bliss.

Feeling good involves first being aware of your feelings. Our feelings are electro chemical impulses that transmit messages. Impulses regardless if they are anger must first be accepted and acknowledged. I'm not advocating suppressing any emotion because what you resist persists. Accept all emotions as energy messages. Get the message and release the messenger.

However, overall we carry a vibrating tone. There is a more long term overarching state of being that most people hold. Where is your vibration dial normally set? What scale on the spectrum do you normally reside?

262

I have seen many activists who are constantly informed about the abuses of the elite few; so much so that it is easy to go into fear and anger. That is where our biological system functions at its lowest, impairing the immune system. In that lower vibration people feel isolated, victimized, and lacking the energy to take action. That is why all oppressive regimes rule by fear, just as this elite group manipulates our economy, exposes us to chemicals, and bombards us with fear-inspiring messages on TV. Dwelling on what was wrong was the reason I left protesting 9/11/2001 and began serving community needs which was more uplifting and fulfilling.

However, if we feel bad about the encroaching police state, you often talk about it with others. If that fills your thoughts, the elite have won. If you are frustrated, fearful, hopeless most of the time, the elite have won. For what you think about most of the time is what you will attract.

By inviting joy and love as your passengers, you get to ride in a beautiful car that people can't help but admire. Your DNA actually lights up because the higher vibration stimulates more receptor nodes in your DNA strands. When the higher vibration exists, we naturally feel connected to others around us; we feel energized and even become more attractive.

Maintaining a high vibration is a powerful practice and one that is challenging to maintain. Here are a few tools to shift your vibe.

Shift Your Vibration

1. Think what it feels like to be energized, hold uplifting thoughts. Thoughts and energy are entwined. You will feel more energy.
2. Eat organic whole foods, without pesticides, GMO, or hormones. Eat at the Common Good Table.
3. Walk or play outside for one hour daily, gaze into long distances and observe nature. Connect with the expansive beauty around you.
4. Have a sport or exercise routine. Try to make it regular, get your cardiovascular system moving.
5. Practice yoga and meditate. It will greatly aid you to still your mind and relieve stress. It also increases your intuitive capacity.
6. Practice gratefulness and think about reaching your goals. The little brother of love is gratefulness. Acknowledge friends, family, nature ...
7. Learn how to access positive energy through relationships. Avoid irritating others, read the book *"How to Win Friends and Influence People."*
8. Change your physiology from slouching to straight, from a frown to a smile. Access the patterning of feeling good. Take long deep breaths expanding you abdomen and lungs with each inhalation. Joy is expansive.
9. See circumstances as opportunities to grow, to get feedback, to discover that your "unhelpful baggage" is not failure. Use the feedback skills provided.
10. Read books or listen to tapes that are uplifting, that make you feel good.
11. Play or listen to music, sing, and dance. Get out of your framework into a melodious one.
12. Change your environment, organize and clean, remove clutter
13. Participate in a high energy group where energy's nature is part of the culture.
14. Complement someone, lend a helping hand, do something positive.

High-Energy Zone

We've all experienced high-energy gatherings. We get there when people pull together in the face of a tough challenge. We feel it when a creative idea yields extraordinary results. A sizzling jam session takes place in the high-energy zone as does singing and dancing. So does an intimate relationship when partners maintain a loving vibration.

In these moments, we feel buoyed and uplifted by our companions. We're more creative, more responsive, more engaged and more comforted. In these moments, the contribution of every individual in a group merges into a collective energy, a synergistic force around which anything seems possible—and often is. These are magic moments.

I first experienced the high-energy zone with my family as a child. Every Sunday for over a decade the whole tribe—some sixty people including aunts, uncles, and cousins—would congregate at my parents' beach house on Narragansett Bay, Massachusetts. The adults would have horseshoe tournaments with plenty of hooting and cheering. Badminton and croquet would fill the backyard. By the water, clusters of family would relax in lawn chairs and discuss the latest news. At low tide about ten of us would pile into our boat and motor out to the sandbar, where we used rakes to harvest quahogs and clams. In the afternoon we'd have a feast, and everyone would contribute—my aunt would provide her legendary potato salad; my mother, her great clam cakes, and stuffed quahogs.

Now, fifty years later, the family still talks about those times, and when they do they get a gleam in the eye and they laugh. Just the memory alone creates a physical sensation of uplift. That's the lasting power of the high-energy zone. Decades later, with just a thought, it lives again.

We all want what my family discovered on the shore of Narragansett Bay. We want to create it with a few people as we support the Common Good; we want to share it at church services, sporting events, social events and in the neighborhood cafe. We seek it without knowing what it is, other than the feelings it elicits—vitality, openness, and a profound sense of connection.

The rejuvenation of our spirit can occur through group endeavors. Any group or person has the potential to resonate in the high-energy zone and thus become a conduit of love and potential.

Through holding that higher vibration we transcend the energies dragging down our spirit.

Realize that tyranny is not the natural state of humanity. It vibrates at a low level driven by greed and fear. Survival of the fittest is the lower evolved ecosystem versus mutually supportive systems. It is time again for people the world over to ask themselves if they still stand with the ideals enshrined in systems created by people who oppose the interest of the Common Good.

It is time to become aware of how we can participate directly in this great transformation process, inside of ourselves and in our shared world. It is a time for a higher expression.

The higher expression gets established within an individual character or a group's held values. High vibrating cultures provide the optimum environment to develop dreams and provide support.

The outline of the ideal culture is found in our essence. Our essence is energy that has characteristics described in Chapter 7. When we develop systems that align with energy's nature we are developing a synergy that resonates with the universe. The culture and environment that results is ideal to develop our potential because it is modeled after potential energy.

The high-energy zone is a vibrational state that aligns with a higher dimension. Our bodies are like tuning forks. When we vibrate at the same frequency as this other dimension, we experience a harmonious match. We link up, or "yoke," with this universal energy. The word *yoke* has the same origin as the word yoga, whose entire purpose is to help us make a harmonious connection with this high vibration. When that happens, the energy rejuvenates our spirits.

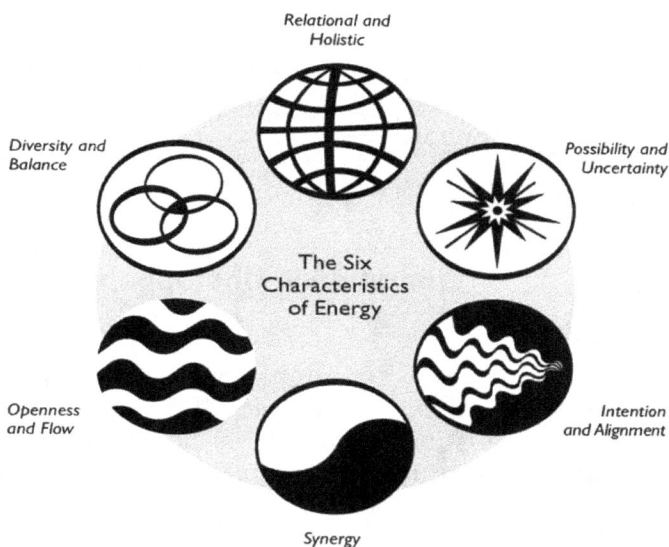

The Six Characteristics of Energy

- Relational and Holistic
- Possibility and Uncertainty
- Intention and Alignment
- Synergy
- Openness and Flow
- Diversity and Balance

Symbols represent the quantum behavior of energy.

Like the Law of Attraction it is the nature of things. When there is synergy with universal energy, a group becomes more empowered and vibrant. Any group has the potential to resonate in the high-energy zone and thus become a conduit of rejuvenation and creativity. Group energy fields provide real sustainable power to make initiatives happen outside of the Elite Systems.

Quantum physics suggests, and six-thousand-year-old yoga teachings assert, that energy is shaped by consciousness. Could there be a Universal Consciousness shaping the energy of the universe? Could this be the consciousness of God, Yahweh, Allah, and so on? Could this higher consciousness be speaking to us directly through every particle in the universe? If our own consciousness can shape energy, then why can't we assume that a consciousness beyond our dimensions is constantly shaping potential energy?

The US Constitution declares God's nature as a basis of our inalienable rights. We can declare this nature as part of the foundation of the Common Good Systems, but you can't find them in the structure and operations of the Elite Systems.

When we align—and help others in our groups to align—with this Universal Consciousness, we bring in something much bigger than the assembled participants. We tap into a wellspring of potential energy. It is real, not imagined; it's an experience, not a concept. It is accessible to any group. It can power grassroots initiatives on the Common Good Road.

Liberation is Unstoppable

Although emerging spontaneously and without leadership, this grassroots movement brings with it a very advantageous set of strategy characteristics. That is, it is non-violent, decentralized, self-propagating, liberating, inclusive, territory-capturing, adaptive, flexible, minimally confrontational, and uplifting. Such a widespread movement is impossible for the .01% to suppress or co-opt.

The distinctive characteristic of the Elite system is its consolidation, centralization and control of power wired into the hands of the few. The hierarchical structure is slow to respond and often inefficient. When the Common Good systems spread local empowerment to the many, there can be rapid and diverse responses. They generate a greater ownership and participation in the local community. Common Good systems would be too dispersed to shut down.

High-energy grassroots systems are developing all around us and are strengthening regional resources, exchanges, and investments. The systems consist of neighbors, municipalities, and counties working together to resolve issues impacting local residents. They involve taking responsibility for the Commons. A grassroots group can be part of a business, a family, community, or marriage, it is the next frontier. It is an evolution we are now living.

Start new purchasing habits. Look at the behemoth corporations like Proctor and Gamble, Wall Mart, Monsanto … if you support them then you support their agenda. Switch to local purchases and support grassroots systems. You don't even have to leave your home, switch your beliefs. Send emails to help others expand their awareness and understanding of what we are dealing with and what is possible. If you inform ten people and each of them informs ten, and that continues, Liberation becomes unstoppable.

We can choose to be a conscious part of an uplifting revolution. We can choose to create an optimum environment for growth and development. We can choose greater fulfillment and community. We can choose to be uplifted in our group endeavors and by one another. So this becomes an evolution!

Our Liberty is not a vague concept that we can reaffirm on occasion as it suits us. It is a choice that we make each and every day. Our purchasing power, our group power, and individual creative power can light the torch of freedom. Even a choice of what we think about and how we feel can liberate us from the Elite Systems. When we take action to unplug from this tyranny, every day is Independence Day; every day is an expression of Liberty.

"You assist an evil system most effectively by obeying its orders and decrees. An evil system never deserves such allegiance. Allegiance to it means partaking of the evil. A good person will resist an evil system with his or her whole soul."

Mahatma Gandhi

Free ongoing Support

www.LiberateGuide.com

Weekly guide for grassroots organizing

and system change. Post questions for author.

Be part of the evolution underway

Appendix

Catalyst for Change

Despite our inalienable and constitutional rights we operate within Elite Systems. In order for us to move into a more uplifting way of being, will require a dramatic shift in the way we are governed, the exchange of Federal Reserve Notes we call "Money", and the military/industrial complex.

What would motivate such a significant change in our societal systems? It might involve becoming aware of the unconstitutional, illegal framework of Elite Systems. Pain and suffering inflicted for staying within these systems is a great motivator. Another could be the prosperity and fulfillment that awaits those who participate in Common Good systems. Another motivator is the system change already underway. There are many inspirational initiatives from which to model.

However, most people don't realize that they are living under an oppressive system. A veil of delusion and crafted media images shade our consciousness and prevent us from seeing the reality of what is being done under the guise of Democracy and Free Trade. The appendix will help lift this veil.

Change also requires breaking deeply engrained personal behaviors formed by beliefs that can be manipulated by propaganda and other forms of social engineering. These beliefs become reinforced to create what is familiar. Individuals and societies will often choose to suffer, instead of letting go of the "known", or the familiar. Even if the familiar is feudalism, or Wage Slavery, many would prefer that over considering a new way of operating. However, when the pain and suffering from a dysfunctional system becomes so great that the human spirit can no longer endure, that pain becomes a catalyst for action and change.

Many recovered from addiction have often shared with me how they had to hit rock bottom before they were ready to change. I often would hear stories of suffering, abuse, and disenfranchisement. However, most times, it is this very suffering that propels them forward to change their circumstances.

Enough of today's population are feeling the strain of higher prices, lower wages, fewer work opportunities, greater debt, and have outrage at seeing banking and corporate interest rule the US government. People are feeling the pain and want to embrace change. Having knowledge can replace fear, concern, and disempowerment with hope, creativity, and empowerment.

Appendix A

The Head of the Beast:
The Monetary System

Even before the United States' independence, a battle has been waged by private international Central Banks for the control of money production. They realized that it would eventually lead to the control of the nation, if the ruse was maintained.

An historical perspective of the involvement of Central Banks illustrates the Rothschild Cartel persistent battle to control the production of money. This control provides tremendous purchasing power to create other systems that further enrich the perpetrators of this ruse. Its footprints includes the English colonialism and the New World Order of today, and its trademark is taking the wealth and well being of the many to serve the whims and delusions of an elite few.

The US timeline shows the Central Bank's relentless actions, to the extent of waging war against the US, to get their banks in control of money production. Even the attempts and successes of assassinations of American Presidents all occurred after challenging central bankers and their monopoly on money. They understood from history that the Central Banks artificially create booms and busts that cause people to lose their jobs, homes, and retirements, while the bankers further consolidate wealth and control in their hands.

The accomplishments of the Rothschild's and fellow bankers are nothing short of astonishing. They have literally got the world to give them the right to manufacture money out of debt and then to turn around and lend the mammon back to the world plus usurious interest! Almost single handedly, this small group of men has woven "Elite" systems of control to make this planet their feudal state. Through their efforts to dominate the world they have caused and are presently causing extraordinary pain and agony on a global scale.

Follow the United States timeline of how the Central Bankers sought control of the monetary system. Understand the sequence of events that has allowed this Elite group to flourish at the great expense of the Common Good.

History Timeline of the Hidden War of the Elite
Against the Common Good

1694 – Bank of England Established

This was the first Central Bank established in England whose beneficiaries were the aristocracy and the monarchy. It served as model for most modern central banks.

1743 – Mayer Amschel Rothschild

Founder of the Rothschild Banking Empire, is born in Frankfurt, Germany. Mayer Amschel Rothschild extended his banking empire across Europe by carefully placing his five sons in key positions.

They set up banks in Frankfurt, Vienna, London, Naples, and Paris. By the mid 1800's they dominated the banking industry, lending to governments around the world and people such as the Vanderbilts, Carnegies, and Cecil Rhodes.

1757– Colonial Scrip Issued in US

The American colonies had a chronic shortage of gold and silver coins. When Benjamin Franklin attended an Iroquois Nation powwow, he was very impressed with the distribution of Wampum. This form of exchange was meant to commemorate events and gifts that were distributed during the year. There was always enough Wampum for people to make the transactions they wanted to.

Benjamin became an advocate for fiat paper money called Colonial Scrip and attributed the scrip to the prosperity of colonists who used it. They were able to issue paper money at no interest. As a legitimated government, they could both spend and lend money into circulation.

Debt free, fiat currency was printed in the public interest to address this need. As Benjamin Franklin said, "In the colonies we issue our own money. It is called colonial scrip. We issue it in proper proportion to the demands of trade and industry to make the products pass easily from the producers to the consumers. In this manner, creating for ourselves our own paper money, we control its purchasing power and we have no interest to pay no one."

Soon enough however, the Bank of England had Parliament impose restrictions on the colonies issuance of Colonial Scrip. Restrictive measures on the use of Scrip were set in place by 1763. The British Parliament declared that all taxes could only be paid in coin. Poverty and unemployment began to plague the colonies because the operating medium had been cut in half. There were insufficient quantities of money to pay for products and services.

This was a grievance that added onto other grievances on the ruling elite. Benjamin Franklin put the bank's action in perspective, *"The Colonies would have gladly borne the little tax on tea and other matters had it not been the poverty caused by the bad influence of the English bankers on the Parliament, which has caused in the colonies hatred of England and the Revolutionary War."*

1776 – American Independence

Our founding fathers saw the ravage caused by the Central Bank in England. The government focused on the public owning and benefiting from this medium of exchange.

Article 1, section 8, of the Constitution reads: *"The Congress shall have the Power.....To coin Money, regulate the Value thereof,"*....

Secretary of State Thomas Jefferson was adamantly opposed to the idea of a privately owned federal bank and said, *"And I sincerely believe that the banking establishments are more dangerous than standing army; and the principle of spending money to be paid by posterity under the name of funding, is but swindling futurity on a large scale. Bank-paper must be suppressed and the circulating medium must be restored to then nation to whom it belongs." --*

"If the American people ever allow the banks to control the issuance of their currency... the banks and corporations that will grow up around them will deprive the people of all property, until their children wake up homeless on the continent their fathers conquered."

From 1776 to 1790 there was Free Banking; there were no formal central bank. The 13 states had their own banks, currencies and financial institutions.

1776 – Rothschild's Plan for World Dominance

The same year as the Declaration of Independence a Jesuit Professor Adam Weishaupt who was retained by Rothschild's completes a world dominance plan.[41] It was a long term plan that mapped the destruction of nation states, the abolition of private property, and the creation of a World Government of absolute despotism under a World Dictator, with a World Police Force to crush all opposition.

1791 – Congress chartered the Bank of the United States

In 1790 Hamilton persuaded Congress to pass the Assumption Act where the Federal Government assumed States debts. This would assure the ruling class get full dollar return on bonds they purchased pennies on the dollar. He then argued the need for a central US bank. He then persuaded Congress to create the First US Bank – a private company, partly owned by Foreigners including the Rothschild– to handle the financial needs of the new central government. It was for a twenty year charter. Hamilton resigned as Secretary of the Treasury in 1793.

In 1811 Congress refused to renew the charter for the Bank of the United States. They did so under grave threats of retaliation from Central Bank in England. They closed the bank.

1812-1815 – War breaks out with Britain and the US

Threatened by Rothschild for not renewing the charter, Rothschild and the Bank of England financed a war against the United States. The idea was to bankrupt the nation or get their bank in. They got the latter. 1815 President James Madison proposed a second privately owned Bank of the United States. The war ends.

1817 – The Privately Owned Second Bank of the US

The Second Bank was chartered in 1816 for twenty years and opened in 1817. The owners again included the Rothschild and the Bank of England. It served as the Main Depository for Government Revenue, making it a highly profitable bank.

1832 – Andrew Jackson campaigns against private Central Banks

Jackson denied the Second Bank of the US and vetoes the bank charter renewal. Andrew Jackson was skeptical of the central banking system and believed it gave too few men too much power and caused inflation. He was also a proponent of gold and silver. President Jackson issued an Executive Order to Stop Depositing Government Funds into the Bank of US. By September 1833, government funds were being deposited into state chartered banks.

President Andrew Jackson said regarding bankers: *"The bank, is trying to kill me, but I will kill it!" "You are a den of vipers and thieves. I intend to rout you out, and by the eternal God I will rout you out."*

"Paper is poverty... it is only the ghost of money, and not money itself."

In December of 1834, President Jackson declared that the national debt will be paid off. The next month there was an assassination attempt on Jackson. Jan 30, 1835 two guns misfired and he escaped.

1833 – 1837 Artificial Bubble

The Central Banks retaliated and created a manufactured "bubble" through too much money in the system. During that period the money supply increased 84%. Spurred by the 2nd Bank of the US the total money supply rose from $150 million to $267 million.[42]

1836 – Bank of the United States is closed.

Jackson closed the Bank of the United States overriding Congress, commenting: *"The bold effort the present bank had made to control the government are but premonitions of the fate that* await the American people should they be deluded into a perpetuation of this institution or the establishment of another like it."

1837-1843 – Depression

The depression was inevitable with the previous bubble. 343 of the 850 banks in the US closed entirely as the largest banks consolidated wealth and power. Thus they take more real wealth with expansion and contraction of the currency they controlled. It is a theme repeated when the private Central Banks control the monetary flow.

1861 – American Civil War

The war was fought on two fronts. Lincoln said, "*The money*

powers prey upon the nation in times of peace and conspire against it in times of adversity. The banking powers are more despotic than a monarchy, more insolent than autocracy, more selfish than bureaucracy. They denounce as public enemies all who question their methods or throw light upon their crimes. I have two great enemies, the Southern Army in front of me and the bankers in the rear. Of the two, the one at my rear is my greatest foe. Corporations have been enthroned, and an era of corruption in high places will follow. The money power of the country will endeavor to prolong its reign by working upon the prejudices of the people until the wealth is aggregated in the hands of a few, and the Republic is destroyed."

In February 1863, Congress established another National

Banking system. The bankers were intending to charge between 24% and 36% interest rates for money to finance the war. To avoid the interest, Lincoln ordered the printing of $450 million in bank notes guaranteed by the U.S. government.

"*The government should create, issue, and circulate all the currency. Creating and issuing money is the supreme prerogative of government and is its greatest creative   opportunity. Adopting these principles will save the taxpayers immense sums of interest and money will cease to be the master and become the servant of*

278

humanity." Lincoln. The notes were called "Greenbacks" and effectively eliminated the interest the private banks charged on notes they issued.

April 15, 1865 – Lincoln Assassinated and National Banking Act

The associates of the President Lincoln's assassin were according to many, on the payroll of bankers[43]. After his death Congress revoked the Greenback Law and enacted, in its place, the National Banking Act supporting privately owned national banks. The Nation was thrown into a state of constant debt, paying interest to bankers who created cash.

1881– President James Garfield, Staunch Proponent of "Honest Money"

Garfield opposed fiat currency (money that was not backed by any physical object) and was a strong advocate of a bi-metal monetary system, backed by gold and silver.. *President James A. Garfield was inaugurated in 1881, he said "Whoever controls the volume of money in any country is absolute master of all industry and commerce".* He had the second shortest Presidency in history. On July 2, 1881 Garfield was shot, he died from the wound on September 19.

1907– Banking Panic

The New York Stock Exchange dropped dramatically as everyone tried to get their money out of the banks at the same time across the nation. This banking panic spurred debate for banking reform. JP Morgan and others gathered to create an image of concern and stability in the face of the panic, a panic they themselves induced, which eventually led to the formation of the Federal Reserve. They misled the public into believing that the Federal Reserve would help to regulate bankers when in fact it really gave even more power to private bankers, but in a less transparent way.

In 1908 JP Morgan, a Rockefeller relative, and Senator Nelson Aldrich, head of the new National Monetary Commission studied the banking panic. Their efforts were to get a private Central Bank to control the money supply. If they controlled that, it would open the nation's vault to them.

1910 – Bankers Meet Secretly on Jekyll Island

Over the course of a week, some of the nation's most powerful bankers met secretly off the coast of Georgia, drafting a proposal for a private Central Banking system that would become the Federal Reserve. Those in attendance included Nelson Aldrich, A.P. Andrew (Assistant Secretary of the Treasury), Paul Warburg (Kuhn, Loeb, & Co.), Frank Vanderlip (President of National City Bank of New York), Charles D. Norton (president of the Morgan-dominated First National Bank of New York), Henry Davidson (Senior Partner of JP Morgan Co.), and Benjamin Strong (representing JP Morgan).

Paul Warburg   Sen. Nelson Aldrich   Frank Vanderlip   Benjamin Strong

Henry Davidson   Charles Norton   Abe Andrews

Even before the Fed was formed John F. Hylan, then mayor of New York, said in 1911 that *"the real menace of our republic is the invisible government which, like a giant octopus, sprawls its slimy length over our city, state and nation. At the head is a small group of banking houses, generally referred to as 'international bankers.'"*

Dec 23, 1913 – Federal Reserve Act Passed

In exchange for financial support for his presidential campaign, Woodrow Wilson's signed the Federal Reserve Act. In December 1913, while many members of Congress were home for Christmas, the Federal Reserve Act was rammed through Congress and signed by President Wilson.

The Fed became law the day before Christmas Eve, in the year 1913. It was one of those backdoor deals making sure those who opposed it were not present. Shortly afterwards, the German International bankers, Kuhn, Loeb and Co. sent one of their partners there to run the Fed.

The Federal Reserve Act allowed the Central Bankers to win a long fought battle. Now they were able to loan money out at interest, make decisions without government approval, and control the amount of money in circulation, creating bubble and busts at their will.

The Primary Owners of the Federal Reserve Bank Are: Rothschild's of London, Berlin Lazard Brothers of Paris Israel, Moses Seaf of Italy; Kuhn, Loeb & Co. of Germany and New York; Warburg & Company of Hamburg, Germany; Lehman Brothers of New York; Goldman, Sachs of New York; Rockefeller Brothers of New York

Congressman Charles Lindberg, Sr., in 1913 had this to say regarding the powers of the newly created Federal Reserve System. *"When the president signs this Act, the invisible government, by the money power -proven to exist by The Monetary Trust Investigation- will be legalized. The new law will create inflation whenever the Trust wants inflation. From now on, depressions will be scientifically created." "This is the strangest, most dangerous advantage ever placed in the hands of a special privilege class by any Government that ever existed. The system is private, conducted for the sole purpose of obtaining the greatest possible profits from the use of other people's money. They know in advance when to create panics to their advantage, they also know when to stop panic. Inflation and deflation work equally well for them when they control finance."*

1913 – Income tax established

The Constitution only allowed direct apportioned taxation amongst the States, so indirect Income Tax was initiated through the 16th Amendment. The 16th Amendment was pushed through without proper ratification of the states, in February of 1913.

The 16th Amendment stated: *"The Congress shall have power to lay and collect Federal taxes on incomes, from whatever source derived, without apportionment among the several States,*

and without regard to any census or enumeration." Congress actually does not have the power.

According to the two volume work by Bill Benson and Red Beckman, "The Law That Never Was" the 16th amendment, which created the IRS, was never properly ratified, not even by one state![44] The researchers traveled the then 48 states to verify that fact. So in a very real sense the income tax and IRS isn't legal, as many have proclaimed.

1914 – World War I Starts

The primary beneficiaries of WWI were the owners of the Federal Reserve Bank. World War I had turned the United States from a debtor nation into a creditor nation. In the aftermath of the war, both the victorious Allies and the defeated Central Powers owed the United States enormous sums of money. The Republican administrations of the 1920s insisted on payments in gold bullion, but the world's gold supply was limited and by the end of the 1920s, the United States, itself, controlled much of the world's gold supply.

1921-1929 – The "Roaring 20's"

The Federal Reserve Floods the Economy with Cash and Credit.

From 1921 to 1929 the Federal Reserve increased the money supply by $28 billion, almost a 62% increase over an eight-year period.[45] This artificially created another "boom" a financial bubble bound to bust with a sudden contraction. There are Elites like the Rockefellers who miraculously position their investments right before the crash to get maximum profit from the impending misery on the masses.

1929 – Federal Reserve Contracts the Money Supply

In 1929, the Federal Reserve began to pull money out of circulation as loans were paid back. 1929-1933- Federal Reserve reduced the money supply by 33%.[46] With significantly less money to go around, businessmen could not get new loans and could not even get their old loans renewed, forcing many to stop investing. The Federal Reserve, especially the New York branch[47] created a "bust" which was inevitable after issuing so much credit in the years before. The Federal Reserve's actions triggered the banking crisis, which led to the Great Depression.

October 24, 1929, The Great Depression

"Black Thursday", is the most devastating stock market crash in history. Within 15 years of the creation of the Federal Reserve Bank the U.S. experienced it's worst depression. This depression initiated by the Federal Reserve Bank transferred billions of dollars into the private banker's hands at the expense and the impoverishment of on nearly everyone else. That wasn't enough so the Fed demanded all of the gold in the US as further payment.

April 5th 1933, President Franklin D. Roosevelt gets the gold

The president ordered citizens to hand their gold and gold certificates to the private Federal Reserve Bank: Executive Order 6102: "Section 2. *All persons are hereby required to deliver on or before May 1, 1933, to a Federal Reserve Bank or a branch or agency thereof or to any member bank of the Federal Reserve System all gold coin, gold bullion and gold certificates now owned by them or coming into their ownership on or before April 28, 1933"*.

"Section 9. Whoever willfully violates any provision of this Executive Order or of these regulations or of any rule, regulation or license issued there under may be fined not more than $10,000, or, if a natural person, may be imprisoned for not more than ten years, or both"

1933 Enslavement of the United States Citizens

The private bankers of the Federal Reserve took all the gold in the United States. But there wasn't enough to discharge the debt that they claim had accumulated up to 1933. What did this nation do to deserve such debt accumulation, why are we indebted?

Since the U.S. went bankrupt in 1933, all new money has to be borrowed into existence. All states started issuing serial-numbered, certificated "warehouse receipts" for births and marriages in order to pledge the people as collateral against those loans and municipal bonds taken out with the Federal Reserve's banks. The "Full faith and credit" of the American people is what pays back the nation's debt.

In order to catalog its laborers to pay the debt the government needed an efficient, methodical system of tracking its property to that end. Humans today are looked upon merely as "human resources". The people are resources to the Central Bank; their birth certificates are a security on the New York Stock Exchange. That is why if you look at all birth certificates in the United States at the bottom, you will have a series of red numbers printed on the birth certificate, the following birth certificate had its red number in the lower, bottom, left circle. These numbers are a security stock exchange number on the World Stock Exchange, an accounting of your worth in this elite system.

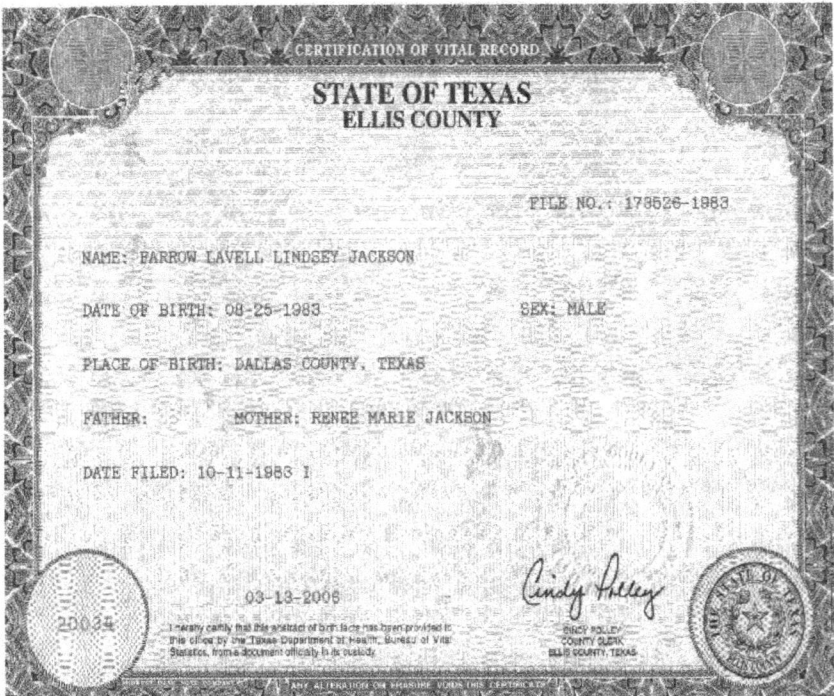

Henry Ford once said *"It is well enough that people of the nation do not understand our banking and monetary system, for if they did, I believe there would be a revolution before tomorrow morning"*.

1950 and 1960 The growth of the Middle Class

One bread winner could earn enough to purchase a nice home, send three rids to college and one of the partners didn't work outside to develop home life. There were good paying jobs, a strong manufacturing base. People became educated. We had equal rights protest, the Vietnam War protests, and new social organizations like the Black Panthers. The Elite were losing their grip, then they clamped down.

1963, November 22 – Kennedy Assassinated

His exposure of a ruthless conspiracy did not go very far. Issues such as the Bay of Pigs, and a verbal exposure of the power behind the government displeased factions of the Elite. The banker controlled CIA should be investigated for the assassination as they are high on a list of suspects.

1970's – The dismantling of the middle class

Move manufacturing jobs offshore, have corporate profits feed stockholders, lower worker's wages, bust up unions, bring the tax burden to the masses excluding the elite, and create huge profits based on financial maneuvers versus producing anything of value. Also, they vastly increased debt gouging interest.

1999 – The Financial Services Modernization Act

The law partially deregulated the financial industry. It allows companies working in the financial sector to integrate their operations and invest in each other's businesses and consolidate. This includes businesses such as insurance companies, brokerage firms, investment dealers, commercial banks etc. This provided a doorway to one of their key strategic objectives, to manipulate and consolidate.

2000-2003 – The Federal Reserve Extends "Easy Credit"

The Fed lowers the Federal Fund Rate from 6.5% to 1% and sets up another financial "Boom".[48]

2004 – Investment Banks and the SEC Cut a Deal

Up until 2004, the amount of debt the banks could take on was limited. However, in 2004, the Securities and Exchange Commission (SEC), agreed to let banks regulate themselves taking on as much debt as they wanted, therefore unleashing billions of dollars for high-risk investment packages.

2004-2006 – Federal Reserve Sets Off New "Bust"

By making loans and adjustable rate mortgages more expensive, they raised Fed rate to 5.25% while reducing the money in the circulation.[49] This contracted the market and the bubble burst, as it has done in every depression.

Our present financial woes are because in part by the Fed's own figures show that the money supply (M3) has shrunk by $3 trillion since 2008. [50]

2007-2011 – Worst Financial Crisis since the Great Depression

The financial crisis impacted people around the world – millions lost their homes, jobs, and retirement funds. Many of the smaller banks were absorbed by others, which allowed the biggest banks to further consolidate wealth and eliminate competition. In 2008, J.P. Morgan Chase & Co. bought up both Washington Mutual (the biggest bank to "fail" in the history of the United States) and Bear Stearns (the fifth largest investment bank). The Fed keeps on paying billions into their system through bailouts and other scams. They loan money to big banks that play the commodities market that results in higher gas and food prices for Main Street.

2010 – Corporate Profits

- JP Morgan Chase reports record profits made a record profit of $17.4 billion. In 2010, James Dimon, CEO, received $20,816,289 in total compensation. The bank turned a $19 billion profit in 2011, up 9 percent.

- Exxon Mobil had a record profit of $40 billion in 2008 due to record oil prices. In 2010, R. W. Tillerson received $28,952,558 in total compensation. Exxon and Mobil had $41.1 billion in 2011 profit.

- General Electric claimed a $3.2 billion tax benefit. Though it made a $14.2 billion profit in 2010. They paid $0 in US taxes. In 2010, Jeffrey R. Immelt received $21,428,765 in total compensation.

- Goldman, Sachs revealed a 90% leap in profits in spite of accusations of dishonesty while providing multimillion dollar bonuses. They posted a 2.7 billion profit in the first quarter of

2011. For the first nine months of 2012, Goldman Sachs reported revenue of $24.9 billion and reported a net profit of $4.6 billion.

2017 – People are Waking Up

- President Trump's actions are a wakeup call where the volume is turned up. People are more clearly seeing the lies and manipulation, appointments, budgets, and priorities. A growing population is realizing that the primary mechanisms of the US Federal Government are controlled by a small group of banking/oil elite.

- Now is the time to end this 100 year banking scam, there is a growing movement to end and audit the Federal Reserve, and model the transition after the state run North Dakota Bank or debt free monetary systems.

- There are many inspirations, strategies, and tips in this book to develop grassroots initiatives in your community; it is a time for action.

Appendix B

The Limbs of the Beast: Government, Military, Corporate, Media Systems

A small group of corrupt elite are waging a war on 99% of the population. Most people are not aware of the dangers that exist. A top-down, undemocratic, globalization process is effectively removing local controls and cultural freedoms. The primary instrument of the rule by the few is private, interest-bearing debt that affords the manipulation of our sub-conscious. As a result of this regime, nations, states, and families around the world are virtual prisoners of a private Central Bank system, and its debt money instruments and policies.

The Central Banks has global reach as the International Monetary Fund (IMF). In the year of 2000 there were seven countries without a Rothschild owned Central Bank: Afghanistan, Iraq, Sudan, Libya, Cuba, North Korea, and Iran. The first four have all had regime change by CIA insurgents, US troops or US air attacks. In 2012 three countries are resisting the Central Bank presence: Cuba, North Korea, and Iran. The limbs of the beast stretch throughout the world. It is a global network of a New World Order.

Major players are the Rothschild Cartel, the Rockefellers and the Royal British Family. It is beyond the grasp of most people to imagine the wealth they have accumulated. Forbes magazine poses lower ranking billionaires like Bill Gates and Warren Buffet as the richest men in the World. British law prevents the disclosure of assets for the Royal British Crown so those figures are not available. The combined wealth of the Rockefeller family, depicted here, in 1998 was approx (US) $11 trillion and the Rothschild's (U.S.) $100 trillion.[51] That wealth has escalated since.

With seeming unlimited wealth at their fingertips the owners of the Central Banks have the resources and connections to fund all sorts of schemes to further their personal enrichment. It has taken colonialism to a more subtle level in the form of bank/corporate rule and monetary indebtedness.

Now you can understand why the Central Bankers began their quest to control America's money production well before the Declaration of Independence and was a prime reason for separating from the British Monarchy and their banking cartel in 1776. These bankers knew that if they won the battle of money production they would eventually control the nation.

For one hundred years they have developed and refined economic, government, corporate, and media systems. Their operation is covert, subversive, and highly efficient utilizing compartmentalization and the illusion to hide their objective.

Our nation's health was severely compromised when Woodrow Wilson betrayed the citizens and gave his cronies one of our biggest strengths, our ability to issue money. In turn, our nation became infected with a terrible virus that has turned it into an unrecognizable beast.

The Beast's Appendages

The primary controlling mechanism in the United States is the monetary system directed by the owners of the Federal Reserve. Its primary limbs are government, corporations, and the media. There are other appendages like health care, food supply, education, and infrastructure. But they are under the direction of the primary limbs.

Government: Our political system has been taken over by money and the media controlled by the Elite. For elections they chose who they will display to the public; only candidates who will do their bidding will progress, otherwise they get no money and plenty of bad press. Through their vast interests in corporations they control lobbying groups which shapes law and policy. They have the power to form government committees that do their bidding, changing laws that benefit the 1%.

We think we have a choice between our two party systems, but they are two hands of the same body. The policies and direction are almost indistinguishable between the Bush and Obama administration. Now Trump is the same, just more in your face. But what we are fed are politicians who claim "hope" to stop the corruption and end war. These are false hopes spun by actors who continue to do the bidding of those who control the money. Regardless of party affiliation they take us further down the path of control by the Elite few under the illusion of choice.

Corporations: The declaration of corporate personhood and the ability to provide unlimited campaign contributions further empowered the Elite who control the corporations. Citizens United should be rightly named Disenfranchisement of Citizens. It gives leaders and boards of large multinational corporations and the lobbyists they employ great influence. It also provides a shield and a form of insurance for the high level players. Because of consolidated power and shield, it allows them to disengage from the 99%.

The Elite has shaped the labor market for example, by moving manufacturing offshore and making the US dependent on foreign manufacturing and shipping that they manage on some level. This separation provides another level of control.

Acquisitions and consolidation is the signature of corporate development under the Elite's control. Organizations like Monsanto are a swinging door between the Federal Government. Many of the committees where the real government policies are set come from these corporate leaders.

Media: Since the mid 1980's the Federal Communication Commission (FCC) has been changing the laws to allow consolidation of media ownership. They relentlessly chipped away the laws that prevented these mergers. Presently five corporations control main street media.

These corporations select specific stories that support the Elite agenda. Even some stories are made up, "Fake News" get displayed like a Hollywood production, to represent the news. They determine what to show the public and what to emphasize. There is also great opportunity for diversionary tactics that prevents citizens from seeing beyond this fabricated veil. Their veil keeps the 99% from the truth allowing the Elite to manipulate our economy, health, and prosperity behind their curtain. The manufactured chaos of Trump's reign provides another screen for dismantling democracy.

Through the layers of front people it allows the super elite to stay out of the limelight. But one thing is for certain that their control, power and influence allows them to dictate policy and decisions in such a way that directly benefits them at the cost of others. It is the primary reason for the financial havoc, unemployment, foreclosures, and hardships.

A Game of Manipulation

In strict hierarchy, the few who have and utilize the primary control, power, and influence shape the organization. Not only their decisions are amplified throughout, their consciousness is also shaping the consciousness of the system. Their personal values shape the values and culture of the organization. Another word when they have strict control, the organization's values align with their personal values.

In this hierarchy the Elite set the tone for the values. They make the other systems in their image and likeness in terms of how decisions are made, where resources go. The leaders in a strict hierarchy are true monarchs. Values and operating principles often come from its founders. So it is interesting to note what principles established their staggering fortune. Also what are the values they embrace? Is there a repeated strategy used?

One consistent strategy is the gathering and manipulation of information for personal gain. As the wealth and power of the Rothschild grew in size and influence so did their intelligence gathering network. By 1835 they had their 'agents' strategically located in all the capitals and trading centers of Europe, gathering intelligence.

Their unique spy system started out when the Rothschild brothers began sending messages to each other through a network of couriers linking their Frankfurt, Vienna, London, Naples, and Paris banks. Soon it developed into something much more elaborate, effective and far reaching. It was a spy network par excellence. Its stunning speed and effectiveness gave the Rothschild a clear edge in all their dealings with news on international level.

And there was no news more precious than the outcome at the

Battle of Waterloo. There were vast fortunes to be made -- and lost -- on the outcome of battle. The Stock Exchange in London was at fever pitch as traders awaited news of the outcome of this battle. If Britain lost, English consuls would plummet to unprecedented depths. If Britain was victorious, the value of the consul would leap to new heights.

Arriving at the Exchange amid frantic speculation on the outcome of the battle, Nathan Rothschild knowing the outcome from his agents took up his usual position at the exchange.[52] Rothschild agents immediately began to dump consuls on the market. As hundreds of thousands of dollars worth of consuls came onto the

market their value started to slide. Then they began to plummet. Word began to sweep through the Stock Exchange: "Rothschild knows." "Wellington has lost at Waterloo."

After several hours of feverish trading the consul was selling for about five cents on the dollar. Nathan's cue released dozens of Rothschild agents made their way to the order desks around the Exchange and bought every consul in sight. A short time later the 'official' news arrived in the British capital. England was victorious.

Nathan Rothschild

Within seconds the consul skyrocketed to above its original value. As the significance of the British victory began to sink into the public consciousness, the value of consuls rose even higher. Napoleon had 'met his Waterloo.' Nathan had bought control of the British economy. Overnight, his already vast fortune was multiplied twenty times over. It also provides insight into the operating strategies of Rothschild that is still operating today.

Their spy network developed into three primary locations where they had strong Central Banks and control of the government. The three primary spy/messenger networks have morphed into the CIA in the US, the Mossad of Israel, and MI-6 in England.

Since the Battle of Waterloo in 1815 the Rothschild clan has dominated the economies of the industrial nations. The clan promised to secrecy, and to marry within the family. The closeness of the Rothschild brothers is seen in a letter from Soloman (Salmon) Rothschild to his brother Nathan on Feb. 28, 1815. *"We are like the mechanism of a watch: each part is essential."* This closeness is further seen in that of the 18 marriages made by Mayer Amschel Rothschild's grandchildren - 16 were contracted between first cousins.

The inbreeding and secrecy creates a disconnect from humanity. For generations they have been sequestered behind their vast wealth, their sense of privilege for generations creates a view of humanity from a high perch. It allows them to not have compassion for the suffering under them.

One example how this works can be illustrated by a yoga teacher I knew who had a large ashram and thousands of disciples. After 30 years he fell from grace when his lies about sex and money were revealed. I asked him how he could be so loving and wise and be deceptive at the same time. His response was revealing. "I separate myself above everyone else; the rules didn't apply to me. I could do what I please."

When you take that disconnect even further it becomes Psychopathy. It is distinguished as "emotional deafness" — a biochemical inability to experience normal feelings of empathy for others. There is an insular focus on personal desires. This shark-like fixation on self-interest means that psychopaths often feel a clear detachment from other people, viewing them more as sheep to be preyed upon than fellow humans to relate to.

Systems based on deception, manipulation, back door deals, and thievery create an environment well suited for individuals with these traits. Psychopaths by their mental wiring are able to advance rapidly in these systems. I'm not implying that all leaders in these systems are psychopaths; all it takes is a few in the right positions.

The CIA and Military Industrial Complex

"When a government is dependent upon bankers for money, they and not the leaders of the government control the situation, since the hand that gives is above the hand that takes. Money has no motherland; financiers are without patriotism and without decency; their sole object is gain." Napoleon Bonaparte

What we are dealing with is what Eisenhower in his farewell speech termed the Military/Industrial/Complex. It is that, a complex networking of government and industry to secretly support a hidden agenda. It is the banking interest that feeds this complex. This agenda only serves the Elite at the cost of the masses. It is a network that encompasses the globe, and the level of suffering, thievery, and death this group has orchestrated over a span of one hundred years is unmatched in history.

The Rothschild catalyst for accumulation of their enormous wealth was in large part based on the activities of spies and information gatherers. Their taking over of the British economy in 1850 was due to information agents able to relay vital information that was integral in the deception. Likewise having the best access to and manipulation of information is integral to their plan. Prior to World War 2 the Office of Naval Intelligence carried out Black Ops and covert operations to solely benefit US private corporate interests like the Banana Republic. So based on the successes in intelligence gathering in World War II they felt justified in pushing their legislatures to form the National Security Council.

Under the provisions of the National Security Act of 1947, the National Security Council (NSC) and the Central Intelligence Agency (CIA) were created. The Act charged the CIA with coordinating the nation's intelligence activities and correlating, evaluating, and disseminating intelligence that affects national security. They were also authorized to conduct clandestine operations.

Their control is through the inner government also connected with the MOSSAD in Israel, and MI-6 in Great Britain, who become their eyes and ears and a channel to carry out covert operations ... operations that always are in the interest of the elite few. It is reminiscent of the powerful spy network they built in 1835 and so much of their empire is built on manipulation of information and covert operations.

The 1947 Act also prohibited the CIA from engaging in law enforcement activity and restricted its internal security functions. In the last sixty years the CIA has overthrown more than 30 democratically elected leaders, either by coup, assassination or clandestine operations designed to subvert the will of the people. In place of democracy, America installs right-wing, conservative tyrants, dictators, puppets, proctors and kings, all supported, financially and politically, by whichever party retains power in America. This take over can be done through war, if need be, or through clandestine pressure.

The Elite's control of groups within the CIA and US military and private mercenary contractors, allows them the spying and covert operation cover that has been the downfall of many foreign democratically elected leaders. The CIA, IMF, or other Elite group determines the next leaders who consistently seem to replace them with harsh dictators who exploit the country for the banking and business interests they represent. As we will see their agenda of regime change to pilfer and control resources is a key strategy. Successful methods of overthrow used 60 years ago are still being used today.

But before they bring in the CIA, the IMF men try to steer that country onto the road of Elite control. This version of the destabilization program is less messy, offering plausible deniability for the western powers who are overthrowing a foreign government. It starts when the IMF moves in to offer a bribe to a dictator in a third world country. He gets 10% in exchange for taking out an exorbitant loan for an infrastructure project that the country does not need or can't afford.

When the country inevitably defaults on the loan payments, the IMF begins to take over, imposing a restructuring program that eventually results in the full scale looting of the country's resources for western business interests. This program, too, was run in country after country, from Jamaica to Myanmar, from Chile to Zimbabwe. The source code for this program was revealed in 2001, however, when former World Bank chief economist Joseph Stiglitz went public about the scam. 53

More detail was added in 2004 by the publication of John Perkin's *Confessions of an Economic Hitman*, which revealed the extent to which front companies and complicit corporations aided, abetted and facilitated the economic plundering and overthrow of foreign governments. 54

Although still an effective technique for overthrowing foreign nations, the fact that this particular scam had been exposed meant that the architects of global geopolitics would have to find a new way to get rid

CIA operations follow the same recurring script. First, Elite business/banking interests abroad are threatened by a popular or democratically elected leader. The people support their leader because he or she intends to conduct land reform, strengthen unions, redistribute wealth, nationalize foreign-owned industry, and regulate business to protect workers, consumers and the environment.

The CIA mobilizes the opposition. First it identifies right-wing groups within the country (usually the military), and offers them a deal: "We'll put you in power if you maintain a favorable business climate for us." The Agency then hires, trains and works with them to overthrow the existing government (usually a democracy). It uses every trick in the book: propaganda, stuffed ballot boxes, purchased elections, extortion, blackmail, sexual intrigue, false stories about opponents in the local media, infiltration and disruption of opposing political parties, kidnapping, beating, torture, intimidation, economic sabotage, death squads and even assassination.

These efforts culminate in a coup, which installs a right-wing dictator. The CIA trains the dictator's security apparatus to crack down on the traditional enemies of big business, using interrogation, torture and murder. The victims are said to be "communists," and now "terrorists" but almost always they are just peasants, liberals, moderates, labor union leaders, political opponents and advocates of free speech and democracy. Widespread human rights abuse follow. Brutal dictators who then suppress the citizens, enslave them through cheap labor, and steal their natural resources—all to benefit the Elite. There are over thirty cases where such subjugation has occurred starting in 1953, as they recently did in Libya under the guise of a "humanitarian cause" sanctioned by the UN.

Even more disturbing is that much of this funding for covert operations comes from the drug trade as illustrated by the Iran/Contra scandal. The CIA is an integral part of this opiate epidemic. I have witnessed the devastating effects these drugs have on our community. There have been whistle blowers, but nothing happens.

The first CIA overthrow described below was considered a great success. It has served as a template for the overthrow of many democratically elected governments.

1953 Iran and the CIA

The CIA's first coup d'état was the overthrow of the democratically elected government of Iran. Prime Minister Mohammad Mosaddeg began nationalizing the countries oil reserves in 1953 following through on his election promises. The oil industry of Iran was then controlled by the Anglo-Iranian Oil Company, whose refinery is shown here. The banking and corporate interests did not share the citizen's joy.

The CIA was sent into the country to bring an end to Mosaddeg 's government.[55] The coup was orchestrated by the intelligence agencies of the United Kingdom and the United States. The CIA bribed street thugs, clergy, politicians and Iranian army officers to take part in a propaganda campaign against Mosaddeg and his government. According to the CIA's declassified documents and records, some of the most feared mobsters in Tehran were hired by the CIA to stage pro-Shah riots on 19 August. Other CIA-paid men were brought into Tehran in buses and trucks, and took over the streets of the city. They began a campaign of terror, staging bombings and attacks on Muslim targets in order to blame them on Mosaddeg. They fostered and funded an anti- Mosaddeg campaign amongst the radical Islamist elements in the country. 800 people were killed during and as a direct result of the conflict. Finally, they backed the revolution that brought their favored puppet, the Shah, into power.[56]

Within months, their mission had been accomplished: they had removed a democratically elected leader who threatened to build up an independent, secular Persian nation and replaced him with a repressive tyrant whose secret police would brutally suppress all opposition.

Mosaddeg was arrested, tried and convicted of treason by the Shah's military court. He was sentenced to three years in jail, and then placed under house arrest for the remainder of his life. Mosaddeg's supporters were rounded up, imprisoned, tortured or executed. The tangible benefits the Elite reaped from overthrowing Iran's elected government included a share of Iran's oil wealth. Washington continually supplied arms to the unpopular Shah, and the CIA-trained SAVAK, his repressive secret police force. The Shah ruled as an authoritarian monarch for the next 26 years, until he was overthrown in a popular revolt in 1979.

The campaign according to the CIA was a success and the after-action report describing the operation in glowing terms. The pattern was to be repeated time and time again in country after country. Guatatemla, Loas, Dominican Republic, Ecuador, Brazil, Indonesia, Greece, Bolivia ... the list goes on.

The Association for Responsible Dissent estimates that by 1987, 6 million people had died as a result of CIA covert operations. Former State Department official William Blum correctly calls this an *"American Holocaust."*

The Overthrow Formula

In foreign countries CIA operations follow a recurring script. First, Elite business/banking interests abroad are threatened by a popular or democratically elected leader. The people support their leader because he or she intends to conduct land reform, strengthen unions, redistribute wealth, nationalize foreign-owned industry, and regulate business to protect workers, consumers and the environment.

The CIA mobilizes the opposition. First it identifies right-wing groups within the country (usually the military), and offers them a deal: "We'll put you in power if you maintain a favorable business climate for us." The Agency then hires, trains and works with them to overthrow the existing government (usually a democracy). It uses every trick in the book: propaganda, stuffed ballot boxes, purchased elections, extortion, blackmail, sexual intrigue, false stories about opponents in the local media, infiltration and disruption of opposing political parties, kidnapping, beating, torture, intimidation, economic sabotage, death squads and even assassination.

These efforts culminate in a coup, which installs a right-wing dictator. The CIA trains the dictator's security apparatus to crack down on the traditional enemies of big business, using interrogation, torture and murder. The victims are said to be "communists," and now "terrorists" but almost always they are just peasants, liberals, moderates, labor union leaders, political opponents and advocates of free speech and democracy. Widespread human rights abuse follows. Brutal dictators then suppress the citizens, enslave them through cheap labor, and steal their natural resources—all to benefit the Elite. There are over thirty cases where such subjugation has occurred starting in 1953.

CIA Operations Serving the Elite

1954 Guatemala — CIA overthrows the democratically elected Jacob Arbenz in a military coup. Arbenz has threatened to nationalize the Rockefeller-owned United Fruit Company, in which CIA Director Allen Dulles also owns stock. Arbenz is replaced with a series of right-wing dictators whose suppressive policies will kill over 100,000 Guatemalans in the next 40 years.

1954-1958 North Vietnam — CIA officer Edward Lansdale spends four years trying to overthrow the communist government of North Vietnam. The CIA also attempts to legitimize a tyrannical puppet regime in South Vietnam, headed by Ngo Dinh Diem. These efforts fail to win the hearts and minds of the South Vietnamese because the Diem government is opposed to true democracy, land reform and poverty reduction measures. The CIA's continuing failure results in escalating American intervention, culminating in the Vietnam War.

1957-1973 Laos — The CIA carries out approximately one coup per year trying to nullify Laos' democratic elections. The problem is the Pathet Lao, a leftist group with enough popular support to be a member of any coalition government. In the late 50s, the CIA even creates an "Armee Clandestine" of Asian mercenaries to attack the

Pathet Lao. After the CIA's army suffers numerous defeats, the U.S. starts bombing, dropping more bombs on Laos than all the U.S. bombs dropped in World War II. A quarter of all Laotians will eventually become refugees, many living in caves.

1959 Haiti — The U.S. military helps "Papa Doc" Duvalier become dictator of Haiti. He creates his own private police force, the "Tonton Macoutes," who terrorize the population with machetes. They will kill over 100,000 during the Duvalier family reign. The U.S. does not protest their dismal human rights record.

1961 The Bay of Pigs — The CIA sends 1,500 Cuban exiles to invade Castro's Cuba. But "Operation Mongoose" fails, due to poor planning, security and backing. The planners had imagined that the invasion will spark a popular uprising against Castro -- which never happens. A promised American air strike also never occurs. This is the CIA's first public setback, causing President Kennedy to fire CIA Director Allen Dulles.

Dominican Republic — The CIA assassinates Rafael Trujillo, a murderous dictator Washington has supported since 1930. Trujillo's business interests have grown so large (about 60 percent of the economy) that they have begun competing with American business interests.

Ecuador — The CIA-backed military forces the democratically elected President Jose Velasco to resign. Vice President Carlos Arosemana replaces him; the CIA fills the now vacant vice presidency with its own man.

Congo (Zaire) — The CIA assassinates the democratically elected Patrice Lumumba. However, public support for Lumumba's politics runs so high that the CIA cannot clearly install his opponents in power. Four years of political turmoil follow.

1963 Dominican Republic — The CIA overthrows the democratically elected Juan Bosch in a military coup. The CIA installs a repressive, right-wing junta.

Ecuador — A CIA-backed military coup overthrows President Arosemana, whose independent (not socialist) policies have become unacceptable to Washington. A military junta assumes command, cancels the 1964 elections, and begins abusing human rights.

1964 Brazil — A CIA-backed military coup overthrows the democratically elected government of Joao Goulart. The junta that replaces it will, in the next two decades, become one of the most bloodthirsty in history. General Castelo Branco will create Latin

America's first death squads, or bands of secret police who hunt down "communists" for torture, interrogation and murder. Often these "communists" are no more than Branco's political opponents. Later it is revealed that the CIA trains the death squads.

1965 Indonesia — The CIA overthrows the democratically elected Sukarno with a military coup. The CIA has been trying to eliminate Sukarno since 1957, using everything from attempted assassination to sexual intrigue, for nothing more than his declaring neutrality in the Cold War. His successor, General Suharto, will massacre between 500,000 to 1 million civilians accused of being "communist." The CIA supplies the names of countless suspects.

Dominican Republic — A popular rebellion breaks out, promising to reinstall Juan Bosch as the country's elected leader. The revolution is crushed when U.S. Marines land to uphold the military regime by force. The CIA directs everything behind the scenes.

Greece — With the CIA's backing, the king removes George Papandreous as prime minister. Papandreous has failed to vigorously support U.S. interests in Greece.

Congo (Zaire) — A CIA-backed military coup installs Mobutu Sese Seko as dictator. The hated and repressive Mobutu exploits his desperately poor country for billions.

1967 Greece — A CIA-backed military coup overthrows the government two days before the elections. The favorite to win was George Papandreous, the liberal candidate. During the next six years, the "reign of the colonels" — backed by the CIA — will usher in the widespread use of torture and murder against political opponents.

Operation PHEONIX — The CIA helps South Vietnamese agents identify and then murder alleged Viet Cong leaders operating in South Vietnamese villages. According to a 1971 congressional report, this operation killed about 20,000 "Viet Cong."

1968 Operation CHAOS — The CIA has been illegally spying on American citizens since 1959, but with Operation CHAOS, President Johnson dramatically boosts the effort. CIA agents go undercover as student radicals to spy on and disrupt campus organizations protesting the Vietnam War. They are searching for Russian instigators, which they never find. CHAOS will eventually spy on 7,000 individuals and 1,000 organizations.

Bolivia — A CIA-organized military operation captures legendary guerilla Che Guevara. The CIA wants to keep him alive for interrogation, but the Bolivian government executes him to prevent worldwide calls for clemency.

1969 Uruguay — The notorious CIA torturer Dan Mitrione arrives in Uruguay, a country torn with political strife. Whereas right-wing forces previously used torture only as a last resort, Mitrione convinces them to use it as a routine, widespread practice. "The precise pain, in the precise place, in the precise amount, for the desired effect," is his motto. The torture techniques he teaches to the death squads rival the Nazis'.

1970 Cambodia — The CIA overthrows Prince Sahounek, who is highly popular among Cambodians for keeping them out of the Vietnam War. He is replaced by CIA puppet Lon Nol, who immediately throws Cambodian troops into battle. This unpopular move strengthens once minor opposition parties like the Khmer Rouge, which achieves power in 1975 and massacres millions of its own people.

1971 Bolivia — After half a decade of CIA-inspired political turmoil, a CIA-backed military coup overthrows the leftist President Juan Torres. In the next two years, dictator Hugo Banzer will have over 2,000 political opponents arrested without trial, then tortured, raped and executed.

1973 Chile — The CIA overthrows and assassinates Salvador Allende, Latin America's first democratically elected socialist leader. The problems begin when Allende nationalizes American-owned firms in Chile. ITT offers the CIA $1 million for a coup (reportedly refused). The CIA replaces Allende with General Augusto Pinochet, who will torture and murder thousands of his own countrymen in a crackdown on labor leaders and the political left.

1974 CHAOS exposed — Pulitzer prize winning journalist Seymour Hersh publishes a story about Operation CHAOS, the domestic surveillance and infiltration of anti-war and civil rights groups in the U.S. The story sparks national outrage. Congress holds hearings on the illegal domestic spying efforts of James Jesus Angleton, the CIA's chief of counterintelligence. His efforts included mail-opening campaigns and secret surveillance of war protesters. The hearings result in his dismissal from the CIA.

1975 Australia — The CIA helps topple the democratically elected, left-leaning government of Prime Minister Edward Whitlam. John Kerr, a longtime CIA collaborator, exercises his constitutional right to dissolve the Whitlam government. The Governor-General is a largely ceremonial position appointed by the Queen; the Prime

Minister is democratically elected. The use of this archaic and never-used law stuns the nation.

Angola — Eager to demonstrate American military resolve after its defeat in Vietnam, Henry Kissinger launches a CIA-backed war in Angola. The CIA supports the brutal leader of UNITAS, Jonas Savimbi. This polarizes Angolan politics and drives his opponents into the arms of Cuba and the Soviet Union for survival. This entirely pointless war kills over 300,000 Angolans.

Nicaragua — Anastasios Samoza II, the CIA-backed dictator, falls. The Marxist Sandinistas take over government, and they are initially popular because of their commitment to land and anti-poverty reform. Samoza had a murderous and hated personal army called the National Guard. Remnants of the Guard will become the Contras, who fight a CIA-backed guerilla war against the Sandinista government throughout the 1980s.

1980 El Salvador — The Archbishop of San Salvador, Oscar Romero, pleads with President Carter "Christian to Christian" to stop aiding the military government slaughtering his people. Carter refuses. Shortly afterwards, right-wing leader Roberto D'Aubuisson has Romero shot through the heart while saying Mass. The country soon dissolves into civil war, with the peasants in the hills fighting against the military government. The CIA and U.S. Armed Forces supply the government with overwhelming military and intelligence superiority. By 1992, some 63,000 Salvadorans will be killed.

1981 Iran/Contra Begins — The CIA begins selling arms to Iran at high prices, using the profits to arm the Contras fighting the Sandinista government in Nicaragua. President Reagan vows that the Sandinistas will be "pressured" until "they say 'uncle.'"

1989 Panama — The U.S. invades Panama to overthrow a dictator of its own making, General Manuel Noriega. Noriega has been on the CIA's payroll since 1966, and has been transporting drugs with the CIA's knowledge since 1972. By the late 80s, Noriega's growing independence and intransigence have angered Washington... so out he goes.

1990 Haiti — Competing against 10 comparatively wealthy candidates, leftist priest Jean-Bertrand Aristide captures 68 percent of the vote. After only eight months in power, however, the CIA-backed military deposes him. More military dictators brutalize the country, as thousands of Haitian refugees escape the turmoil in barely seaworthy boats. As popular opinion calls for Aristide's return, the CIA begins a disinformation campaign painting the courageous priest as mentally unstable.

2011 Libya — Another example of the CIA conducting training in that country for a year to create a subversive group. They bring in mercenaries from South Africa and start killing citizens. The mainstream media portrays Kaddafi as a self deluded mad man, a crazed person who is killing his people. So that justifies the US with their allies to bomb the cities and kill civilians, then invade it and take its wealth. Interesting that even before the regime fell a Central Bank was set up in Southern Libya.

Eisenhower's Warning to the American People

The citizens of the U.S. were warned by Dwight Eisenhower during his presidential farewell speech to the nation on January 17, 1961. It appears that the rogue military industrial complex that Eisenhower warned did grasp far reaching powers.

"We face a hostile ideology--global in scope, atheistic in character, ruthless in purpose, and insidious in method. Unhappily the danger it poses promises to be of indefinite duration....

This conjunction of an immense military establishment and a large arms industry is new in the American experience. The total influence-economic, political, even spiritual--is felt in every city, every State house, every office of the Federal government. We recognize the imperative need for this development. Yet we must not fail to comprehend its grave implications. Our toil, resources and livelihood are all involved; so is the very structure of our society.

In the councils of government, we must guard against the acquisition of unwarranted influence, whether sought or unsought, by the military-industrial complex. The potential for the disastrous rise of misplaced power exists and will persist.

We must never let the weight of this combination endanger our liberties or democratic processes. We should take nothing for granted. Only an alert and knowledgeable citizenry can compel the proper meshing of the huge industrial and military machinery of defense with our peaceful methods and goals, so that security and liberty may prosper together."

But over the years the power has been misplaced, the only security sought is to secure greater wealth for the ultra wealthy. The citizenry has not been alert or knowledgeable. Under this regime they have been dismantling liberty on a global level. Notice how it doesn't matter if a Democrat or Republican is in power the same policy of global subjugation continues.

In 2012 the U.S. has drone bases across the African Continent are in Djibouti, Seychelles, Ethiopia, and Kenya. Drone strikes occur in Somalia and bases are expanding to the Arabian Peninsula. *"The Obama administration's use of drone strikes to commit war crimes around the world, it is both widespread and systematic,"* says Francis A. Boyle, University of Illinois professor of international law and author of "Tackling America's Toughest Questions". *"Drone strikes therefore qualifies as a Crime against Humanity under the Rome Statute for the International Criminal Court."*

Washington maintains the largest collection of foreign bases in world history: more than 1,000 military installations outside the 50 states and Washington, DC. They include everything from decades-old bases in Germany and Japan to brand-new drone bases in Ethiopia and the Seychelles islands in the Indian Ocean and even resorts for military vacationers in Italy and South Korea.[57] In total, the U.S. military has some form of troop presence in approximately 150 foreign countries, not to mention 11 aircraft carrier task forces -- essentially floating bases -- and a significant, and growing, military presence in space. The United States currently spends an estimated $250 billion annually maintaining bases and troops overseas.

The military has not been a model of accountability with the citizen's taxed income. $2.3 trillion was un-accounted for in 2001 military budget and the short fall was announced the afternoon of September 10, 2001 [58]. Coincidentally many involved in the investigation and their records were destroyed at the Washington Pentagon and in NY City Building 7 on the following day.

The next largest military spender is China with a 2012 budget of about $106 billion compared to the US at over $1,500 billion with all its many defense budgets homeland security, FBI with the department of defense. War and plunder are the elite's most enriching venture.

Militarizing Local Police

The Prisons and local police have increasingly been militarized. Although much less money but just as disturbing is the prison industrial complex. The United States has the highest documented incarceration rate in the world—742 adults per 100,000. There are some 2.2 million adults incarcerated in federal and state prisons and local jails. About 5 million are on probation or parole. Seventy percent of the inmates are nonwhite.[59]

The Omnibus Crime Bill, pushed through the Senate with the help of Joe Biden, appropriated $30 billion to expand the nation's prison program. It gave $10.8 billion in federal matching funds to local governments to hire 100,000 new police officers over five years. It provided $10 billion for the construction of new federal prisons. It expanded the number of federal crimes to which the death penalty applied from two to 58. It eliminated an existing statute that prohibited the execution of mentally incapacitated defendants. It instituted the three-strike proposal that mandates life sentences for anyone convicted of three "violent" felonies. It ordered states to track sex offenders. It permitted children as young as 13 to be tried as adults. It set up special courts to deport non-citizens alleged to be "engaged in terrorist activity" and authorized the use of secret evidence.

The prison population during the Clinton presidency jumped from 1.4 million to 2 million. In 2016 it is at about 2.3 million in prison. There are 3.8 million people on parole. The United States has spent $300 billion since 1980 on the prison system.

These increased military and prison expenditures were made in light of drastic cuts to our social services. It doesn't matter if a Republican or Democrat is in power the results are the same: increased expenditures into ventures that harm and suppress others through invasions, force, and incarceration.

A One Party System

"The real rulers in Washington are invisible and exercise power from behind the scenes." Supreme Court Justice Felix Frankfurter

Politicians and the two party systems provide the illusion of choice. But there is a deeper control of both parties from a single source. Democrats and Republicans are two arms from a single body. The government, banking and the corporate world have fused together, becoming the mechanism controlled by an elite few.

The awakened have been forced to confront the truth that the state has itself stopped serving the people, becoming not our servant, but an adversary. There exists a growing understanding that elected representatives have become the lap dogs of the elite and their interests. The so-called representatives of the people nurture and develop the growing Elite Systems.

These politicians are supported by those who have money to get them in office provided they do the Elite's bidding. The electoral process is shaped by money and the media which the Elite control. Politicians manipulate the masses into being elected, later betraying their voters by pursuing not the will of the people, but the investments of the elite.

There are good politicians like Dennis Kucinich a U.S. Representative, serving from 1997-2013 He stands for the Common Good. However there are very few like him and it is difficult to stay in as they redistricted Dennis out of office.

The Democratic and Republican parties are not government controlled agencies. They are private clubs ruled by those who control the club. They make the rules not the government or citizens. They chose their candidates in a show that makes it appear the citizens have a choice. Through this rigged system only those that represent the elite systems will be elected.

In reality, elections cannot be said to be democratic or free of fraud when only two parties controlled by an Elite with a single agenda in mind is allowed into government power. The Democrat and Republican parties are not government entities but are like clubs that have rules crafted by the elite. It is an illusion that we are allowed to run candidates, are allowed to participate in debates, and we are in control of election results. We are tricked into thinking we have choice, that real differences exist between parties, that elections are democratic and not predetermined through manipulation, omission, and distortion.

Administrations have been supporting these Elite Systems by allowing the Federal Reserve to continue, supporting the activities of the CIA, providing corporations more rights than people, passing banking reform to increase the flow of wealth to the elite few. Giving billions in bail out money to bankers with no enforceable directives on how that money should be allocated.

By sending manufacturing jobs overseas, the only source of credit creation remaining was mortgage fraud, wars overseas, speculation in oil and food commodities to drive up consumer prices and bailing out the banks. All of this money creation leads to unpayable debts being burdened on taxpayers with declining incomes.

In 2009 the Supreme Court opened the doors of our electoral process and democracy to shadowy, undisclosed, unlimited corporate spending in our elections. In his dissent Justice Stevens remarked "The Court's ruling threatens to undermine the integrity of elected institutions across the Nation."

The funding of our electoral contests has a direct effect on who controls our political process. Corporations are overwhelming our political system with massive contributions leading directly to corporate control of the government. Cost for the 2012 US election is approximately $6 Billion.[60] The cost exceeded $6.6 Billion in 2016.This must end if the US government is to be truly responsive to the public interest; the election system requires public financing if it is to represent public interest.

The Elite's leadership, based in the United States, is woven into multi-national corporations, the aero-defense industry, large media companies, huge banks, lobbyists, politicians, government

agencies, and think tanks. Look at the interchangeable leadership at Monsanto, Lockheed, Halliburton, Wall Street, Central Banks and you can see how they are a part of a larger interconnected plan run behind the scenes.

David Rockefeller, the third generation, illustrates the influence this family has in this country. David has been the main architect for the free trade agreements of the Americas. He is the chairman of the American Society; he is the founder of the Forum of the Americas. He is the founder and board member of the institute for the International. He is the honorary chairman of the Trilateral Commission. He is the founder of the Council of Foreign Relations. He is also one of the family members who own the Federal Reserve.

Linda Fisher, seven years executive director of Monsanto, who because Deputy Minister for EPA and actually switched back and forth three times. Justice Clarence Thomas was Monsanto's lawyer for regulatory affairs, who became Supreme Court Justice. Mickey Kantor was Secretary of Commerce and became a board member for Monsanto. Michael Freedman was a senior VP of Monsanto and became commissioner for the FDA. William Rickelshaus became the Chief Administrator for the EPA then became a Monsanto Board member. Daniel Rumsfield was Secretary of Defense and was president of Monsanto's subsidiary.

We have become a one party system ruled by banking and corporate interests. But the irony is that we are allowing ourselves to be ruled in this way by traveling the Elite Road.

The truth, as always and in every society, is that the people hold all the power. No amount of illegal surveillance or police state gadgets could ever hold back an engaged, informed public that recognized their own power over the public officials. The citizens support the government with their tax dollars; the citizens control the elections and the elected representatives. It is the 99% that buy from the corporate giants every single day. The power is within us to demand election reform.

It is similar to Community ReStart's members getting together to prevent its overthrow. Once that illusion of empowerment is shattered, the people will realize they hold the power cord. The Elite Systems lose their power when we unplug.

Actions

Election reform: Dennis Kucinich introduced a Constitutional Amendment, H.J. Res. 100, which would require that all federal campaigns be financed exclusively by public funds and prohibit expenditures from every other source. Let us change our campaign financing system so that we can truly claim to be a government of the people, by the people, and for the people.

Public financing of federal elections is critical to the restoration of our American democracy. How we fund our elections is not an academic argument. We must restore the voice of the citizens.

We must also reform the recording device of our voice. The ballot system has been compromised through electronic digital systems that make them too vulnerable to manipulation. We need to go back to paper ballots for reliable counts.

The Constitution is a living, breathing document and it is up to us to claim its power to deal with the threats to our government, our nation and our way of life.

- Election Reform public funded, including media coverage
- No electronic ballots, that are easily manipulated, use printed ballots.
- End corporate lobbying practices
- Rescind Corporate Personhood
- End the CIA

Appendix C

Social Engineering

A question haunts me as my awareness of injustice and abuse from parasitic elites increases. How can fractions of 1% of the population get away with perpetrating these atrocities on the 99%? What allows them to elicit control? What weaves this curtain of deceit that blocks our view of the truth?

A science has been exploring these questions for over one hundred years. The primary funding source for this science was the Rockefeller Foundation. They explored how to mold society for a certain function, aspiration, and achievement; and also how to prevent the population from protesting the loss of their rights, or accept the growing class divides.

Social engineering can influence invisible control mechanisms in all of us. Through behavior modification experiments that stem from B F Skinner and Pavlov's dogs that unconsciously wagged their tails and began to salivate when a bell rang. Experimenters on humans began in earnest with John B Watson. These scientists found they could employ a variety of techniques to get people to do what they want and stop people from doing what you don't want them to do. It is the scientific reproducibility, the control, and the unawareness of the person being manipulated that makes it an important tool of the Elite.

Humans can then be seen as machines that can be manipulated by the 1% and create the illusion of a democracy. People can be programmed for certain action by the push of a button or the sound of a bell; we are malleable and can be redesigned and shaped without our awareness. You may not be aware of how pervasive social engineering is.

Virtually all law and governance has the effect of seeking to change behavior and could be considered "social engineering" to some extent. Proscription on murder, rape, theft, and littering are all policies aimed at discouraging undesirable behaviors. Governments also influence behavior more subtly through incentives and disincentives built into economic policy and tax policy, for instance, and have done so for centuries.

Social engineering is often more apparent in countries

with authoritarian governments. In the 1920s, the government of the Soviet Union embarked on a campaign to fundamentally alter the behavior and ideals of Soviet citizens, to replace the old social frameworks of Tsarist Russia with a new Soviet culture to create the New Soviet man. The Soviets used newspapers, books, film, mass relocations, and even architectural design tactics to serve as "social condenser" and change personal values and private relationships.

Тов. Ленин ОЧИЩАЕТ землю от нечисти.

Similar examples are the Chinese "Great Leap Forward" was

an economic and social campaign of the Communist Party of China (CPC), reflected in planning decisions from 1958 to 1961. The aim was to use China's vast population to rapidly transform the country from an agrarian economy into a modern communist society through the process of rapid industrialization and collectivization. Mao Zedong led the campaign based on the Theory of Productive Forces. Chief changes in the lives of rural Chinese included the introduction of a mandatory

process of agricultural collectivization. Private farming was prohibited, and those engaged in it were labeled as counter revolutionaries and persecuted.

The Nazis themselves were no strangers to the idea of influencing political attitudes and re-defining personal relationships. The Nazi propaganda machine under Joseph Goebbels was a synchronized, sophisticated and effective tool for creating public opinion. *"If you tell a lie big enough and keep repeating it, people will eventually come to believe it. The lie can be maintained only for such time as the State can shield the people from the political, economic and/or military consequences of the lie. It thus becomes vitally important for the State to use all of its powers to repress dissent, for the truth is the mortal enemy of the lie, and thus by extension, the truth is the greatest enemy of the State"*, Joseph Goebbels.

Non-authoritarian regimes tend to rely on more sustained social engineering campaigns that create more gradual, but ultimately far-reaching, change. By shaping beliefs, they shape perception, underneath that haze of false perception the leaders behind the scene can plunder all they want.

The "War on Terror" has shaped much of our foreign policy and fear in the United States. The manipulation of the media plays a large role in this engineering of deceit. In an Elite/Corporate run "democracy" power brokers influence the public to agree with the Administrations decisions. Integral is the control of perception. On the Elite Road it is not the truth that counts but perception. This means control of the media is integral to their strategy of engineering consent.

Media Consolidation and Control

When I was a business consultant I worked closely with 28 TV broadcasting stations from 1987 to 1993. I would often dine with broadcasting executives who often expressed their concerns about the FCC regulation changes. There were an alarming number of mergers and buyouts, and they were seeing the repercussions in their industry. The only groups to win these merger bids were large corporate entities run by right wing extremists. These executives knew that when that diversity is lost, and the group controlling the media has an extremist agenda, our ability to get to the truth will be greatly diminished.

In 1983, 50 corporations controlled the vast majority of all

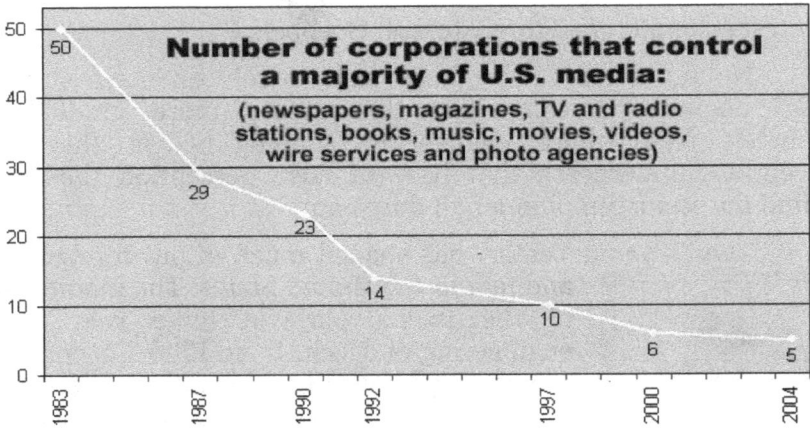

Number of corporations that control a majority of U.S. media:

(newspapers, magazines, TV and radio stations, books, music, movies, videos, wire services and photo agencies)

Year	Number
1983	50
1987	29
1990	23
1992	14
1997	10
2000	6
2004	5

news media in the U.S. At the time, Ben Bagdikian was called "alarmist" for pointing this out in his book, *The Media Monopoly*. These corporations own and operate 90% of the mass media -- controlling almost all of America's newspapers, magazines, TV and radio stations, books, records, movies, videos, wire services and photo agencies. In 2004, Bagdikian's revised and expanded book, *The New Media Monopoly*, shows that only 5 huge corporations -- Time Warner, Disney, Murdoch's News Corporation, Bertelsmann of Germany, and Viacom (formerly CBS) -- now control most of the media industry in the U.S. General Electric's NBC is a close sixth.

Critics of media deregulation and the resulting concentration of ownership fear that such trends will only continue to reduce the diversity of information provided, as well as to reduce the accountability of information providers to the public. The ultimate consequence of consolidation, critics argue, is a poorly-informed public, restricted to a reduced array of media options that offer only information that does not harm the Elite's growing range of interests. There are even more sinister uses of media control.

The Elite's most profitable venture, war and the resulting control of nations' resources is greatly aided by propaganda. This goes on as concerned citizens are asking how a world so sick of bloodshed and a population so tired of conflict could be led to more wars.

The Propaganda Machine

The Elite greatly prosper through war, and the media becomes a platform to justify actions that result in the plunder of countries, all at US taxpayer expense. A centuries-long history[61] of how media has been used to justify wars is well documented in the Corbett Report, January 2012.

The media generates wartime frenzy, dehumanizes the supposed enemies, and manipulates the public into believing in a war that later was found untrue.

Newspapers like William Randolph Hearst's New York Journal widely implied that the sinking of the Maine was the work of the Spanish. Whipped into an anti-Spanish frenzy by stories depicting Spanish forces' alleged torture and rape of Cubans, and pushed over the edge by the Maine incident, the public had their justification for the US-Spanish war. Although it is now widely believed that the explosion on the Maine was due to a fire in one of its coal bunkers, the initial reports of Spanish involvement stuck and the nation was led into war.

The US was drawn into World War I by the sinking of the Lusitania, a British ocean liner carrying American passengers. The ship was torpedoed by German U-boats off the coast of Ireland, killing over 1,000 of its passengers. What the public was not informed about at the time was that just one week before the incident, then-First Lord of the Admiralty Winston Churchill had written to the President of the Board of Trade that it was *"most important to attract neutral shipping to our shores, in the hopes especially of embroiling the United States with Germany."* Nor did reports of the attack announce that the ship was carrying rifle ammunition and other military supplies. Instead, emphasized that the attack was an out-of-the-blue strike by a maniacal enemy, and the public was led into the war.

The US involvement in World War II was likewise the result

of deliberate disinformation. Although the Honolulu Advertiser had even predicted the attack on Pearl Harbor days in advance, the Japanese Naval codes had already been deciphered by that time, intelligence knew. Actually the US provoked it through naval blockades on Japan. They then allowed the attack to happen on unsuspecting citizens to catapult the country into another war. Yet the history books still portray Pearl Harbor as an example of a surprise attack.

In 1991, the world was introduced to the emotional story of

Nayirah, a Kuwaiti girl who testified about the atrocities committed by Iraqi forces in Kuwait, such as removing babies from incubators to die on the concrete floor. This justified the first war with Iraq. What the world was never told was that the incident had in fact been the work of a public relations firm, Hill and Knowltown, and the girl had actually been the daughter of the Kuwaiti ambassador with aspirations of being an actress. Once again, the public was whipped into a frenzy of hatred for the Hussein regime, on the basis of an imaginary story told to the public via their televisions, orchestrated by a pr firm.

In the lead-up to the final war on Iraq, the American media

infamously took the lead in framing the debate about the Iraqi government's weapons of mass destruction not as a question of whether or not they even existed, but as a question of where they had been hidden and what should be done to disarm them. NBC Nightly News asking "what precise threat Iraq and its weapons of mass destruction pose to America", and Time debating whether Hussein was "making a good-faith effort to disarm Iraq's weapons of mass destruction."

We now know that in fact the stockpiles did not exist, there were no weapons of mass destruction except the US military and their coalition that laid out mass destruction on this sovereign country. The administration premeditatedly lied the country into yet another war, but the most intense opposition the Bush administration ever received over this documented war crime was some polite correction on the Sunday political talk show circuit. Look at the cost in lives and wealth of those nations. Trillions of dollars have been spent and trillions unaccounted for, most to the pockets of the Elite. The suffering caused is unimaginable. All based on a lie.

They do not broadcast what they don't want you to hear. "Project Censored" suppressed news stories of 2009. It is a remarkable fact that more than 1 million deaths of Iraqi civilians are directly attributable to the U.S.-British led invasion begun in March 2003. This tally is garnered from research conducted by a prestigious British polling group, http://www.opinion.co.uk/ and serves to further confirm figures from a scientific study published in Lancet, a leading British medical journal.

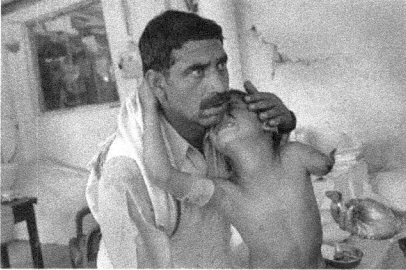

In 2005, the Bush White House admitted to producing videos that were designed to look like news reports from legitimate independent journalists, and then feeding those reports to media outlets as prepackaged material ready to air on the evening news. When the Government Accountability Office ruled that these fake news reports in fact constituted illegal covert propaganda, the White House simply issued a memo[62] declaring the practice to be legal.

Similarly in Libya 2011 year, shortly after Obama admitted the presence of covert operatives on the ground in Libya, identified as CIA agents by the New York Times, he admitted the goal of destabilizing the Gadhafi government. Foreign mercenaries were brought in to kill civilians and then the media blamed the Libyan government for killing its own citizens. They were able to use propaganda to justly an invasion by UN allies for "humanitarian reasons". Now the entire country is being ransacked, but that does not make the media.

It is not only that the top down control of the news that make up or distort stories, it is that journalists are being complicit. As the vehicle through which information from the outside world is captured, sorted, edited and transmitted into our homes, the mass media has a huge responsibility. It shapes and informs our understanding of events to which we don't have first-hand access. The reporters, producers, and directors have a great responsibility to report the most important news in the most objective way. Aside for a few pockets of truth reporters, a major portion of main street media is shaped by the Elite and their agenda.

An informed and engaged public is far less likely to go along with wars waged for power and profit for the Elite few, at the tax payers' expense. And as the public becomes better informed about the very issues that the media has distorted for so long, they realize that the answer to all of the manipulation is to drive off this road. Instead, get your news from independent reliable sources such as the Corbett Report (www.corbettreport.com) or Boiling Frog Post (www.boilingfrogpost.com).

TV Hypnosis and Diversion

On several occasions I asked active members in my local 9/11 Truth Movement, or Community ReStart members (over 100) how many watch TV. I received a consistent response, 90% did not watch main stream TV. They did not want to fill their head with made up stories and propaganda. They didn't want to waste their time numbing out in front of a flickering tube. They didn't want to get diverted from the true task at hand. They rely on other news sources through primarily the internet and radio. It is interesting that those who renounce main stream TV have time to get involved. But this is far from the case for most Americans.

According to the A.C. Nielsen Co., the average American watches more than 4 hours of TV each day (or 28 hours/week, or 2 months of nonstop TV-watching per year). In a 65-year life, that person will have spent 9 years glued to the tube.

- Number of TV sets in the average U.S. household: 2.2 [63]

- Number of hours per day that TV is on in an average U.S. home: 6 hours, 47 minutes

- Number of hours of TV watched annually by Americans: 250 billion

- Number of minutes per week that parents spend in meaningful conversation with their children: 3.5

- Number of minutes per week that the average child watches television: 1,680

- Percentage of local TV news broadcast time devoted to advertising: 30% about crime, disaster and war: 53.8%

- Percentage of local TV news broadcast devoted to public service announcements: 0.7%

Televisions transmit hypnotic flashing lights in a dark room, ideal for generating an Alpha Mind state. The state of mind you go into a trance. Our brain uses its 8 to 13 cycles per second Alpha waves to idle itself, to rest areas not actively processing and acting on incoming sensory and motor information. While this idling is a normal and favorable phenomenon, if Alpha wave activity occurs too often, then it becomes more difficult to stay focused and be active. TV can cause unfocussed daydreaming and inability to concentrate. Researchers have said that watching television is similar to staring at a blank wall for several hours.

Dr. Erik Peper, another influential brain wave researcher and writer, once said, "The horror of television is that the information goes in, but we do not react to it. It goes right into our memory pool and perhaps we react to it later, but we do not know what we are reacting to. When you watch television you are training yourself not to react and so later on, you're doing things without knowing why you're doing them or where they came from."[64]

Under the influence of television, the frontal lobe cannot function at its full capacity. The brain does record information: sight, memory, and emotions are all functioning well. Nevertheless, the brain no longer critically analyzes the information. Terrible scenes can be depicted, but the viewer tends only to laugh or shrug them off. Normally, if those kinds of events happened in real life the individual would be appalled. Even this is changing as people become more desensitized through exposure.

The same hypnotizing brain activity that occurs while watching television also occurs while playing video games. In a survey conducted by Akio Mori, a professor in Nihon University's College of Humanities and Sciences, it was found that the longer people spent playing video games, the less activity they showed in the prefrontal region of their brains, which governs emotion and creativity. What is even more worrying is that according to the study, brain activity in the people who continually played games did not recover in the periods when they weren't playing games.[65]

We take in the news and stories that shape our awareness. We absorb it in a hypnotic state. It provides emotional pabulum and escape, influencing our society in many ways. It shapes our values and cultural norms. Consider the effect that the growing amount of televised sexual content is having on American young people. Documentation shows that television's and internet's erotic influence is so pervasive that it increases sexual activity in teens and younger children. Studies show that the age of first sexual intercourse significant decreases due to the influence of TV. The more television watched the lower the age for that first sexual encounter. Not only do studies show it, children themselves report that television encourages them to take part in sexual activity at a young age.[66]

The combination of becoming less sensitive to violence, non - responsiveness, and stimulating a state of low brain response further explains why US citizens are not reacting to some of the scandals occurring in the banking, corporate, government, and legal sectors.

Education System and the Loss of Critical Thinking

Children are taken from families during their formative years and provided a certain type of education that reinforces beliefs about Elite Systems, teaches obedience to authority, and reduces critical thinking. The education system can actually be seen as a factory to create indifference to intellectual things and ideas. It is a factory for obedient workers.

In school students are given a stream of information they must memorize in unrelated segments. Like Pavlov's dogs, students then respond to bells and move on to the next class. Different subjects are taught in different classrooms by different teachers, further enhancing segmentation. Segmentation prevents grasping the big picture and is integral to Elite Systems. This does not create an environment to really think about and explore a topic from many perspectives.

Not given the opportunity for critical thinking, the teacher's job is to convey small bits of information that should not be challenged. Then they show how to connect the information by memorizing someone else's conclusions. Not participating and doing it yourself, provides a more superficial learning experience.

Teachers often use fear to get students to participate or create an emotional dependency for approval and good grades, often distancing students from connecting with the lesson itself. Provisional self esteem is reinforced if you are approved by the teacher. One is allowed to feel good about yourself only if an authority gives you the right signal. If you are not approved by the teacher, the way to boost self esteem is to be a rebel. If you rebel you often don't really participate in the lessons.

When grades are paramount, research has found that the interest for learning actually decreases. People think less deeply and are not able to retain knowledge for very long, because it is memorized for a test. In addition, students will accept easy assignments because of the higher probability of getting a higher grade.

The Federal Government gets to mandate what schools teach and testing required by funding just enough of the school operation to make their monies make or break the school. In western Massachusetts it is 18% of the school budget. If they don't comply with the "No Child Left Behind" testing, they will be forced to close their doors as federal funds would be withdrawn.

The standardized testing from the federal government further reinforces this departure from effective education. With a "no child left behind" theory, these tests tend to measure what matters least. The truth is that the deeper thinking kids don't do as well as someone who has better memorizing skills but who may never have an original idea in their life. Under the present U.S. educational system, there is an absence of critical thinking. Students are taught to regurgitate what they are told. They are not encouraged to question "facts". We need educated, critical thinkers if we are to sustain a functional democracy.

Competition is often part of the schooling as it builds character, so they say. But in truth, it often creates neurosis that can inhibit growth. Species survive because they can adapt to surroundings and the best mechanism for this adaptation is cooperation. If we look at most species, they use social collaboration as an effective means for survival. The notion of competition and survival of the fittest usually occurs during mating rituals. It has been consistently found that the more difficult a task within any group, the more dependence upon collaboration and team work, and that competition disrupts the cohesive achievements in a group project.

A functioning democracy requires people to work with each other, yet that is not taught in school. While conducting hundreds of workshops in teambuilding I would ask how many received training, or even had discussions about listening skills in school. Out of thousands of people asked I only found eight participants who had some listening training and six of those were from private schools. I would scratch my head in wonder. The skill you use the most in life is interpersonal skills. If you want to advance in a job interpersonal skills are essential. Yet it doesn't even enter the curricula?

The goal of education should be to create lifelong learners and critical thinkers, to develop interpersonal skills and collaboration;

324

however, the educational system is designed to do the opposite. If you produce students who memorize what they are told, take action when authority tells them, and compete among themselves, then they are well suited for the Elite Systems, but not for life.

Chemical Control

There are many strategies being used to further the trance and the control by the Elite. For they know that if the masses wake up, the scam is over for the 1%. So another method is chemicals that affect our capacity to comprehend, respond, and be active. Four methods of chemical ingestion the elite use: the water we drink the air we breathe, the food we eat, and the medicines we take.

The most widely used chemical in creating subjugation to authority is sodium fluoride. The very first occurrence of purposefully

putting sodium fluoride into drinking water was in the German ghettos and in Nazi Germany's infamous prison camps. The Gestapo had little concern about sodium fluoride's 'supposed' effect on children's teeth; instead, their reason for mass-medicating water with sodium fluoride was to sterilizing them and force the people in their concentration camps into calm, bovine, submission.[67]

In the 1930's Hitler and the German Nazis envisioned a world to be dominated and controlled by a Nazi philosophy of pan-Germanism. The German chemists worked out a mass-control through medication of drinking water supplies. By this method they could reduce population by water medication that would produce sterility in women, and make them docile. In this scheme of mass-control, sodium fluoride occupied a prominent place.[68] Fluoride not only makes people docile it also dumbs them down.

A Harvard University analysis of 27 epidemiological studies of Fluoride in the main water supply concluded that "children in high fluoride areas had significantly lower IQ scores than those who lived in low fluoride areas.[69] The adverse health effects of fluoridated water include: brain damage, and infertility. This practice amounts to forced medication of the population without their consent.

Sodium Fluoride is used as rat and cockroach poison and Sarin Nerve Gas. The American public needs to understand the fact that Sodium Fluoride is a hazardous waste by-product of the nuclear and aluminum industries. Fluoride is also a main ingredient in anesthetic, hypnotic, and psychiatric drugs! Why, is it allowed to be added to the toothpastes and drinking water?

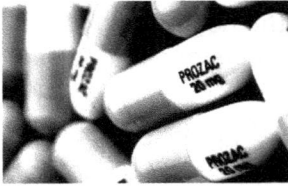

Fluoride is a psychoactive drug that numbs the mind. It is also a basic ingredient in the most popular drug being prescribed Prozac. Prozac, scientific name Fluoxetine, is 94% fluoride. In 2011 over 30% of the US population is on some form of Prozac. How does this affect our health?

Independent scientific evidence over the past 50 plus years has shown that sodium fluoride shortens our life span, promotes various cancers and mental disturbances, and most importantly, makes humans stupid, docile, and subservient.[70] There is increasing evidence that aluminum in the brain is a causative factor in Alzheimer's Disease, and evidence points towards sodium fluoride's strong affinity to 'bond' with this dangerous aluminum (remember it is a byproduct of aluminum manufacturing) and also it has the ability to 'trick' the blood-brain barrier by imitating the hydrogen ion thus allowing this chemical access to brain tissue.

We are also being attacked by chemicals through the air; most of the United States is being sprayed nearly daily in most regions with long trails of chemicals from high flying military planes. It is related to HAARP (High Frequency Active Auroral Research Program), a US military weather modification program. The composition of the spray is primarily aluminum oxide, barium, among other ingredients. The aluminum does have long term impacts on health and mental clarity.

To verify all you need do is go outside and look up. The long white streaks are not Con Trails if they remain longer than 5 min, usually the crystallized water dissipate in less than a minute.

Chemtrails linger, after an hour, depending on the wind turbulence, it will spread to form fake cirrus clouds, and then a haze covers the sky. Why are they spraying us like annoying bugs? Learn about the growing data on weather modification and HAARP on the internet.

Another form of attack is the foods we eat, especially genetically modified and chemically treated foods. There is a wide range of research on the topic. But the simple solution is to first grow your own produce if possible. The second best is to support local farms that grow healthy and nutritious produce. But the point is if we utilize the elite's food chain we are taking in foods low in nutrition. Most importantly the foods can harm us because of their altered genes, and also the chemical sprays and hormones added. Adding harmful chemicals and modified genes in the food supply lowers people's energy, immune system, and increases obesity, and makes the population more docile. *Buy local*!

The Use of Debt and Fear

"When the people fear their government, there is tyranny; when the government fears the people, there is liberty." — *Thomas Jefferson*

In behavioral studies the driving force scientists used to motivate response was fear. Social engineering is much about influencing a target to take an action. Many actions are taken due to an emotion that is felt. Instead of talking just about how to manipulate, they cause a target to feel the emotion. Once we can trigger that emotion we can trigger an action to follow it up.

In the mid-20th century people in the United States where made to fear the "communist menace". They urged citizens to be on the lookout for "communist sympathizers", university professors were arrested for discussing Marx's philosophy in their lectures. Hollywood actors who expressed sympathy with socialism or the poor where arrested. Many were jailed. Unions were destroyed because Washington said they were "hotbeds of communism". People's homes were ransacked by FBI and police looking for "communist writings". People were imprisoned for "thought crimes" such as thinking Marx may have had a few good ideas. The lives of many people were destroyed, and the majority of the population, under the manipulation of U.S. Senator Joe McCarthy, was kept in a state of perpetual fear.

The anger and fear that people are feeling because of the exploitation, stress, and disenfranchisement often gets redirected at other people. In the south poor, uneducated white people were being told that their problems were due to black people. Their anger and frustrations were then vented into the KKK. At other times the scapegoat is abortion or gay marriage. Presently, the scapegoat du jour is the immigration issue.

The growing disenfranchisements, economic stress, diminishing options, are making many people feel an emotional volcano that wants to erupt. Some vent through gangs and violence against other similar disenfranchised youth. Now, even people who have paid their monies to the Social Service System, and who have had much of their savings taken away are now told that they are a burden to the system because of their "entitlement". So that even those who are receiving social services, become scapegoats saying they are the reason why our country is impoverished. It is just more talking lines to divert attention and generate divisiveness, fear and hate.

"Oderint dum metuant (Let them hate so long as they fear)" – Caligula, Roman Emperor

Now that they have a war on terror, that gives them the delusional framework to generate a state of continual fear. People's state of anxiety of pervasive fear, a sense of what is looming, is even worse than the event itself. The war on terror provides a coercive environment that perpetuates fear and anxiety. They can ratchet up the level of fear through media hype like the terror alerts registering yellow, orange, and red.

Fear is a useful means to suppress information. National Security is the excuse to hide treason. One of the simplest ways to ensure universal fear and mistrust is to announce that 'there are enemies amongst us' and have everyone spy on everybody else. In a society where there is such spying, there is universal mistrust - which is simply a form of fear.

As a counter measure it is important that local law officials become educated about the threat to the towns and cities they have sworn to protect. A growing number of law enforcement agents have taken oaths to defend their families, community, and Constitution over Federal or State Actions that may harm what they have sworn to defend. Oath Keepers organization is geared towards active duty, retired, and veterans of the military, law enforcement, firefighters; and concerned citizens.[71]

The answer is to educate local law officials who will be called upon to enforce the elite's decisions which are often against the Common Good.

Actions

- Turn off the TV and video games

- Become active in your community

- Question the debts and interest imposed from this Elite System, eliminate as much debt as possible.

- Be aware of the water you drink, eliminate Sodium Fluoride

- Inquire about Chemtrails, look in the sky

- Minimize pharmaceutical use of fluoride in drugs you use

Appendix D

False Flag Attacks

Before exposing the darkest and most horrific strategy used by the parasitic elite, it is important to put this information in its proper perspective. The following facts are meant to expose a strategy and a consistent pattern of harm, deception, and reprisals. The parasitic elite are able to extract tremendous wealth, and enslave populations to a life of suffering through this strategy. It has been their main mechanism for capturing peaceful countries to pillage the population and resources. It is an inhuman crime that can only be attributed to psychopaths and the systems they create in their own image.

This strategy loses its potency when the truth is exposed. Therefore this information is meant to nullify one of their main weapons. It is a weapon of great darkness; this darkness cannot exist in the presence of light and truth. The Sword of Light needs to burn bright. Actually, exposing the truth exposes the perpetrators and the entire house of cards that the Elite have so cleverly constructed will collapse.

The False Flag Formula

Create violence, blame it others, and use it to gain more power. This is why there are hundreds of documented examples of governments staging attacks in order to blame them on their political enemies.[72] In every civilization, in every culture, in every historical period, authoritarians have known that spectacular acts of violence help to further consolidate their own power and control. It can be used to overtake an entire nation, look at the repercussions from 9/11/2001.

In Germany a new Reichstag election was scheduled for early

March 1933. Only a few days before the election, on February 27, the Reichstag building was partially destroyed by fire. The Nazis set the blaze, but they blamed the Communists, charging that the Communists were plotting to seize power. Hitler convinced Hindenburg to take strong action against the supposed Communist threat, and the president suspended freedom of speech and the press and other civil liberties. Later elections swept the Nazis into power. On March 23, 1933, the German Government passed the Enabling Act, which gave dictatorial authority to Hitler's cabinet for four years. Armed with full powers, Hitler moved to eliminate all possible centers of opposition subordinating all independent institutions to the authority of Hitler and the Nazi Party.

The Russian FSB was caught planting bombs in Moscow in the 1990s during a terror scare that swept Putin into power and stirred the public into supporting the Second Chechen War. [73]Their autocratic President came to power campaigning on the graves of those his old FSB cronies had killed.

The British SAS officers were caught dressing up as Arabs in

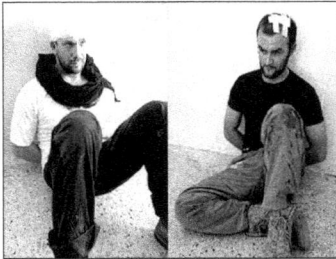

Iraq, driving around with trucks full of munitions, shooting at police to stir up ethnic tensions and insure that permanent bases could be built in the region. The captured British agents shown here, staged themselves as Sunni's to stir ethnic unrest that would justify their continued occupation.[74] Haroon Aswat, the supposed mastermind behind the 7/7 London bombings, was working for British Intelligence. British military intelligence took part in IRA bombings.

The Israeli's Mossad has been caught time and again posing as the very Muslim terrorists they claim to be opposing. Israel uses the specter of terror to further extend their blank check drawn on American funds to expand their police state at home and maintain their hard line stance against Palestine.

The United States has taken the most brazen and destructive path. Some of the greatest destruction of human life and property this

332

world has ever seen has been perpetrated by the Bankster's covert strong arm. The CIA has sponsored terrorism in the 30 countries using this false flag strategy. However there are two false flag attacks that still have a profound impact on our US society today, and the world. Vietnam and the War on Terror exemplify the harm they will do to meet selfish goals.

There were smaller incidents associated with legislation.

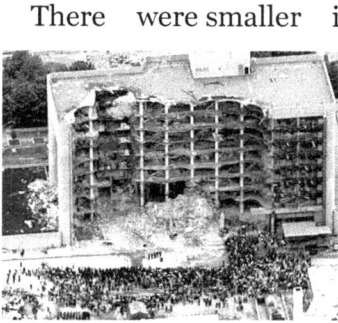

Multiple bombs were found, dismantled and taken out of the Alfred P. Murrah building on April 19, 1995.[75] This expands the investigation beyond a truck bomber, but was never pursued. Timothy McVeigh had written a letter to his sister in which he claimed to be in the Special Forces for the U.S. Army. They are learning the bombing was being directed by FBI informants, just as the 1993 World Trade Center bombing was. McVeigh's body was never recovered from his suppose execution.

In February 1995, Joe Biden introduced a bill called the Omnibus Counterterrorism Act of 1995. Proposing sweeping changes to American law enforcement, it allowed for secret evidence to be used in prosecutions, expanded wiretapping by the government, and the creation of "terrorism" as a federal crime that could be invoked to allow the use of US military in domestic law enforcement in direct violation to long-standing laws against such measures.

The Clinton Administration was unable to get the bill passed in the wake of the Oklahoma City Bombing tragedy, but it returned in 2001 as the Patriot Act. Senator Biden even bragged that his 1995 bill was in large part the Patriot Act's forerunner. In the wake of the Patriot Act, all crimes and even misdemeanors could be treated as acts of terrorism, and civil liberties were greatly eroded.

Operation Northwoods and their own Army Counterinsurgency Manuals teach officers how to commit false flag attacks to blame on their enemies.

9/11/2001 Truth

What happened in New York and Washington DC on that day in September? The reasoning and identified perpetrators the government presents does not add up. If we stick with the facts versus repeated stories of a former CIA operative named Osama held up in a cave in Afghanistan brought down the military and financial centers of the United States. If you believe their conspiracy theory than their story and facts do not coincide.

9/11 Facts; The World Trade Towers

- The three-tower collapses each exhibited the eleven classic characteristics of pre-planned, well-engineered building demolitions such as collapsing at nearly free fall speed and falling into its foundation. Fire has never, before or after 9/11, caused steel-frame buildings to collapse. This is the only time that a sky scraper collapsed by a fire, and three occurred on the same day?

- The collapse of the 47-story World Trade Center Building 7, a  steel framed high-rise, is highly suspicious as no plane hit this building and was the third in history to "collapse from fires alone", the first and second being the WTC Twin Towers. How can a few small fires collapse this building at free fall speed and have the entire building in a pile at its footprint?

- The World Trade Center Towers 1 and 2 center/core areas contained 42 massive vertical support beams. The Commission Report denied their existence to promulgate the now discredited "Pancake" collapse theory.

- The fires in the Twin Towers were not very big, very hot, or very long-lasting compared with fires in several steel-frame buildings that did not collapse.

- Office furniture burns at low temperatures of 600 to 800°F, and that jet fuel, an ordinary hydrocarbon has a maximum burning temperature of 1200°F, but steel melts at 2750°F.

- Over one hundred first responders reported many explosions and flashes of light prior to and during the collapse.

- Mid-air pulverization of 180,000 tons of concrete was not explained. Large volumes of metal decking, floor trusses and "pan caked" floors were also missing.

- Blast pressure front effects: multi-ton steel sections ejected laterally – up to 600 ft. away at 50 mph. How can jet fuel poured on steel create this as the collapse could not account for such projectiles?

- FDNY and others found several tons of "molten steel ...flowing like lava" in the ruins. 1400°F office fires cannot produce 2800+°F molten steel/iron. Thermite incendiaries used in control demolitions can.

- Microspheres formed from molten iron and other elements were found in the WTC dust by USGS, the RJ Lee Group, EPA, and independent scientists. Thermite reactions account for the ubiquitous spheres.

- 'Lucky' Larry Silverstein was awarded 4.68 billion dollars in insurance claims for the Twin Towers which he had just leased six weeks before 9/11.

- Information sites that provide lengthy back up to all statements made in 9/11 facts can be found at: Architects and Engineers for 911truth. www.ae911truth.org, CorbettReport.com. Any books or videos by David Ray Griffin or Richard Gage are recommended.

9/11 Facts in Washington Attacks

- The Pentagon, the most-guarded airspace on planet, with its own multi-billion dollar missile defense system was penetrated on 9-

11-01.

- The 9/11 Commission failed to investigate why the hole in the Pentagon was not even close to resembling the profile of a commercial jet or provide sound scientific evidence of how the large airline engines, along with its passengers and contents, could disintegrate.

- Eyewitness testimony said there were no remains of a Boeing 757 either inside or outside the Pentagon. All objective investigators conclude that a plane did not hit, and that it is impossible for such a plane, its titanium engines, and passengers to vaporize as they claim.

- All 85 video tapes in the Pentagon vicinity were confiscated by the FBI and the few released showed no plane.

- The evidence identifies a missile and or explosives that penetrated the Pentagon.

- Tests have shown that cell phone calls with 2001 technology cannot be made at altitudes over 8,000 feet for any meaningful duration and, that more significantly, United Airlines Flight 93 was proven to be 35000 to 40000 feet high when calls were made?

9/11 Set Up

- In September of 2000 a group known as The Project for A New  American Century (PNAC), many of whom would become key officials in the Bush administration, including Dick Cheney, Donald Rumsfeld, and Paul Wolfowitz were signatories of a radical military plan, which stated that their goals would not be reached unless a "cataclysmic event, like a new Pearl Harbor", occurred in order to get American citizens on-board with their agenda.[76]

- Operation Gladio B, the NATO-directed effort was used to radicalize, enable, and protect Islamic terrorists in the 90's. Also Imam Fethullah Gulen's $25 billion (CIA-supported) Islamic network was part of the Al Qaeda formation.[77]

- President Bush's brother Marvin and his cousin Wirt Walker III were both principals in the company in charge of security for the World Trade Center.

- The 9/11 Commission failed with over 100 other questions, omissions, inconsistencies and implausible scenarios that fall unacceptably short of the 9/11 Commission's original mandate, constituting gross malfeasance in its overriding obligation to the 9/11 victims' families to conduct a thorough investigation.

Think of Bush standing over the smoking rubble of the Twin  Towers declaring a new war on terror, posturing as some hero out to get the bad guy. Still in shock from the horror of the tragedy that has just unfolded before us a nation can be led into the most ruthless despotism, declaring a new age of global war on terror. Despotism that now bears the shroud of "security". Now people are waking up and realizing that the questioning needs to go to the highest level. This delusional veil masked as security needs to be lifted.

You can see the repercussions through the endless war on terror, massive military spending, the growing stress of national and personal debt, the suppression of the middle class, the degradation of our environment, and the extraordinary wealth accumulated by the elite few.

Nowhere in human history has one event; on one day had such reverberations. This one event has justified a perpetual war on terror. Expenditures on that war send trillions of dollars to the military/industrial complex. They have drained the coffers of the US and Iraq. The US had its liberty dramatically taken away by an act of terror on 9/11/2001.

Laws Passed Justified by 9/11 and the Questionable Commission Report

- USA Patriot Act. The most anti constitution legislation ever passed.

- Elevate the President above the law. Argued complete discretion in the exercise of his Commander-in-Chief authority. Barred Congress and the courts from exercising any oversight. Resulted in illegal detentions, disappearances, torture.

- Used to secretly authorize the NSA to wiretap Americans without probable cause or judicial oversight.

- 2006 Military Commissions Act, which insulated military tribunals from any challenge that they violate the Geneva Convention, Revoked habeas corpus rights for "enemy combatants", this includes US Citizens that this commission deems as terrorists.

- July 2007 Executive Order would authorize seizure of property of those accused of supporting the war on terror.

- "Enemy combatants" can be held indefinitely without trial. Including dissenters to the government who they label as terrorist.

- Suspicious organizations can have their assets frozen without notice or hearings.

- Military tribunals can sentence defendants to death on the basis of hearsay and coerced testimony. They can go after them with drones and missals.

- Authorization for use of Military Force, enacted in September 2001, which the President has subsequently used to claim the whole world, including the U.S., is a "battlefield" on the so-called "War on Terror.

- "The overturning of the venerable Posse Comitatus Act of 1878, which barred the use of active duty military inside the U.S. for police-type functions.

- The revision of the Insurrection Act to empower the President to take control of state National Guard units, even over the objections of state governors and authorize federalization of the National Guard to "suppress public disorder" in the event of broadly-stated occurrences.

- The President has greatly reduced hurdles to the declaring of martial law. There was no connection between 9/11 and Iraq. *None.* President Bush himself later admitted this.

- This supposedly endless war has not been declared by Congress.

- This war is making us less safe and bankrupting our future in terms of a failing infrastructure, polluted air and water, inadequate health care, substandard public education, etc.

- World-wide, the majority of people are more terrorized by the actions of the US administration and its state-sponsored terrorism than by any specific terrorist group.

The enacted in 2001 and re-approved in 2011 USA Patriot Act is the most sinister of all, in that it violates the first, fourth, fifth, sixth, seventh, eighth, ninth and tenth amendments of the Bill of Rights. In expansion, it grants the government the right to rifle your mail, tap your telephone and inquire into what you are reading. In a stunning overturn of well-accepted fourth amendment rights a federal court has granted government the right to track your movement with GPS technology, including via cell phones and GPS equipment.

THE PATRIOT ACT:
Turning Citizens into
Suspects Since 2001

The 9/11 attacks resulted in 2,996 casualties, which included 343 firefighters and 59 police officers who were in trying to save victims inside the World Trade Center. A study published in The Lancet medical journal estimated that there were 654,965 deaths between 2003 and 2006 – representing 2.5% of the Iraqi population.[78] This would suggest that today the statistic would be updated to about 1,455,590 casualties in Iraq alone.

But in Iraq this is not the end of the death tolls for those who participated as aggressors or victims; there is also the fallout from exposure to depleted Uranium. The soldiers, civilians and unborn children have already begun to see the scourge that poisons their being and rivals Agent Orange.

Look at the cost to this planet as Libya and other countries fall to this same ruthless tactic. An objective investigation will clearly show the truth behind the most significant one day attack affecting our planet today. To expose it, is to remove its power and grip.

Be a Truth Seeker

It is our civic duty to question our officials if there is dishonesty, and particularly if treason is involved. The evidence to

proceed with an impartial investigation is so compelling that it moves people into action when they realize that nearly two million people have died in Afghanistan and Iraq under the guise of 9/11. They also realize that as US citizens, they are the only ones who can peacefully put an end to this genocide. They realize that to go it alone is futile, and they need each other. Community is vital on the Common Good Road in front of us. Community is needed to expose the full scope of the abuse, and manipulations that are against our Constitution.

Homeland Security Secretary came out and admitted that the Bush administration had made up terror threats[79] in order to scare

340

the people into supporting the government, now we know what the real definition of terrorism is. It is governments scaring their own citizens into following the Elite's self serving agenda.

We must realize the parasitic elite use fear and intimidation. They will create crisis with a solution that further erodes our freedom. We must be vigilant, for these tactics are being used in many arenas.

Question what we are told. False flag can come into our monetary system, like creating booms and busts, and blaming it on the spending habits of the citizens. As in past situations, they will somehow introduce solution like a new currency and austerity measures that allows them to increase their pilfering, control of money and bring about a new form of serfdom.

Questions Fluoride in our drinking water to the chemtrails left in our sky. Question vaccines and what they are really injecting into us. Question the data on global warming and the carbon tax initiative and the impact of HAARP. Question the "official" government data on joblessness, poverty, and inflation. Question, research, help find solutions, and inform others.

Being a truth seeker means accessing literature, videos, and the internet for the real news. A good place to start is podcasts and videos at www.CorbettReport.com. You should question the main stream media and look for more reliable sources of information.

Become a truth seeker: third party supporters and libertarians, anti-war protestors and human rights campaigners, people who are upset with the government giving trillions to the banks that have engineered our current financial crisis in the first place.

Everyone is now a potential terrorist, according to the governmental and media agencies that deign to limit our range of acceptable opinions and control dissent. However that stance is powerless as more people become informed. So increase your circle of influence and be aware of what is best to engage in.

In the marketing realm the idea is to engage a target audience with your message. Marketers found truth does not rule, perception does. Corporations spend billions to make images and words evoke certain emotions and shape perceptions. You will need to deal with perceptions fabricated by this elite media, be patient and patient in the education of others.

Truth Seekers can approach communicating truth in a variety of ways. Having a loving and kind disposition makes the truth more acceptable. Each time we provide a different perspective or opposing view we are confronting the beliefs that our media, educational system, monetary system, and the war machine has spent over one hundred years crafting.

Being a truth seeker means you are willing to break old beliefs and embrace a deeper truth. It means being willing to engage people where they are at and being willing to discuss the truth in conjunction with positive action.

Now is the time to act

Free ongoing Support

www.LiberateGuide.com

Weekly guide for grassroots organizing and system change. Post questions for author.

Be part of the evolution underway

References

[1] In the High Energy Zone: the six characteristics of highly effective groups' Paul Deslauriers

[2] *Beyond Einstein* by M. Kaku,

[3] Helmuth, et al., *In New Techniques and Ideas in Quantum Memory Theory* ed. D. M. Greenberger (New York: New York Academy of Science, 1986)

[4] Foundations of Physics June 1973, Volume 3, Issue 2, pp 139–168
Quantum theory as an indication of a new order in physics. B. Implicate and explicate order in physical law   David Bohm

[5] *The Computer and the Universe*, J. A. Wheelers, The International Journal of Theoretical Physics, (1982)

[6] Provereb

[7] The names were changed, all events are factual.

[8] *The Level and Distribution of Global Household Wealth* April 2008, James B. Davies,1 Susanna Sandström,2 Anthony Shorrocks,2 and Edward N. Wolff3 Economics Dept, University of Western Ontario; 2 UNU-WIDER, Helsinki;

[9] *Wealth and inequality in the US,* http://visual.ly/wealth-and-inequality-united-states

[10] www.taxjustice.net/cms/upload/pdf/The_Price_of_Offshore_Revisited_Presser_120722.pdf

[11] *The Looting of America* by Les Leopold

[12] Productivity and the Workweek by Erik Rauch

[13] *55 Reasons Why The U.S. Economy Is NOT On The Right Track* In 2012 By: ETF Daily News   Friday, February 24, 2012

[14] " The War on Terror Has Cost" Feb 3, 2015 Niall Mc Carthy; Forbes Business

[15] *The Lives of Twelve Caesars*, the Life of Nero, 38 (c. 121); Tacitus, *Annals*, XV (c. 117) Cassius Dio, *Roman History*, Books 62 (c. 229); Suetonius,

[16] *False Flags Don't Fly Anymore* , James Corbett, The Corbett Report , Apr 19, 2010

[17] *Media Manipulation and the Drums of War: How Media is used to Whip the Nation into Wartime Frenzy* By James Corbett Global Research, January 03, 2012

[18] *Weeding Out Corporate Psychopaths* by Mitchell Anderson Published on Thursday, November 24, 2011 the Toronto Star

[19] *"The Corporate Psychopaths Theory of the Global Financial Crisis"* by Clive R. Boddy Oct 26, 2012 –

[20] Dr. Merabian, University of California study

[21] *(YI, 13-8-1925, p. 277)*

[22] *Matthew 25:40*

[23] *A Force More Powerful,* DVD

[24] , *Women of Protest: Photographs from the Records of the National Woman's Party,* Manuscript Division, Library of Congress, Washington, D.C., mnwp 156007

[25] Library of Congress, LC-USZ62-31799 DLC

[26] Smoking restriction: A voluntary mandate that forbids use of tobacco products. Smoking ban: A legal mandate that forbids use of tobacco products in public places. SOURCE: ANRF, 2009.

[27] "In the High-energy zone: 6 Characteristics of Highly Effective Groups" Paul Deslauriers (available at: www.nrgPublishing.com)

[28] Proverb

[29] David Bohm, *Wholeness and the Implicit Order* (Routeledge, New York, 1980)

[30] 2 Wayne Dyer, *Manifest Your Destiny* (Harper Collins Publishers, 1997)

[31] *The Fifth Discipline—The Art and Practice of the Learning Organization* Peter Senge, (Double Day, 1990)

[32] Historical Debt Outstanding - Annual 1900 – 1949, Us Treasury Department.

[33] *From NAFTA To The Collapse Of The Bubble Economy* by Paul Craig Roberts, Posted on July 27, 2012

[34] *End the Fed,* Ron Paul, ISBN: 0446549193

[35] From NAFTA To The Collapse Of The Bubble Economy Paul Craig Roberts: July 27, 2012

[36] *"Facebook Is Trying To Build a Successful Online Marketplace. Here's How One Group Did.". Bloomberg.com. 2016-10-24. Retrieved 2017-08-09.*

[37] Barcelona's barter markets: an antidote to overconsumption

by Kirsten Dirksen on June 16, 2009

[38] Names have been changed, but all incidents occurred.

[39] *War at Home* by Brian Glick.

[40] *Think and Grow Rich.*Hill, Napoleon, 1960, [Revised Edition], Fawcett Books, New York, ISBN 0-449-21492-3

[41] *British History,* The Journal of History, New Source Inc., Summer 2007

[42] http://wiki.mises.org/wiki/Panic_of_1837

[43] *The Rothschilds' International Plot to Kill Lincoln* October 29, 1976, in *New Solidarity.*

[44] *The Law that Never Was, volume I & II by* Bill Benson and Red Beckman http://www.thelawthatneverwas.com

[45] *Free Enterprise Did Not Cause the Market Meltdown* by Tom

DeWeese. The American Policy Center, October, 2008.

[46] *Essays on the Great Depression.* Bernanke, Ben S. (2000). Princeton University Press. p. 7. ISBN 0-691-01698-4. Also *A Monetary History of the United States.*

[47] *The Creature from Jekyll Island: A Second Look at the Federal Reserve.* Griffin, G. Edward (2002). American Media (publisher). ISBN 978-0-912986-39-5.

[48] Open Market Operations Archive, The Federal Reserve:http://www.federalreserve.gov/monetarypolicy/openmarket_archive.htm

[49] www.federalreserve.gov/monetarypolicy/openmarket.htm#2006

[50] *Indentured Servitude for Seniors: Social Security Garnished for Student Debts,* Ellen Brown, May 11, 2012

[51] *Who's Who of the Global Elite* by Gaylon Ross Sr, quote from author.

[52] *Rothschild, Nathan Mayer (1777–1836)* Victor Gray and Melanie Aspey, , Oxford Dictionary of National Biography, Oxford University Press, Sept 2004; online edn, May 2006 accessed 21 May 2007.

[53] *The Globalizer Who Came In From the Cold,* by Greg Palast Wednesday, October 10, 2001

[54] *Confessions of an Economic Hit Man* by John Perkins, 2004

[55] Clandestine Sertvice History: Overthrow of Premier ossadeq of Iran, Mar. 1954: p iii.

[56] *Mohammad Mosaddeq and the 1953 Coup in Iran* Edited by Mark J. Gasiorowski and Malcolm Byrne June 22, 2004

[57] *The Lily-Pad Strategy: How the Pentagon Is Quietly Transforming Its Overseas Base Empire,* David Vine, American University, December,2012

[58] *The War On Waste* By Aleen Sirgany, CBS Evening News, February 11, 2009

[59] *The Unsilenced Voice of a "long Distance" Revolutionary* by Chirs Hedges, Nation of Change December 11, 2012

[60] *Total Cost of Election Could Be $6 Billion* By NICHOLAS CONFESSORE, New York Times, October 31, 2012

[61] An excellent resource www,CorbettReport.com Excerpts used, refer to JAN. 2012
Faking It: How the Media Manipulates the World into War

[62] issued Washington Post Mar 15, 2005

[63] *How to Add Twelve Years to Your Life,* The Donella Meadows Archive

[64] *Four Arguments for the Elimination of Television* E. Peper, as cited in J. Mander, (New York, NY: Quill, 1977): 211.

[65] *Study Suggests: More Game Less Brain,* www.megagames.com (September 7, 2002). http://www.megagames.com/news/study-suggests-

more-game-less-brain

[66] E. Hundt, Chairman of the Federal Communications Commission, delivered before the National Press Club, (Washington, DC: July 27, 1995).

[67] *The Crime and Punishment of I.G. Farben* by Joseph Borkin

[68] *The Truth about Water Fluoridation by* Charles Perkins

[69] *Impact of Fluoride on Neurological Development in Children* A <u>Choi</u> and P <u>Grandjean</u>, Harvard University, Environmental Health Perspectives July 20, 2012

[70] *The Truth About 'Fluoride' (or what every Mother should know)* By Dr. A. True Ott The Journal of History, August 2000

[71] oathkeepers.org

[72] *False Flags Don't Fly Anymore* , James Corbett, The Corbett Report , Apr 19, 2010

[73] *FBI Terrorists, 9/11 Updates, Bad Week to be a Bankster* - Sunday Update, James Corbett, March 2010 , Corbett Report

[74] *British Special Forces Caught Carrying Out Staged Terror In Iraq? Media blackout shadows why black op soldiers were arrested* Paul Joseph Watson | September 20 2005

[75] *Bomb Damage Analysis of Alfred P. Murrah Federal Building.* by Brigadier Gen. Bentin K. Partin, USAF (Ret.), Physics 911

[76] The Project for the New American Century. By William Rivers Pitt, 2/25/03

[77] Interview 598 – Sibel Edmonds on Gladio B, Protected Terrorists and Stifled Investigations. Corbett Report Feb 2013 www.corbettreport.com

[78] *The Human Cost of the War in Iraq: A Mortality Study, 2002–2006* By Gilbert Burnham, Shannon Doocy, Elizabeth Dzeng, Riyadh Lafta, and Les Roberts. A supplement to the October 2006 Lancet study.

[79] Made up terror threats Huffington Post August 20, 2009

Free ongoing Support

www.LiberateGuide.com

Weekly guide for grassroots organizing and system change. Post questions for author.

Be part of the evolution underway

www.ingramcontent.com/pod-product-compliance
Lightning Source LLC
Chambersburg PA
CBHW050451270326
41927CB00009B/1695